SOURCE READINGS IN $\mathcal{M}$USIC
HISTORY

Source Readings in Music History, Revised Edition:

1 GREEK VIEWS OF MUSIC, ed. Thomas J. Mathiesen

2 THE EARLY CHRISTIAN PERIOD AND THE LATIN
   MIDDLE AGES, ed. James McKinnon

3 THE RENAISSANCE, ed. Gary Tomlinson

4 THE BAROQUE ERA, ed. Margaret Murata

5 THE LATE EIGHTEENTH CENTURY, ed. Wye Jamison Allanbrook

6 THE NINETEENTH CENTURY, ed. Ruth A. Solie

7 THE TWENTIETH CENTURY, ed. Robert P. Morgan

Also available in a one-volume composite edition.

SOURCE READINGS IN *Music* HISTORY

OLIVER STRUNK

EDITOR

Revised Edition

LEO TREITLER GENERAL EDITOR

VOLUME 4

The Baroque Era

Edited by MARGARET MURATA

 W · W · NORTON & COMPANY

New York · London

The text of this book is composed in Caledonia
with the display set in Bauer Bodoni and Optima.
Composition by the Maple-Vail Book Manufacturing Group
Manufacturing by Maple-Vail Book Manufacturing Group
Book design by Jack Meserole
Cover illustration by Mary Frank

The Library of Congress has cataloged the one-volume edition as follows:

Source readings in music history / Oliver Strunk, editor. — Rev. ed.
  / Leo Treitler, general editor.
      p.   cm.
  Also published in a 7 v. ed.
  Includes bibliographical references and index.
  ISBN 0-393-03752-5
  1. Music—History and criticism—Sources.   I. Strunk, W. Oliver
(William Oliver), 1901–   . II. Treitler, Leo, 1931–   .
ML160.S89   1998
780′.9—dc20   94-34569
                                                   MN

ISBN 0-393-96697-6 (pbk.)

W. W. Norton & Company, Inc., 500 Fifth Avenue, New York, N.Y. 10110
http://www.wwnorton.com

W. W. Norton & Company Ltd., 10 Coptic Street, London WC1A 1PU

3 4 5 6 7 8 9 0

FROM THE FOREWORD TO THE FIRST EDITION OF *SOURCE READINGS IN MUSIC HISTORY*

*T*his book began as an attempt to carry out a suggestion made in 1929 by Carl Engel in his "Views and Reviews"—to fulfil his wish for "a living record of musical personalities, events, conditions, tastes . . . a history of music faithfully and entirely carved from contemporary accounts."[1] It owes something, too, to the well-known compilations of Kinsky[2] and Schering[3] and rather more, perhaps, to Andrea della Corte's *Antologia della storia della musica*[4] and to an evaluation of this, its first model, by Alfred Einstein.

In its present form, however, it is neither the book that Engel asked for nor a literary anthology precisely comparable to the pictorial and musical ones of Kinsky and Schering, still less an English version of its Italian predecessor, with which it no longer has much in common. It departs from Engel's ideal scheme in that it has, at bottom, a practical purpose—to make conveniently accessible to the teacher or student of the history of music those things which he must eventually read. Historical documents being what they are, it inevitably lacks the seemingly unbroken continuity of Kinsky and Schering; at the same time, and for the same reason, it contains far more that is unique and irreplaceable than either of these. Unlike della Corte's book it restricts itself to historical documents as such, excluding the writing of present-day historians; aside from this, it naturally includes more translations, fewer original documents, and while recognizing that the somewhat limited scope of the *Antologia* was wholly appropriate in a book on music addressed to Italian readers, it seeks to take a broader view.

That, at certain moments in its development, music has been a subject of widespread and lively contemporary interest, calling forth a flood of documentation, while at other moments, perhaps not less critical, the records are either silent or unrevealing—this is in no way remarkable, for it is inherent in the very nature of music, of letters, and of history. The beginnings of the Classical

1. *The Musical Quarterly* 15, no. 2 (April 1929): 301.
2. *Geschichte der Musik in Bildern* (Leipzig, 1929; English edition by E. Blom, London, 1930).
3. *Geschichte der Musik in Beispielen* (Leipzig, 1931; English edition New York, 1950).
4. Two volumes (Torino, 1929). Under the title *Antologia della storia della musica della Grecia antica al' ottocento*, one volume (Torino, 1945).

symphony and string quartet passed virtually unnoticed as developments without interest for the literary man; the beginnings of the opera and cantata, developments which concerned him immediately and deeply, were heralded and reviewed in documents so numerous that, even in a book of this size, it has been possible to include only the most significant. Thus, as already suggested, a documentary history of music cannot properly exhibit even the degree of continuity that is possible for an iconographic one or a collection of musical monuments, still less the degree expected of an interpretation. For this reason, too, I have rejected the simple chronological arrangement as inappropriate and misleading and have preferred to allow the documents to arrange themselves naturally under the various topics chronologically ordered in the table of contents and the book itself, some of these admirably precise, others perhaps rather too inclusive. As Engel shrewdly anticipated, the frieze has turned out to be incomplete, and I have left the gaps unfilled, as he wished.

For much the same reason, I have not sought to give the book a spurious unity by imposing upon it a particular point of view. At one time it is the musician himself who has the most revealing thing to say; at another time he lets someone else do the talking for him. And even when the musician speaks it is not always the composer who speaks most clearly; sometimes it is the theorist, at other times the performer. If this means that few readers will find the book uniformly interesting, it ought also to mean that "the changing patterns of life," as Engel called them, will be the more fully and the more faithfully reflected. . . . In general, the aim has been to do justice to every age without giving to any a disproportionate share of the space.

It was never my intention to compile a musical Bartlett, and I have accordingly sought, wherever possible, to include the complete text of the selection chosen, or—failing this—the complete text of a continuous, self-contained, and independently intelligible passage or series of passages, with or without regard for the chapter divisions of the original. But in a few cases I have made cuts to eliminate digressions or to avoid needless repetitions of things equally well said by earlier writers; in other cases the excessive length and involved construction of the original has forced me to abridge, reducing the scale of the whole while retaining the essential continuity of the argument. All cuts are clearly indicated, either by a row of dots or in annotations.

Often, in the course of my reading, I have run across memorable things said by writers on music which, for one reason or another, were not suited for inclusion in the body of this book. One of these, however, is eminently suited for inclusion here. It is by Thomas Morley, and it reads as follows:

> But as concerning the book itself, if I had, before I began it, imagined half the pains and labor which it cost me, I would sooner have been persuaded to anything than to have taken in hand such a tedious piece of work, like unto a great sea, which the further I entered into, the more I saw before me unpassed; so that at length, despairing ever to make an end (seeing that grow so big in mine hands which I thought to have shut up in two or three sheets of paper), I laid it aside, in full determination to

have proceeded no further but to have left it off as shamefully as it was foolishly begun. But then being admonished by some of my friends that it were pity to lose the fruits of the employment of so many good hours, and how justly I should be condemned of ignorant presumption—in taking that in hand which I could not perform—if I did not go forward, I resolved to endure whatsoever pain, labor, loss of time and expense, and what not, rather than to leave that unbrought to an end in the which I was so far engulfed.[5]

OLIVER STRUNK
The American Academy in Rome

5. Thomas Morley, *A Plain and Easy Introduction to Practical Music,* ed. R. Alec Harman (New York: Norton, 1966), p. 5.

FOREWORD TO THE REVISED EDITION

> *Hiding in the peace of these deserts*
> *with few but wise books bound together*
> *I live in conversation with the departed,*
> *and listen with my eyes to the dead.*
> —*Francisco Gómez de Quevedo*
> *(1580–1645)*

The inclusion here of portions of Oliver Strunk's foreword to the original edition of this classic work (to which he habitually referred ironically as his *opus unicum*) is already a kind of exception to his own stricture to collect in it only "historical documents as such, excluding the writing of present-day historians." For his foreword itself, together with the book whose purpose and principles it enunciates and the readings it introduces, comes down to us as a historical document with which this revision is in a conversation—one that ranges over many subjects, even the very nature of music history.

This principle of exclusion worked for Strunk because he stopped his gathering short of the twentieth century, which has been characterized—as Robert Morgan observes in his introduction to the twentieth-century readings in this series—by "a deep-seated self-consciousness about what music is, to whom it should be addressed, and its proper role within the contemporary world." It is hardly possible to segregate historian from historical actor in our century.

For the collection in each of the seven volumes in this series the conversation begins explicitly with an introductory essay by its editor and continues with the readings themselves. The essays provide occasions for the authors to describe the considerations that guide their choices and to reflect on the character of the age in each instance, on the regard in which that age has been held in music-historical tradition, on its place in the panorama of music history as we construct and continually reconstruct it, and on the significance of the readings themselves. These essays constitute in each case the only substantial explicit interventions by the editors. We have otherwise sought to follow Strunk's own essentially conservative guidelines for annotations.

The essays present new perspectives on music history that have much in common, whatever their differences, and they present new perspectives on the music that is associated with the readings. They have implications, therefore, for those concerned with the analysis and theory of music as well as for students of music history. It is recommended that even readers whose interest is focused on one particular age acquaint themselves with all of these essays.

The opportunity presented by this revision to enlarge the book has, of course, made it possible to extend the reach of its contents. Its broader scope reflects achievement since 1950 in research and publication. But it reflects, as well, shifts in the interests and attitudes that guide music scholarship, even changes in intellectual mood in general. That is most immediately evident in the revised taxonomy of musical periods manifest in the new titles for some of the volumes, and it becomes still more evident in the introductory essays. The collections for "Antiquity and the Middle Ages" have been separated and enlarged. What was "The Greek View of Music" has become *Greek Views of Music* (eight of them, writes Thomas J. Mathiesen), and "The Middle Ages" is now, as James McKinnon articulates it, *The Early Christian Period and the Latin Middle Ages*. There is no longer a collection for "The Classical Era" but one for *The Late Eighteenth Century,* and in place of the epithet "The Romantic Era" Ruth Solie has chosen *The Nineteenth Century*. The replacements in the latter two cases represent a questioning of the labels "Classic" and "Romantic," long familiar as tokens for the phases of an era of "common practice" that has been held to constitute the musical present. The historiographic issues that are entailed here are clarified in Solie's and Wye Jamison Allanbrook's introductory essays. And the habit of thought that is in question is, of course, directly challenged as well by the very addition of a collection of readings from the twentieth century, which makes its own claims to speak for the present. Only the labels "Renaissance" and "Baroque" have been retained as period designations. But the former is represented by Gary Tomlinson as an age in fragmentation, for which "Renaissance" is retained only *faute de mieux,* and as to the latter, Margaret Murata places new emphasis on the indeterminate state of its music.

These new vantage points honor—perhaps more sharply than he would have expected—Strunk's own wish "to do justice to every age," to eschew the "spurious unity" of a "particular point of view" and the representation of history as a succession of uniform periods, allowing the music and music-directed thought of *each* age to appear as an "independent phenomenon," as Allanbrook would have us regard the late eighteenth century.

The possibility of including a larger number of readings in this revision might have been thought to hold out the promise of our achieving greater familiarity with each age. But several of the editors have made clear—explicitly or implicitly through their selections—that as we learn more about a culture it seems "more, not less distant and estranged from ours," as Tomlinson writes of the Renaissance. That is hardly surprising. If the appearance of familiarity has arisen out of a tendency to represent the past in our own image, we should hardly wonder that the past sounds foreign to us—at least initially—as we allow it to speak to us more directly in its own voice.

But these words are written as though we would have a clear vision of our image in the late twentieth century, something that hardly takes account of the link, to which Tomlinson draws attention, between the decline of our confidence about historical certainties and the loss of certainty about our own identities. Standing neck-deep in the twentieth century, surrounded by uncountable numbers of voices all speaking at once, the editor of this newest selection of source readings may, ironically, have the most difficult time of any in arriving at a selection that will make a recognizable portrait of the age, as Morgan confesses.

Confronted with a present and past more strange and uncertain than what we have been pleased to think, the editors have not been able to carry on quite in the spirit of Strunk's assuredness about making accessible "those things which [the student] must eventually read." Accordingly, this revision is put forward with no claim for the canonical status of its contents. That aim has necessarily yielded some ground to a wish to bring into the conversation what has heretofore been marginal or altogether silent in accounts of music history.

The sceptical tract *Against the Professors* by Sextus Empiricus, among the readings from ancient Greece, is the first of numerous readings that run against a "mainstream," with the readings gathered under the heading "Music, Magic, Gnosis" in the Renaissance section being perhaps the most striking. The passage from Hildegard's *Epistle* to the prelates of Mainz in the medieval collection is the first of many selections written by women. The readings grouped under the reading "Glimpses of Other Musical Worlds" in the Renaissance collection evince the earliest attention paid to that subject. A new prominence is given to performance and to the reactions of listeners in the collection from the Baroque. And the voices of North American writers and writers of color begin to be heard in the collection from the nineteenth century.

There is need to develop further these once-marginal strands in the representation of Western music history, and to draw in still others, perhaps in some future version of this series, and elsewhere—the musical cultures of Latin America for one example, whose absence is lamented by Murata, and the representation of the Middle Ages in their truly cosmopolitan aspect, for another.

This series of books remains at its core the conception and the work of Oliver Strunk. Its revision is the achievement of the editors of the individual volumes, most of whom have in turn benefited from the advice of numerous colleagues working in their fields of specialization. Participating in such a broadly collaborative venture has been a most gratifying experience, and an encouraging one in a time that is sometimes marked by a certain agonistic temper.

The initiative for this revision came in 1988 from Claire Brook, who was then music editor of W. W. Norton. I am indebted to her for granting me the privilege of organizing it and for our fruitful planning discussions at the outset. Her thoughts about the project are manifested in the outcome in too many ways to enumerate. Her successor Michael Ochs has been a dedicated and active editor, aiming always for the highest standards and expediting with expertise the complex tasks that such a project entails.

LEO TREITLER
Lake Hill, New York

CONTENTS

NOTES AND ABBREVIATIONS   xiv

INTRODUCTION   3

I   ANCIENT MUSIC AND MODERN

1   Pietro de' Bardi   Letter to Giovanni Battista Doni   15

2   Giovanni Maria Artusi   FROM *Artusi, or, Of the Imperfections of Modern Music*   18

3   Claudio and Giulio Cesare Monteverdi   "Explanation of the Letter Printed in the Fifth Book of Madrigals"   27

4   Pietro della Valle   FROM "Of the Music of Our Time"   36

5   Pierfrancesco Tosi   FROM *Observations on the Florid Song*   43

II   THE PROFESSION AND ITS INSTITUTIONS

6   Heinrich Schütz   Memorandum to the Elector of Saxony   49

7   Francesco Coli   FROM *Pallade veneta*   54

8   Johann Sebastian Bach   "Short but Most Necessary Draft for a Well-Appointed Church Music"   57

9   Geronimo Lappoli and Anna Renzi   Contract for the 1644 Season at the Teatro Novissimo   61

10   Evrard Titon du Tillet   FROM THE First Supplement to *The Parnassus of France*   63

11   Alexandre-Toussaint Limojon, Sieur de Saint-Didier   FROM *The City and Republic of Venice*   66

12   "The Truthful Reporter"   Two Letters on Opera in Rome   70

13   Guillaume Dumanoir   FROM Statutes of the Masters of Dance and Players of Instruments   73

14   Roger North   FROM *Memoirs of Music*   77

15   Roger North   FROM *Notes of Me*   80

III DOMESTIC MUSIC

16   Grazioso Uberti   FROM *The Musical Disagreement*   85
17   Jean Loret   FROM *The Historical Muse*   88
18   Roger North   FROM *Notes of Me*   89

IV PRINCIPLES FOR PERFORMANCE

19   Giulio Caccini   Dedication to *Euridice*   97
20   Giulio Caccini   FROM Preface to *Le nuove musiche*   99
21   Lodovico Viadana   Preface to *One Hundred Sacred Concertos,
     op. 12*   109
22   Agostino Agazzari   *Of Playing upon a Bass with All
     Instruments*   113
23   Anonymous   FROM *The Choragus, or, Some Observations for
     Staging Dramatic Works Well*   121
24   Christopher Simpson   FROM *The Division-Viol, or, The Art of
     Playing* Ex Tempore *upon a Ground*   126
25   Lorenzo Penna   FROM *Musical Daybreaks for Beginners in
     Measured Music*   130
26   Georg Muffat   FROM Prefaces to *Florilegia*   136

V IMITATION AND EXPRESSION

27   Jacopo Peri   Preface to *The Music for Euridice*   151
28   Claudio Monteverdi   Letter to Alessandro Striggio   154
29   Claudio Monteverdi   Preface to *Madrigali guerrieri, et
     amorosi*   157
30   Michel de Pure   FROM *Aspects of Ancient and Modern
     Spectacles*   159
31   François Raguenet   FROM *A Comparison between the French
     and Italian Music and Operas*   162
32   Jean Laurent Le Cerf de la Viéville   FROM *Comparison between
     Italian and French Music*   171
33   Joseph Addison   FROM *The Spectator*   175
34   Pier Jacopo Martello   FROM *On Ancient and Modern
     Tragedy*   178
35   Jean-Philippe Rameau   FROM *Treatise on Harmony*   183
36   Johann Mattheson   FROM *The Complete Music Director*   188

VI DIFFERENCES NOTED

37 Athanasius Kircher FROM *Musurgia universalis, or, The Great Art of Consonances and Dissonances* 199

38 Richard Ligon FROM *A True & Exact History of the Island of Barbados* 204

39 Lady Mary Wortley Montagu FROM Letters of 1717– 1718 208

40 Charles Fonton FROM *Essay on Oriental Music Compared to the European* 213

41 Jean Baptiste Du Halde FROM *Geographical, Historical, Chronological, Political, and Physical Description of the Empire of China and of Chinese Tartary* 216

GLOSSARY OF FOREIGN PERFORMANCE TERMS 223

INDEX 227

NOTES AND ABBREVIATIONS

Footnotes originating with the authors of the texts are marked [Au.], those with the translators [Tr.].

References to other volumes in this series are indicated as follows:

SR Oliver Strunk, ed., *Source Readings in Music History*, rev. ed., Leo Treitler, ed. (New York: W. W. Norton, 1997)

SR1 Oliver Strunk, ed., *Source Readings in Music History*, rev. ed., Leo Treitler, ed., vol. 1: *Greek Views of Music*, Thomas J. Mathiesen, ed. (New York: W. W. Norton, 1997)

SR2 Oliver Strunk, ed., *Source Readings in Music History*, rev. ed., Leo Treitler, ed., vol. 2: *The Early Christian Period and the Latin Middle Ages*, James McKinnon, ed. (New York: W. W. Norton, 1997)

SR3 Oliver Strunk, ed., *Source Readings in Music History*, rev. ed., Leo Treitler, ed., vol. 3: *The Renaissance*, Gary Tomlinson, ed. (New York: W. W. Norton, 1997)

SR5 Oliver Strunk, ed., *Source Readings in Music History*, rev. ed., Leo Treitler, ed., vol. 5: *The Late Eighteenth Century*, Wye Jamison Allanbrook, ed. (New York: W. W. Norton, 1997)

Years in the common era (A.D.) are indicated as C.E. and those before the common era as B.C.E.

Omissions in the text are indicated by five spaced bullets (•   •   •   •   •).

THE
BAROQUE
ERA

INTRODUCTION

*T*he writing of music histories begins as a history of musical scores. The histories of Baroque music that were standard around 1950[1] relied on a number of important musical prints. The earliest of these—the elegant original publications of works by Peri, Caccini, Cavalieri, and Viadana—introduced a shorthand notation for basso continuo accompaniment and announced music that was new in harmony, rhythm, melody, and expression. To present the later phases of the Baroque, however, musicologists turned to the published "monuments" of music undertaken in the nineteenth century, such as Friedrich Chrysander's edition of Handel's works, published between 1858 and 1902; the Purcell Society's series, begun in 1878; the complete works of Corelli that Joseph Joachim and Chrysander edited between 1871 and 1891; Philip Spitta's edition of Schütz, begun in 1885; the Rameau edition begun by Camille Saint-Saëns in 1895; and of course, the original Bach Society collection of J. S. Bach's works, issued between 1851 and 1900. For the first edition of *Source Readings in Music History*, Oliver Strunk chose nineteen readings that dated from the years 1600 to 1725 to show the bases on which knowledge of such scores became part of a broader musical knowledge of the era in which opera and oratorio were invented, large-scale instrumental music evolved, and instruments and voices were indissolubly joined in public and private spaces.

Since the 1950s the repertory of music composed between 1600 and the mid-eighteenth century has been much expanded by the further exploration of musical sources, particularly for opera after 1640 and for keyboard music. These sources, mostly in manuscript, have become increasingly available in facsimile and in professional, recorded performances. The readings that Strunk offered are more meaningful today, when we can hear performances of Lully that give us a convincing idea of what it was that the nobleman Jean Laurent Le Cerf de la Viéville was defending when he championed French music over Italian, and when we can hear a continuo ensemble with the instruments that Agostino Agazzari described—citterns, Baroque harps, and a battery of lutes. We now also have performances of operas by Cesti and Purcell, of French lute and gamba suites, and of church cantatas by Buxtehude.

---

1. For example, Hugo Riemann, *Handbuch der Musikgeschichte*, vol. 2, *Das Generalbasszeitalter*, 2d ed. (Leipzig, 1922); Robert Haas, *Die Musik des Barocks* (Potsdam, 1928), Manfred Bukofzer, *Music in the Baroque Era* (New York, Norton, 1947). The second edition of the *Oxford History of Music* was begun in 1929.

The present collection of readings from what has traditionally been called the Baroque era reflects this increased accessibility to the repertory and includes more texts dating from the years 1650 to 1690 and 1723 to 1751. But the primary aim of this revised selection is not to provide a greater number of documents about a greater number of composers or musical genres and performances. Rather, it gives voice to the wide range of people who were intensely engaged in creating and thinking about music during a period of much change and controversy. The writing of music histories only begins with the study of scores and with accounts of people, places, and performances. The historian also seeks to find out how it came about that musicians did what they did and, if possible, why. The historian also wants to know what listeners of the past thought they were hearing and what it meant to them. The category "listeners," in this regard, always includes professional musicians with their expert ears, such as Pierfrancesco Tosi, a castrato who sang in London beginning in 1693, and Johann Mattheson, *Capellmeister* to a duke, two authors newly included here. But also to be counted as listeners are the gentleman viol player, the Sunday worshiper, the young princess at court eager to gain attention by her dancing, and the nobleman who held a box in a Venetian theater.

We can hear from such listeners because, during the seventeenth and eighteenth centuries, music became on the whole a more public affair and of greater social interest, more a subject for conversation and more likely to be written about, than it had been before. In fact, were the epithet "Baroque" not so common, several developments in musical life in these centuries could justify a label for the era that is less related to style, such as the historians' "early modern."[2] For not only were musical genres for public consumption established, such as opera and the concerto, but with them the foundations were laid for musical institutions such as the public concert and subscription opera theater that we now take for granted. Although many performers continued to serve noble patrons and religious establishments, the scope of the profession expanded considerably, as did its economic base. Several of the readings document these developments: a contract for an opera singer, the revised guild statutes for the instrumentalists of Paris, and a firsthand account of a concert series that began in London in the 1680s. The new public venues fostered the growth of music criticism, that is, writing about music by listeners, as opposed to the treatises by and for composers that had been more common earlier. *Amateurs* and critics are represented here by opera-goers such as François Raguenet, Joseph Addison, and the anonymous Italian "Truthful Reporter." We also hear from Grazioso Uberti, a jurist; Francesco Coli, a priest working for the Inquisition; society reporter Jean Loret; Roger North, once attorney general to the Queen of England; and Lady Mary Wortley Montagu, wife of an ambassador to the Ottoman Empire. Lady Mary excepted, none of these is a

2. For an assessment of what the word "Baroque" has come to mean in recent scholarship and a justification for its continued use, see Rosario Villari's introduction to his *Baroque Personae*, trans. L. G. Cochrane (Chicago: University of Chicago Press, 1995).

writer of recognized literary quality, yet each speaks for passionate listeners and for accomplished nonprofessionals and their private music-making at home.

Listeners have an important place in studies of Baroque music for several reasons. First of all, the ear was considered an important organ of learning, creativity, and judgment by the modernists of Monteverdi's generation. Controversies over the authority of the senses as against the authority of reason (which underlay the rules of musical composition) marked the opening of the era and persisted in diverse forms with different advocates well into the eighteenth century. Equally important was improvisation, which was called for in varying degrees in most Baroque genres, engaging performer and listener on a plane of immediacy. Furthermore, much that was considered modern in the first decades after 1600 arose from improvisational practice, as composers captured in score what had been enjoyed—or just tolerated—as transient or incidental in performance. The new scores, however, still left much unwritten. The twentieth-century's exploration of how to perform Baroque music exposed the range of what was not indicated in vocal scores or in the challenging array of music for many different kinds of instruments. The variability in what a Baroque score can suggest to performers (and to scholars) has delighted the ears of many and irritated those of others.

With the exception of music for unaccompanied solo instruments and for viol consorts, what we now call Baroque music has one element in common, the continuo bass line. Questions about the variety of instruments that played continuo and how harmonies were filled in by continuo players forced modern scholar-performers to seek answers outside of the scores. The search also led to information about tuning and temperament, bowing, rhythm and tempo, voice production, tonguing, and always, the which, how, how much, and when of improvising embellishments. With the information retrieved from the past, modern performers and instrument builders reconstructed and experimented with the same zeal for discovery that had inspired Italians of the early Baroque to try to recover the lost sounds of ancient Greek music. With all the many variables, music that might have been familiar to an audience in 1950 could easily have sounded less so in 1970 and different again in 1995.

Thus the core of any set of readings related to music of the "figured-bass era" and the starting point for any modern performer of its repertory must be the evidence for performance practices of the time. Tracing how this evidence has been transformed into performance over the last seventy years or so demonstrates how very little in the tutorial texts is prescriptive. The pursuit of information about performance practices is often regarded as a search for historical authenticity. Its intellectual value, however, has been in helping to analyze the indeterminate, creative relationship between performer and score—for the score of a Baroque composition is not a set of instructions from composer to performer. Following every rule and recommendation in historical tutors no more makes an accomplished performer of Baroque music than lead sheets and published instruction books on how to play jazz can produce a player who can swing, improvise, and jam. And just as Louis Armstrong and Miles Davis did not share exactly the same rhythmic, melodic, and harmonic language, so suggestions for an ensemble in 1620 do not necessarily apply to one in 1690. Section 4 of this collection, therefore, offers readings that sketch general areas of performance that concern the Baroque repertory and that exemplify some of the basic kinds of initiatives expected of performers. From these the modern reader may gain a sense of the highly articulated and modulated shapes that seventeenth- and eighteenth-century listeners heard. What the music historian Robert Haas had in his ear when he wrote about Monteverdi or Couperin in the 1920s was different from what we may hear on the latest recordings, because modern performers have continually returned to and reinterpreted the basic source readings on performance practices.

Given the multitude of handbooks and tutors that address idioms of performance by genre or national origin (many now available in facsimile and translation), Strunk's original selection of readings on performance practice has been expanded only slightly. In cases where more modern, annotated translations have appeared, for example, Caccini's instructions on singing in *Le nuove musiche,* the reading given here may be shorter than Strunk's. The earliest addition in this area is a set of excerpts from the anonymous treatise *The Choragus,* which came to light only in the 1980s. It is a comprehensive guide to mounting works for the stage before the institution of the Venetian subscription theaters. The treatise covers all conceivable facets of production and gives concrete demonstration of the high level of polish and elegant coordination that the earliest producers of court opera expected to achieve. Gambist Christopher Simpson describes the elements of ensemble improvisation, revealing a concern for the shape of the emerging composition that clearly takes its effect on its listeners into account. Nothing in Lorenzo Penna's 1672 precepts for continuo realization changed Agazzari's advice of sixty-five years earlier, but the new contrapuntal and harmonic styles of the later seventeenth century required additional instructions. To learn the "style, sweetness, ornaments, and graces" of good singing, Penna charged students of voice to listen to good singers. In fact, most of the musicians whose writings appear in this section assumed that what they were explaining could be heard by their readers somewhere in live performance.

This was not the case with Georg Muffat's instructions. Like Schütz before him and unlike the other writers on performance skills, Muffat's musical training was international. He provided his anthologies of suites for string ensembles (with continuo) with detailed instructions for their stylish execution in a manner of playing that he knew was still foreign in the Germany of the 1690s. His specific demonstrations of bowing indicate a highly articulated mode of delivery that may also be foreign to students of the modern violin but that helps us hear string compositions of his time in something like their varied original voices. Knowing that the same rhythmic figure aims for a different musical effect in Caccini than it does in Schubert or that a series of pitches can be taken in six bow strokes rather than with one change of the bow alters one's conception of the physical quality of the musical rhythm and phrasing. Such differences affect many aspects of performance, from the possible tempos for a composition to its dynamic shaping, and they influence the perceived expressive content of a score.

Arousing the passions through music was one of the aims of Baroque performers and composers alike. Pietro de' Bardi described how Jacopo Peri "sweetened" the "roughness and excessive antiquity" of the earliest examples of the new Florentine *stile rappresentativo* and in so doing "made it capable of moving the affections in a rare manner." In 1616 Claudio Monteverdi expressed little desire to compose music for a libretto that he felt did not bring him "in a natural progression to a conclusion that moved" him. Nearly a century later, Le Cerf de la Viéville spoke of the musician's "rekindling" the fire of feelings and of burning passions "with tones of quickening precision." For Tosi, writing in 1723, a pathetic aria rendered by a fine singer could cause "a human soul . . . to melt into tenderness and tears, from the violent motion of the affections." Though he criticized the succession of arias in the Italian operas he heard in 1697 as incoherent, the Frenchman François Raguenet acknowledged that they were declarations "of happy lovers, or complaints of the unfortunate; protestations of fidelity, or stings of jealousy; raptures of pleasure or pangs of sorrow, rage, and despair." Mattheson's statement in *The Complete Music Director* of 1739 that "the true goal of all melody can only be a type of diversion of the hearing through which the passions of the soul are stirred" would have been agreeable to almost all the writers represented here. For Rameau, even single chords and progressions of chords could express sadness, tenderness, gaiety, and surprise.

For some composers and listeners, music gained expressive force when it imitated speech. Rhythm and pitch, along with the emphases and phrasing produced by chord changes (and which are absent from speech), were considered resources for creating the oratorical delivery of a text. Their expressive effectiveness was tied to the aural cues specific to the language of the text and its literary genre. The readings by Peri and Le Cerf de la Viéville and a few comments by librettist Pier Jacopo Martello illustrate this theory, which exploits both the verbal efficacy of poetry and the musical power of its poetic rhythms and implied vocal intonations. The Frenchman avows that "the single secret is to apply such proportionate tones to the words [in an opera] that the verse is indistinguishable from and lives again in the music. This carries the feeling of all that the singer says right to the heart of the listener." In commenting on two lines from Lully's opera *Armide,* he exclaims, "What a passage! Each tone so fits each word that together they create an unmistakable impression on the soul of the listener."[3]

Other composers sought musical figures that could suggest or communicate a state of being by imitating aspects of human behavior other than vocal com-

---

3. In his letter to Monsieur de la °°° in the *Comparaison de la musique italienne et de la musique françoise* (Brussels, 1705), pp. 169, 173–74.

munication. Monteverdi's preface to his eighth book of madrigals of 1638 expresses his satisfaction at finding a musical equivalent of the *concitato,* or "excited," species of emotion by using rapidly repeating sixteenth notes in the instruments, which were accompanied by "words expressing anger and disdain." Modern listeners take the expressiveness of such kinesthetic imitation in music so much for granted that it is difficult to think of it as an accomplishment of the age, or to hear in Monteverdi a prefiguration of the improvisations for silent film by theater organists three centuries later. Instrumental music also came to portray feelings, as dance in the seventeenth century became increasingly imitative of character. A skilled dancer, wrote Abbé Michel de Pure in 1668, should be able "to give someone enraged an abrupt and fiery dance from which one can perceive the disorder of the character and his distraction." To portray a lover, the dancer would express "the various alterations that love, infirmity, chagrin, or joy can cause on the face or on other parts that seem the most affected by interior feelings." De Pure described how movements "pass through the body according to the disquiets and various agitations of the soul, which signify, against our own will, the interior feelings that we strive to hide and to keep secret."[4] The dancer then coordinates these movements to the concept of the dance and to the rhythm of the music. (For de Pure, this would have been music that Louis XIV's ensemble of "Twenty-Four Violins" played for the court ballets.) Resemblance or imitation, then, is the adaptation in art of those movements that proceed from feelings, which in France were identified as the passions and in Italy as the affections. These passions are within us—in the soul or the mind—and so can be detected or perceived only when they "move," causing the body to move.[5] A reciprocal mechanism occurs when an imitation or resemblance "arouses" the passions and causes the receiver to sense that excitation as a motion, or, in other words, as an emotion.

Modern science seeks these "motions" in electrochemical patterns of neurons firing in the brain. In the seventeenth century, the passions were associated with the four liquid humors of the body: phlegm, black bile, choler (also called yellow bile), and blood. These were held to correspond to four principal temperaments, or personalities: the phlegmatic, or slow and stolid person; the melancholy; the choleric, or hot-tempered; and the sanguine or cheerful. Yet though the sources of expression were fixed, their variety was not. Mattheson, for example, is able to characterize even "little, disesteemed dance melodies" with a happy assortment of moods: tender longing, dogged seriousness, pomp and conceit, agreeable joking, contentment and pleasantness, vacillation and instability, ardor and passion, and so forth. The different proportions, furthermore, of the four humors in each individual were considered to influence what motions would be perceived as pleasing or displeasing to a person. Athanasius Kircher illustrated some musical preferences, most of which, but not all, sound

---

4. The brief, localized ornaments of the French style perhaps behave as momentary betrayals of these "disquiets."

5. See also the discussion of imitation and expression by Wye Jamison Allanbrook in the introduction to *SR* 5.

utterly commonplace today. "That the melancholy love settings that are grave, dense, and mournful" remains a recognizable stereotype. Why "phlegmatics are affected by high women's voices, inasmuch as the high sound affects the phlegmatic humor favorably" is less obvious. The theory of the time, as Kircher expounded it, also extended from individuals to nations, as location and climate were thought to influence the balance of humors. The Germans, for example, being "born under a frozen sky . . . acquire a temperament that is serious, strong, constant, solid, and toilsome." Accordingly, they favor a musical style that is "serious, moderate, sober, and choral." Raguenet, ecstatic over what he heard as the boldness of Italian music in the late 1690s, attributed its style to the Italian national character, which, "being much more lively than the French," was capable of being moved to express passions in what was for him an extreme fashion.

> If a storm or rage is to be described in a symphony, their notes give us so natural an idea of it that our souls can hardly receive a stronger impression from the reality than they do from the description; everything is so brisk and piercing, so impetuous and affecting, that the imagination, the senses, the soul, and the body itself are all betrayed into a general transport. . . . A symphony of furies shakes the soul; it undermines and overthrows it, in spite of all; the violinist himself, whilst he is performing it, is seized with an unavoidable agony; he tortures his violin; he racks his body; he is no longer master of himself, but is agitated like one possessed with an irresistible motion.

Such reasoning extended to non-Western music as well. In a comparison between the music of Europe and that of the Ottoman court, the essayist Charles Fonton acknowledged that the Persian, Turkish, and Arabic music that he heard in Istanbul was passionate and moving. But, "adapted to the Asiatic genius, it is like the nation, soft and languorous, without energy and strength." Fonton asserted that "European ears require the strongest impressions, the most manly sounds and the most muscular, less of the melancholy and more of the gay. The people of the Orient are susceptible to the opposite sentiments."

Such general notions of how the era understood feelings to be expressions of character are essential for us to imagine their translation into music; for not to be found in this set of readings is any presentation of *Affektenlehre* as a musical "doctrine of the affections" more specific than the general beliefs about the perception of emotion. George Buelow convincingly demonstrated in 1983 that "this frequently misused word is apparently unknown in the musical literature of the Baroque."[6]

The seventeenth century faced many philosophical and moral issues with regard to representation and expression. Does an emotion generated by the operation of an imitation have a different status from one aroused by some other means? At the beginning of the seventeenth century, even language itself could be distrusted as a mode of representation. Philosophers and poets alike

---

6. George J. Buelow, "Johann Mattheson and the Invention of the *Affektenlehre*" in *New Mattheson Studies*, ed. George J. Buelow and Hans Joachim Marx (Cambridge: Cambridge University Press, 1983), pp. 393–407.

wrestled or played with the unreliability of language, treating it as a form of presentation not always congruent with reality.[7] Monteverdi's great critic Artusi believed that the senses were fallible. He disprized the new music for its appeal to and dependence on the senses and its attempt to be one, as it were, with poetic language. But the main fault of the new music, in his view, was its divergence from a rational system of harmony and counterpoint that was self-contained and not a representation of anything. If Renaissance counterpoint was correct, it was true.[8] The task that presented itself to the Baroque was to remove the uncertain status of representation, to turn it as closely as possible into "the real." Early science would do this by eventually converting perception into mathematical "proof." Raguenet wrote of a musical storm that made as much of an impression on the senses as a real storm, an impression that carried away "the imagination, the senses, the soul and even the body." In short time, *opera seria* would obviate any such betrayal of the senses, by offering such vivid musical portrayals within a higher ordering.[9] In *opera seria,* the representations of passions were collected and presented together in any opera as if each aria were a reference, an infinitely reproducible citation of a representation akin to a mathematical term, and not the thing itself. With this status, the arias could be safely acknowledged as "real," that is, as real portraits. Furthermore, the mechanism that was the libretto structure of the *opera seria,* based on the placement of arias within it, constituted its own discourse, free of any requirement to resemble "the real." When the librettist Martello described entrance, intermediate, and exit arias, his comment on the exit aria was "whether it is verisimilar is not material." Musical and, to an extent, narrative representation was thus subsumed in a methodical process that could lead no one astray. Moreover, after Rameau's proofs of their rational foundations, the procedures of tonal harmony restored the certainty of system to musical composition. Artusi's dilemma may be considered resolved in a statement such as

7. As expressed by Louis Marin: "Did not words, written or oral, interpose their own opacity between the reader and his visual experience of the world?" See his essay "Mimésis et description, ou de la curiosité à la méthode de l'âge de Montaigne à celui de Descartes" in *Documentary Culture: Florence and Rome from Grand-Duke Ferdinand I to Pope Alexander VII,* Villa Spelman Colloquia, vol. 3 (Bologna: Nuova Alfa Editoriale, 1992), pp. 23–47. In the first half of the century dissemblance and dissimulation are persistent topics. They are the weapons and defenses of the courtier, the illusions that keep human souls from God's grace. Many plays and operas turn on the unmasking of disguises or unknown identities. The importance of distrust was encapsulated in Descartes's first rule from his *Discourse on Method:* "The first rule was never to accept anything as true unless I recognized it to be evidently such."

8. See *Artusi, or the Imperfections of Modern Music* (Venice, 1600), especially p. 44; also Gary Tomlinson's introduction to *SR* 3. For the seventeenth century, it took a Descartes to set aside the unreliability of both sense and reason and invent (or reinvent) the possibility of a nearly closed system of certainties.

9. The distinction between the reality of imitation and its intermediary status as representation is more marked in the language of Raguenet's translator, who renders "que souvent la réalité n'agit pas plus fortement sur l'ame" as "that our Souls can hardly receive a stronger Impression from the Reality than they do from the Description," and "que l'imagination, les sens, l'ame, & le corps même en sont entraînez d'un commun transport" as "that Imagination, . . . and the Body it self are all betray'd into a general Transport."

"Sweetness and tenderness are sometimes well enough expressed by prepared minor dissonances" from Rameau's *Treatise on Harmony*.

On its way from Artusi to Rameau, the Baroque was highly conscious of musical change and dealt with it in polemical exchanges, in the writing of music histories, and by the revival and maintenance of the music of its own past. The articulate and informative defenses of the moderns by Pietro della Valle and others that appeared in the 1640s[10] indicate that the most recent battle between the ancients and moderns in Italy had long since been won. In 1649 Marco Scacchi averred that "abandoning this modern style would be to destroy a large part of music, and indeed, it would be reduced to its first poverty."[11] Subsequent changes in musical style can be marked as each new cohort of moderns took hold. In the 1690s Muffat helped introduce the French ballet style of Lully to his German-speaking colleagues. In France itself, Le Cerf de la Viéville rose to defend Lully in 1704 against the proponents of contemporary Italian music. (The first French history of music appeared soon after, in 1715.)[12] By 1739, however, Mattheson is warning German composers that many of their French counterparts imitate the Italians too closely and that models of the newest *modern* style of melody, which was simple and natural, should be found by looking *back* to Lully.[13] Tosi in 1723 declared that the first composers "which pleased on the stage and in the chamber" were Piersimone Agostini (d. 1680) and Alessandro Stradella (d. 1682). These were Tosi's "ancients"; after them, he believed that his own generation had achieved a classic musical perfection against which he harshly criticized modern, contemporary singers and those who composed for them. Tosi in fact became a member of the first Academy of Ancient Music in London, whose first session indeed programmed a composition by Stradella, along with even more "ancient" works by Luca Marenzio.[14]

The treatment of differences in European music extended to the ways in which music of non-Europeans could be regarded. Fonton's essentialist explanation of why music of the East differed from the Europeans' has already been cited, but it is an "ancients versus moderns" perspective that underlay many comparative judgments between them. Both Fonton and Lady Mary Wortley Montagu heard and saw traces of pagan antiquity in Ottoman music. In Fonton's modernist view, the presence of these traces symptomized the slowness

10. Such as Della Valle's discourse arguing that "The music of our ages is not all inferior, but rather is better, than that of the past age," excerpted in No. 4 below, and the *Breve discorso sopra la musica moderna* by Marco Scacchi (Warsaw, 1649), translated by Tim Carter in *Polemics on the 'Musica Moderna'* (Cracow: Musica Jagellonica, 1993), pp. 31–69.
11. Scacchi, *Breve discorso*, ibid., p. 65.
12. The *Histoire de la musique et de ses effets depuis son origine jusqu'à present*, published by Jacques Bonnet from materials collected by Pierre Bourdelot and Pierre Bonnet-Bourdelot (Paris, 1715).
13. Mattheson, *Der vollkommene Capellmeister*, trans. Ernest Harriss (Ann Arbor: UMI Research Press, 1981), pt. 2, 5:60–63.
14. Marenzio died in 1599. For an account of the Academy see William Weber, *The Rise of Musical Classics in Eighteenth-Century England, A Study in Canon, Ritual, and Ideology* (Oxford: Clarendon Press, 1992), especially pp. 56–74.

of development in that region of the world. When Jean-Baptiste Du Halde related how the Chinese imperial court first encountered Western music notation, he could not hide his belief that notation is a practical invention of a creative civilization. In one aspect, however, he was forced to place China ahead of Europe on the wheel of progress. Because he considered the lack of counterpoint a defect in Chinese music, he speculated that its monophonic state could have resulted from the *degeneration* of Chinese music over the ages. For the Englishman Richard Ligon, the music of the African slaves that he heard on Barbados lacked melody. Though he was clearly taken by the drum ensembles, he nonetheless felt that he could have given the Africans "some hints of tune, which being understood, would have serv'd as a great addition to their harmony." Lady Mary's writing serves as an antidote to such views of cultural progress. We recognize what a quick ear she must have had, as she tells of joining in Greek dances as if participating in ancient rites, recognizes the spirituality of Sufi religious dancing, and compares the artful singing she heard in the chambers of Istanbul to the English air and Italian aria—not always to London's advantage. Writing in the form of letters, she was not obliged to edify her readers and offer descriptions intended to serve as exemplars. Nonetheless the vividness and sense of presentness in her accounts succeed in making her points of view seem to be the only ones possible for an enlightened and educated individual to hold. This gives Lady Mary no less a didactic responsibility than the authors in this collection who were teachers, proponents, and persuaders, whether ancient or modern.

•   •   •

The work of many scholars and scholar-performers has influenced this revision of *Source Readings* for the Baroque era. Among those who helped with translation and gave firm advice about particulars in the sources are Claude V. Palisca, Tim Carter, Giuseppina La Face, Luigi Rovighi, Eleanor Selfridge-Field, Beth Glixon, T. Frank Kennedy, Thomas J. Mathiesen, Dinko Fabris, John Hill, Rebecca Harris-Warrick, Ernest Harriss, Richard Charteris, Frederick Lau, Theodore N. Foss, and Judy Ho. Of those who helped with the search for the new contents, I wish also to acknowledge Laurence Dreyfus, who first undertook this project, Lowell Lindgren, Suzanne Cusick, Linda Austern, Robert Garfias, and Richard Crawford. Thanks for assistance are also due to the staffs of the William Andrews Clark Memorial Library at the University of California, Los Angeles, and the Interlibrary Loan Department and the Thesaurus Linguae Graecae at the University of California, Irvine.

I apologize to Hispanists for the continued absence of historical sources from Spain and its far-flung colonies. Other omissions and all errors are attributable to this editor's oversight or intransigence. For inspiration and encouragement I am in debt to Leo Treitler, the general editor of this series, and owe him a thousand thanks for his patience and unfailing acumen. The emphasis in this set of readings on music as an art of performance pays tribute to my late teacher but everpresent guide, Howard Mayer Brown.

1

$\mathcal{A}$NCIENT MUSIC AND MODERN

1 Pietro de' Bardi

In the 1570s, a circle of nobles, scholars, and musicians of Florence, Italy began to formulate a theoretical concept of expressive music through their study of the musical thought of the ancient Greeks and Romans, against which they measured the music of their own time and found it lacking. This group, or "camerata," met at the home of Giovanni de' Bardi, Count of Vernio (1534–1612), who became a promoter of reforms in singing, musical composition, and the staging of tragedy. Beginning in the 1580s, the group's theories of ancient music helped produce such new works as the monodies of Giulio Caccini and the first operas.

One of the earliest historians of this new music was the antiquarian and scholar Giovanni Battista Doni (1594–1647), who asked for a firsthand account of the Florentine Camerata from Bardi's son, Pietro. Born before 1570, son like father had been a member of an academy, the Alterati, with strong musical interests. As one of the founders of another academy, the Accademia della Crusca, he oversaw the first editions of the frequently revised and most authoritative dictionary of the Italian language. He continued his writing and other activities into the 1640s and died shortly after 1660. It should be noted that Bardi's reply to Doni recalls events that had occured almost half a century earlier.

Letter to Giovanni Battista Doni
(1634)

My Most Illustrious and Revered Patron, the most honored Giovan Battista Doni:

My father, Signor Giovanni, who took great delight in music and was in his day a composer of some reputation, always had about him the most celebrated men of the city, learned in this profession, and inviting them to his house, he formed a sort of delightful and continual academy from which vice and in particular every kind of gaming were absent. To this the noble youth of Florence were attracted with great profit to themselves, passing their time not only in pursuit of music, but also in discussing and receiving instruction in poetry, astrology, and other sciences which by turns lent value to this pleasant conversation.

Vincenzo Galilei, the father of the present famous astronomer and a man of certain repute in those days, was so taken with this distinguished assembly that, adding to practical music, in which he was highly regarded, the study of musical theory, he endeavored, with the help of these virtuosi and of his own frequent

TEXT: Angelo Solerti, *Le origini del melodramma* (Turin, 1903; repr. Bologna, 1969), pp. 143–47; translation by Oliver Strunk. Solerti also lists earlier editions. Doni made extensive use of this letter in chapter 9 of his *Treatise on Theatrical Music* (Florence, 1763, also in Solerti).

vigils, to extract the essence of the Greek, the Latin, and the more modern writers and by this means became a thorough master of the theory of every sort of music.

This great intellect recognized that, besides restoring ancient music insofar as so obscure a subject permitted, one of the chief aims of the academy was to improve modern music and to raise it in some degree from the wretched state to which it had been reduced, chiefly by the Goths, after the loss of the ancient music and the other liberal arts and sciences. Thus he was the first to let us hear singing in *stile rappresentativo,* in which arduous undertaking—then considered almost ridiculous—he was chiefly encouraged and assisted by my father, who toiled for entire nights and incurred great expense for the sake of this noble discovery, as the said Vincenzo gratefully acknowledges to my father in his learned book on ancient and modern music.[1] Accordingly he let us hear the lament of Count Ugolino, from Dante,[2] intelligibly sung by a good tenor and precisely accompanied by a consort of viols. This novelty, although it aroused considerable envy among the professional musicians, was pleasing to the true lovers of the art. Continuing with this undertaking, Galilei set to music a part of the Lamentations and Responds of Holy Week, and these were sung in devout company in the same manner.

Giulio Caccini, considered a rare singer and a man of taste, although very young, was at this time in my father's *camerata,* and feeling himself inclined toward this new music, he began, entirely under my father's instructions to sing ariettas, sonnets, and other poems suitable for being heard, to a single instrument and in a manner that astonished his hearers.

Also in Florence at this time was Jacopo Peri, who, as the first pupil of Cristofano Malvezzi, received high praise as a player of the organ and the keyboard instruments and as a composer of counterpoint, and he was rightly regarded as second to none of the singers in that city. This man, in competition with Giulio, brought the enterprise of the *stile rappresentativo* to light, and avoiding a certain roughness and excessive antiquity that had been felt in the compositions of Galilei, he, together with Giulio, sweetened this style and made it capable of moving the affections in a rare manner, as in the course of time was done by them both.

By so doing, these men acquired the title of the first singers and inventors of this manner of composing and singing. Peri had more science, and having found a way of imitating familiar speech by using few sounds,[3] and by meticulous exactness in other respects, he won great fame. Giulio's inventions had more elegance.

The first poem to be sung on the stage in *stile rappresentativo* was the *Story*

1. Vincenzo Galilei, *Dialogo della musica antica e della moderna* (Venice, 1581).
2. *Inferno,* canto 33, lines 4–75.
3. "Ricercar poche corde," which implies restriction to a narrow range of notes, can be understood as applying to the melodic range of the vocal line.

of Daphne by Signor Ottavio Rinuccini, set to music by Peri with a limited range of pitches, in short scenes, and recited and sung privately in a small room.[4] I was left speechless with amazement. It was sung to the accompaniment of a consort of instruments, an arrangement followed thereafter in the other comedies.[5] Caccini and Peri were under great obligation to Signor Ottavio but under still greater to Signor Jacopo Corsi,[6] who, becoming ardent and discontent with all but the superlative in this art, directed these composers with excellent ideas and marvelous doctrines, as befitted so noble an enterprise. These directions were carried out by Peri and Caccini in all their compositions of this sort and were combined by them in various manners.

After the *Dafne,* many stories were represented by Signor Ottavio himself, who, as good poet and good musician in one, was received with great applause, as was the affable Corsi, who supported the enterprise with a lavish hand. The most famous of these stories were the *Euridice* and the *Arianna;*[7] Besides these, many shorter ones were set to music by Caccini and Peri. Nor was there any want of men to imitate them, and in Florence, the first home of this sort of music, and in other cities of Italy, especially in Rome, these gave and are still giving a marvelous account of themselves on the dramatic stage. Among the foremost of these it seems fitting to place Monteverdi.

I fear that I have badly carried out Your Most Reverend Lordship's command, not only because I have been slow to obey Your Lordship, but also because I have far from satisfied myself, for there are few now living who remember the music of those times. Nonetheless I believe that as I serve You with heartfelt affection, so will the truth be confirmed of my small selection from the many things that might be said about this style of *musica rappresentativa,* which is in such esteem.

But I hope that I shall in some way be excused through the kindness of Your Most Excellent Lordship, to whom I wish a most happy Christmas and pray that God, father of all blessings, grant perfect felicity.

Florence, December 16, 1634
Your Very Illustrious and Reverend Lordship's most humble servant,
Pietro Bardi, Count of Vernio

---

4. For the involved history of this work, see Warren Kirkendale, *The Court Musicians in Florence during the Principate of the Medici* (Florence: L. S. Olschki, 1993), pp. 194–204. Peri himself sang the role of Apollo. Six excerpts from the score survive; see Kirkendale, p. 200.
5. "Comedy" was a general term during the period for any staged work with words, whether spoken or with music, whether serious, allegorical, humorous, etc.
6. See further reference to this influential patron and amateur by Peri in No. 27 below,
7. The separate settings of Rinuccini's *Euridice* by Peri and by Caccini, and Monteverdi's *Arianna* of 1608.

2 Giovanni Maria Artusi

Music theorists of the Renaissance traditionally wrote about the physics of sound, tuning, and musical composition in terms of pitch relations and drew upon examples of sacred polyphonic music for illustration. But at the end of the sixteenth century, new musical practices that were flourishing in polyphonic as well as in solo genres had gone beyond the foundations established by the Renaissance contrapuntists. In a set of dialogues published in 1600, Giovanni Maria Artusi (1546–1613), an Augustinian monk, attempted to point out the imperfections in the modern music he was hearing. The responses from the defenders of modern music forced him to issue a second part to his treatise, which he published in 1603. Artusi may also have been the "Antonio Braccino da Todi" who wrote two further critiques of the moderns. The first of these is lost; the second, published in 1608, addresses Giulio Cesare Monteverdi's defense of his brother Claudio's music (see No. 3 below) in response to Artusi's scrutiny in 1600 of Claudio's modernist "errors" in the five-voice madrigal "Cruda Amarilli."

In this part of the dialogue, the speaker Luca understands certain free, modern dissonances as examples of the kind of expressive graces that singers or instrumentalists often improvised in performance. The conservative Vario examines the voice leading in Monteverdi's madrigal and argues that no amount of looking for such musical figures as *accenti* or *portar la voce* can reveal any underlying contrapuntal structure that is regular and in conformance with good harmonic ratios. He accuses the moderns of relying on the ear alone, which, without intellect, may be fooled in its judgment. Although this is but one aspect of his extensive arguments, and though Luca's observations were written by Artusi, the examination of "Cruda Amarilli" reveals the profound difference in how the old and new practices regarded the nature of the musical object. In Artusi's view, much of modern music was defective, irrespective of its aims.

FROM *Artusi, or, Of the Imperfections of Modern Music*

(1600)

SECOND DISCOURSE

LUCA: Yesterday, sir, after I had left Your Lordship and was going toward the piazza, I was invited by some gentlemen to hear certain new madrigals.

TEXT: *L'Artusi overo Delle imperfettioni della moderna musica* (Venice, 1600; facs. Bologna, 1968), fols. 39–44. Translation by Oliver Strunk, revised by Margaret Murata.

Delighted by the amiability of my friends and by the newness of the compositions, I accompanied them to the house of Signor Antonio Goretti, a nobleman
of Ferrara, a young virtuoso and as great a lover of musicians as any man I
have ever known. I found there Signor Luzzasco and Signor Hippolito Fiorini,[1]
distinguished men, with whom had assembled many noble spirits, versed in
music. The madrigals were sung and repeated, but without giving the name of
the author. The texture *(tessitura)* was not unpleasing, even if, as Your Lordship
will see, it introduces new rules, new modes, and new turns of phrase. These
were, however, harsh and little pleasing to the ear, nor could they be otherwise;
for so long as they violate the good rules—in part founded upon experience,
the mother of all things, in part observed in nature, and in part proved by
demonstration—we must believe them deformations of the nature and propriety of true harmony, far removed from the musician's goal, which, as Your
Lordship said yesterday, is delectation.

But, in order that you may see the whole question and give me your opinion,
here are the passages, scattered here and there through the above-mentioned
madrigals, which I wrote out yesterday evening for my amusement.[2]

VARIO: Signor Luca, you bring me new things which astonish me not a little.
It pleases me, at my age, to see a new method of composing, though it would
please me much more if I saw that these passages were founded upon some
reason which could satisfy the intellect. But as castles in the air, chimeras
founded upon sand, these novelties do not please me; they deserve blame, not
praise. Let us see the passages, however.[3]

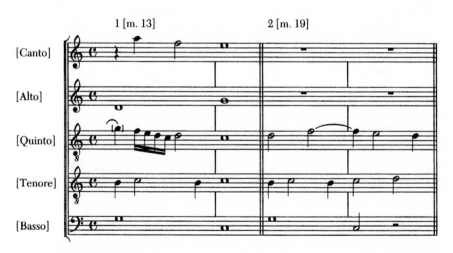

1. Goretti, Luzzaschi and Fiorini were, of course, real persons, prominent in the musical life of
   Ferrara. Luzzaschi, in particular, is cited by Monteverdi as one of those who "renewed" the
   "Second Practice." See No. 3 below. p. 32.
2. Luca put separate parts into score.
3. These musical examples are from "Cruda Amarilli," later published in 1603 in Claudio Monteverdi's *Fifth Book of Madrigals a 5.* Artusi's excerpts differ in a few minor points from the
   published version.

LUCA: Indeed, in the light of what little experience I have in this art, these things do not seem to me to be things with which their authors or inventors could or should construct even a four-story house, as they say, seeing that they are contrary to what is well and good in the institution of harmony. They are harsh to the ear, rather offending than delighting it; and to the good rules left by those who have established the order and the bounds of this science, they bring confusion and imperfection of no little consequence. Instead of enriching, augmenting, and ennobling harmony by various means, as so many noble spirits have done, they bring it to such estate that the beautiful and purified style is indistinguishable from the barbaric. And all the while they continue to excuse these things by various arguments in conformity with the style.

VARIO: You say well. But how can they excuse and defend these imperfections, which could not possibly be more absurd?

LUCA: Absurd? I do not know how you can defend that opinion of yours. They call absurd the things composed in another style and would have it that this is the true method of composition, declaring that this novelty and new order of composing is about to produce many effects which ordinary music, full of so many and such sweet harmonies, cannot and never will produce. And they will have it that the sense, hearing such asperities, will be moved and will do marvelous things.

VARIO: Are you in earnest or are you mocking me?

LUCA: Am I in earnest? It is rather they who mock those who hold otherwise.

VARIO: Since I see that you are not joking, I will tell you what I think, but take note that I shall not be so ready to yield to their opinion. And, for the first argument against them, I tell you that the high is a part of the low and arises from the low and, being a part of it, must continue to be related to it, as to its beginning or as the cloud to the spring from which it is derived. That this is true, the experiment of the monochord will show you. For if two strings of equal length and thickness are stretched over one and the same equal space and tuned perfectly in unison (which is regarded by the musician as a single sound, just as two surfaces which are throughout in contact with each other are regarded by Vitello[4] as a single surface), and if you cut off a part from one of these or bring out a high sound from it by placing a bridge under it, I say that beyond doubt the high will be a part of the low. And if you would know that a part produces the high sound, strike the whole and then the part which is high with respect to the whole, and it will necessarily be related to the low, as the part to the whole or as to its beginning. At the lowest note of the complete system, or of any composition, there may be represented an eye, sending forth various visible rays and regarding all the parts, observing in what proportion they correspond to their beginning and foundation. How then will the first, second, fourth, fifth and the other examples stand, if the higher part has no correspondence or harmonic proportion to the lower?

LUCA: They claim that they do observe harmonic relation, saying that the semiminim [A] in the first example, which is taken after the rest of the same value and which forms a sixteenth[5] with the lower part, would already be dissonant if the cantus were to sing as follows:

for then the tenor, singing the first semiminim an octave lower, would cause the second one, which forms the dissonance, to be heard with it above. Aside from this, they say, since the third of the four semiminims is consonant, what difference can it make if we cause a little more harshness to be heard by con-

4. Erasmus Vitello (Erazm Ciolek), Polish mathematician of the thirteenth century.
5. A major ninth.

verting two semiminims, one consonant, the other dissonant, into one minim wholly dissonant,[6] this is as though we were to sing four semiminims, alternately consonant and dissonant, following the rule for such figures. In this way they make all that they do more gross.

VARIO: Good! I follow you perfectly, and answer that the sense of hearing does not perceive what it does not hear and, not perceiving it, cannot present it to the intellect, there being nothing in the intellect that has not first been perceived by the senses. How absurd it is to say that the tenor sustains a note in one register while the soprano, immediately afterward in a higher register, produces the effect the tenor should have produced! Especially after the rest, how much more evident it is to the ear that the soprano sings a sixteenth and then a fourteenth![7] It is one thing that the ear should hear a dissonance in one part after a rest, another that, when several semiminims are successively taken by step, one after another, one is perceived to be consonant, another dissonant; one thing to hear two semiminims taken by step in the natural way, another to hear a minim, and that taken by leap, in place of the dissonant semiminim. This last offends the ear; the others do not, for the movement is by step.

LUCA: Well said. But they say that all this is called grace and is accented singing.[8]

VARIO: I do not remember having read in any author—and countless excellent ones have written of music—that there is such a thing as accented music. I shall welcome it if you will tell me what it is, according to the pretension of these modern composers.

LUCA: They say that the accents in compositions have a remarkable effect and that these accents occur only when a part ascends to a high note; for example, that when four notes ascend by step, the accent is made on the last note and not on the others, the voice beginning a third lower than the note on which the accent is to be produced and being carried gracefully to its level. But to produce good accord always, this demands the greatest discretion and judgment in the singer for its execution. Here is an example:[9]

6. F against G.
7. Sings a ninth and then a seventh.
8. For a discussion of this musical example in terms of the ornaments called *accenti,* see Claude V. Palisca, "The Artusi-Monteverdi Controversy," in *The New Monteverdi Companion* (London: Faber and Faber, 1985), pp. 130–32. See also the Glossary of Foreign Performance Terms, p. 223.
9. In Artusi's illustration of the *accento,* the ornament appears to "rob" time from the duration of the note to be accented, that is, it is "on the beat." In early seventeenth-century illustrations,

VARIO: I will tell you two things. First, that these words do not explain in clear terms the nature, the peculiarity, and the essence of this manner of accented singing, but seem to be a circumlocution calculated to show, not that they are disposed to regulate all things with rules founded on truth, but rather that they wish to confuse them. We must define what this accent is; then, we shall see whether the parts of our definition are mutually in accord, a thing which I do not know that any serious author has so far done. Second, this manner of singing that you call accented does not assume that the composers will employ barbarisms such as are seen in the examples you show me. It requires that the composers produce good accord (a point which you must note well and above all else) and that the singer use great discretion and judgment in "carrying the voice" *(nel portar la voce)* on such occasions.[10]

And if you tell me that the effect which the tenor produces in the seventh example tends to demonstrate this manner of accented singing, I will reply that since it does not make a good chord and therefore the singer does not know where he can "carry the voice" according to the opinion and will of the moderns, there must of necessity be an error in grammar. It would be better if, when they mean that the singer should, with judgment and discretion, "carry the voice," they were to introduce at that point some sign indicating their wish, in order that, perceiving the need, he might produce better accord and more pleasing harmony than he produces by singing along at his own will.

LUCA: Such an indication would not be unprofitable if one could reasonably discover a universal sign to indicate this manner of "carrying the voice" to the singer. But while these new inventors are exhausting themselves in new inventions to make this manifest, they go on scattering these passages through their compositions, which, when sung or sounded on different instruments by musicians accustomed to this kind of accented music, full of "suppositions,"[11] yield a not unpleasing harmony at which I marvel.

---

the *portar la voce* (see note 10 and the Glossary, p. 225) is also notated as a subdivision of the previous tone, that is, sounding "before the beat." The two effects are different but could be difficult to distinguish, depending on the tempo. Luca's fourth example [d] differs from his others, in that the new *accento* begins on the tone E, a step lower than the previous tone.

10. *Portar la voce,* literally "to carry the voice," is the name of the embellishment, which in other Italian treatises also involves rising pitches and unequal subdivision of a lower tone. Compare the French *port de voix,* and the example above. The Italian term does not seem to have entered the common vocabulary; it is not to be confused with the modern *portamento.* See the Glossary, p. 225.

11. *Suppositi* in Artusi refer to substitute notes. Compare *Artusi,* pt. 2 (1603), pp. 45–47: "But how many melodies have been written using sharps, flats, *fiori, fioretti, accenti,* and *suppositi,* and things against nature?" He rails against unnatural accidentals, intervals of sevenths in place

VARIO: This may result from two things. First, that the singers do not sing what is written, but go ahead "carrying the voice" and sustaining it in such a way that, when they perceive that it is about to produce some bad effect, they divert it elsewhere, taking it somewhere where it seems it will not offend the ear. The second thing is, that sensuous excess corrupts the sense, meaning simply that the ear is so taken up with the other parts that it does not fully perceive the offense committed against it (as it would if the composition were for two, three, or four voices), while reason, which knows and distinguishes the good from the bad, perceives right well that a deception is wrought on the sense, which receives the material only in a certain confused way, even though it border on truth. This manifestly is clearly seen when the organist adds to his other registers that of the twelfth; here it is reason and not the ear that discovers the many dissonances which occur among them.

LUCA: It is known that the ear is deceived, and to this these composers, or new inventors, apply themselves with enthusiasm. They seek only to satisfy the ear and with this aim toil night and day at their instruments to hear the effect which passages so made produce. The poor fellows do not perceive that what the instruments tell them is false and that it is one thing to search with voices and instruments for something pertaining to the harmonic faculty, another to arrive at the true and the exact by means of reason, seconded by the ear.

. . . But tell me if this science can be advanced by new modes of expression. Why is it that you are unwilling to augment it, or that augmenting it displeases you or does not seem good to you? The field is large; everyone is occupied with new things. Musicians too should expand their art, for making all compositions after one fashion sickens and disgusts the ear.

VARIO: I do not deny that discovering new things is not merely good but necessary. But tell me first why you wish to employ these dissonances as they employ them? If you do it in order to say, "I wish them to be plainly heard, but so that the ear may not be offended," why do you not use them in the ordinary way, conformable to reason, in accordance with what Adriano and Cipriano, Palestrina, Porta, Claudio, Gabrieli, Gastoldi, Nanino, Giovanelli,[12] and so many others in this academy have written? Have they perhaps failed to cause asperities to be heard? Look at Orlando Lasso, Filippo di Monte, Giaches Wert, and you will find full heaps of them. If you do not wish the ear to be so much offended by them, you will find the manner and order of their use in the same authors. Now, even if you wish dissonance to become consonant, it

---

of octaves, and certain harmonic relations that arise from figures created by *inganni*, that is, groups of tones that do not have the same pitch intervals but represent the same solmisation syllables. What he considers "true" as opposed to "false" *suppositi* appear to be substitutions that come under the practice of *musica ficta* (though he does not use the term), octave substitutions, and perhaps more diatonic forms of *inganni*.

12. Adrian Willaert, Cipriano de Rore, Giovanni Pierluigi da Palestrina, Costanzo Porta, Claudio Merulo, Giovanni or Andrea Gabrieli, Giovanni Gastoldi, Giovanni Maria or Giovanni Bernardino Nanino, Ruggiero Giovanelli.

remains necessary that it be contrary to consonance; by nature it is always dissonant and can hence become consonant only when consonance become dissonant. This brings us to impossibilities, although these new composers may perhaps so exert themselves that, in the course of time, they will discover a new method by which dissonance will become consonance, and consonance dissonance. And it is no great matter for lofty intelligences like these to be doing and inventing things of this kind exclusively.

LUCA: Their aim is precisely to temper to some degree the harshness of dissonance in another way than that used by their predecessors, and to this they devote their efforts.

VARIO: If the purpose can be attained by observing the precepts and good rules handed down by the theorists and followed by all the experts, what reason is there to go beyond the bounds to seek out new extravagances? Do you not know that all the arts and sciences have been brought under rules by scholars of the past and that the first elements, rules, and precepts on which they are founded have been handed down to us in order that, so long as there is no deviation from them, one person shall be able to understand what another says or does? And just as, to avoid confusion in the arts and sciences, it is not permitted to every schoolmaster to change the rules bequeathed by Guarino,[13] nor to every poet to put a long syllable in verse in place of a short one, nor to every arithmetician to corrupt the processes and proofs which are proper to that art, so it is not permitted to everyone who strings notes together to deprave and corrupt music, introducing new modes of composing with new principles founded on sand. Horace says:

> Est modus in rebus, sunt certi denique fines
> Quos ultra citraque nequit consistere rectum.[14]

LUCA: The truth is that all the arts and sciences have been brought under rules. But still, since dissonances are employed in harmonies as nonessentials, it seems that musicians are entitled to use them as they like. . . .

These musicians observe the rule that the part forming the dissonance with the lowest part has a harmonic correspondence with the tenor, so that it accords with every other part, while the lowest part also accords with every other part. Thus they make a mixture of their own.

VARIO: I see that this rule of theirs is observed in the first, fourth, fifth, sixth, and seventh examples. But in the sixth example, the eighth notes *(crome)* have no harmonic relation, either with the bass or with the tenor. With what sort of rule do you think they can save themselves?

LUCA: I do not know how they can help themselves here. I see the observance of no rule, although I believe that the eighths are the result of perceiving,

13. The grammatical *Regulae* of the humanist Guarino Veronese (1374–1460), a resident of Ferrara after 1429.
14. "There is a measure in all things. There are, in short, fixed bounds, beyond and short of which right can find no place," *Satires* 1.1. 106–7 (trans. Fairclough).

with instruments, that they do not greatly offend the ear because of their rapid movement.

VARIO: Are you not reminded of what Aristoxenus says of such men as these? Yesterday I gave you the substance of this thought; now I shall give you his very words. In the second book of his *Harmonics* he says: "It is therefore a very great and altogether disgraceful sin to refer the nature of a harmonic question to an instrument."[15] As regards the point that, because of their rapid movement they do not offend the ear, the intellect, recognizing the deception wrought upon the sense, declares that since these intervals are not consonant, but dissonant and placed at random, they can in no way be in a harmonic relation; that they can therefore cause no harmony pleasing to the ear; and that their rapidity, accompanied by so many parts making noise together, is nothing else than the sensuous excess which corrupts the sense.

LUCA: They think only of satisfying the sense, caring little that reason should enter here to judge their compositions.

VARIO: If such as these had read the ninth chapter of the first book of Boethius, and the first chapter of his fifth book,[16] and the first chapter of the first book of Ptolemy,[17] they would beyond doubt be of a different mind. . . . Through ignorance a man is unable to distinguish which activities are better and which worse, and as a result of this inability he commonly embraces many things from which he should flee and flees from many which he should follow and embrace. Of ignorance, then, are born compositions of this sort, which, like monstrosities, pass through the hands of this man and that, and these men do not know themselves what the real nature of these compositions is. For them it is enough to create a tumult of sounds, a confusion of absurdities, an assemblage of imperfections; and all springs from that ignorance with which they are beclouded. . . . Our ancients never taught that sevenths may be used absolutely and openly, as you see them used in the second, third, fourth, fifth, sixth, and seventh examples, for they do not give grace to the composition and, as I said a little while ago, the high part has no correspondence to its whole, beginning, or foundation.

LUCA: This is a new paradox.

VARIO: If this new paradox were reasonably founded on some reason, it would deserve much praise and would move onward to eternal life. But it is destined to have a short life, for demonstration can only show that truth is against it.

---

15. See Oliver Strunk, *Source Readings in Music History* (New York: Norton, 1950), p. 31. Artusi quotes Aristoxenus in the Latin translation of Antonio Gogava (Venice, 1562), much decried by sixteenth-century scholars of Greek.
16. From his *Fundamentals of Music* (1.9), "Not every judgment is to be pronounced by the senses, but reason is rather to be believed: wherein of the fallibility of the senses" and (5.1), "Of the nature of harmony, and what the means of judging it are, and whether the senses are always to be believed."
17. Claudius Ptolemaeus, *Of Harmonies*, chap. 1, "Of harmonic criteria."

3 Claudio and Giulio Cesare Monteverdi

By 1605 Claudio Monteverdi had served as musician to the Duke of Mantua for some fifteen years and had published sacred music, a volume of canzonets, and four books of polyphonic madrigals. In his fifth book of madrigals (1605), the first of his publications to indicate a *basso continuo,* he acknowledged Giovanni Maria Artusi's criticisms of his music with a brief announcement that he would produce a written explanation of the modern, or "second," practice. No such explanation was ever published and none is known to exist. But Giulio Cesare Monteverdi published a defense of his brother Claudio's new style in the form of an "explanation" of the 1605 announcement, which he issued in Claudio's *Scherzi musicali* of 1607. Giulio Cesare repeatedly takes great pains to demonstrate that recognized authorities such as Gioseffo Zarlino allowed for the existence of music composed in manners other than those treated in learned writings and that other sixteenth-century composers recognized as great had already anticipated many aspects of Claudio's madrigals that Artusi deemed faults. The Artusi-Monteverdi controversy centered on the combining of polyphonic lines. The key distinction that is often quoted from Monteverdi's defense is that harmony is said to control the contrapuntal lines in the older, "first" practice but obeys the words in the second practice. This did not mean, however, that in 1607, harmony should be subordinate to a single, dominating vocal line. Giulio Cesare adopted Plato's threefold definition of *melodia* as harmonic relation, rhythm, and text; that is, *melodia* signifies the totality of a composition (as it did for ancient music). He argues that these three components of music stand in different relationships to each other in different musical styles. The brothers also challenge Artusi to justify his opinions—not with words but with musical compositions of his own. Their challenge illustrates the esthetic belief of Baroque artists that the senses have a role in judging art, as Claudio himself wrote in 1605.

Giulio Cesare presented his defense in the form of annotations to Claudio's letter, which is reproduced first below.

Explanation of the Letter Printed in the Fifth Book of Madrigals

CLAUDIO MONTEVERDI'S LETTER
(1605)

Studious Readers,

Be not surprised that I am giving these madrigals to the press without first replying to the objections that Artusi made against some very minute portions of them. Being in the service of this Most Serene Highness of Mantua, I am not master of the time I would require. Nevertheless I wrote a reply to let it be known that I do not do things by chance, and as soon as it is rewritten it will see the light under the title *The Second Practice, or, the Perfection of Modern Music.* Some will wonder at this, not believing that there is any practice other than that taught by Zarlino. But let them be assured concerning consonances and dissonances that there is a different way of considering them from that already determined, one that defends the modern manner of composition with the assent of reason and of the senses. I wanted to say this both so that the expression "second practice" would not be appropriated by others and so that men of intellect might meanwhile consider other second thoughts concerning harmony. And have faith that the modern composer builds on foundations of truth.

Live happily.

GIULIO CESARE MONTEVERDI'S EXPLANATION OF THE LETTER
(1607)

Some months ago a letter of my brother Claudio Monteverdi was printed and given to the public. A certain person, under the fictitious name of Antonio Braccini da Todi,[1] has been at pains to make this seem to the world a chimera

---

TEXT: Claudio Monteverdi, *Il quinto libro de madrigali a cinque voci* (Venice, 1605), "Studiosi lettori," translated by Claude V. Palisca, "The Artusi-Monteverdi Controversy" in *The New Monteverdi Companion*, ed. Denis Arnold and Nigel Fortune (London: Faber and Faber, 1985), pp. 151–52, reprinted by permission; and Giulio Cesare Monteverdi, "Dichiaratione della lettera stampata nel quinto libro de' suoi madregali" in *Scherzi musicali a tre voci di Claudio Monteverde*, ed. Giulio Cesare Monteverdi (Venice, 1607), translation by Oliver Strunk. The Italian texts are available in Domenico de' Paoli, *Claudio Monteverdi: Lettere, dediche e prefazioni* (Rome, 1973), pp. 391–92 and 394–407. Giulio Cesare's annotations were originally interlined with Claudio's text, as they are below.

1. A first text by "Braccino" is unknown and may not have been published. Its author replied to Giulio Cesare Monteverdi in Antonio Braccino, *Discorso secondo musicale per la dichiaratione*

and a vanity. For this reason, impelled by the love I bear my brother and still more by the truth contained in his letter, and seeing that he pays attention to deeds and takes little notice of the words of others, and being unable to endure that his works should be so unjustly censured, I have determined to reply to the objections raised against them, declaring point for point in fuller detail what my brother, in his letter, compressed into little space, to the end that this person and whoever follows him may learn that the truth that it contains is very different from what he represents in his discussions. The letter says:

Be not surprised that I am giving these madrigals to the press without first replying to the objections that Artusi made

By "Artusi" is to be understood the book bearing the title, *L'Artusi, or, Of the Imperfections of Modern Music*, whose author, disregarding the civil precept of Horace, *Nec tua laudabis studia, haud aliena reprendes*[2] and without any cause given to him, and therefore unjustly, says the worst he can of certain musical compositions of my brother Claudio.

against some very minute portions of them.

These portions, called "passages" by Artusi, which are seen so lacerated by the said Artusi in his Second Discourse, are part of my brother's madrigal "Cruda Amarilli," and their harmony is part of the melody of which it is composed; for this reason, in respect of everything that constitutes "melody," he [Claudio] has called them portions and not "passages."

Being in the service of this Most Serene Highness of Mantua, I am not master of the time I would require.

This my brother said not only because of his responsibility for both church and chamber music, but also because of other extraordinary services; for, serving a great prince, he finds the greater part of his time taken up, now with tourneys, now with ballets, now with comedies and various concerts, and lastly in an ensemble of two *viole bastarde,* which responsibility and study are perhaps not so usual, as his adversary could have understood. And my brother has bided his time and continues to bide his time, not only for the reason and valid excuse set forth, but also because he knows that *properante omnia perverse agunt* [the hasty do all things badly], that excellence and speed are not companions in any undertaking whatsoever, and that perfect excellence requires the whole man, the more so in attempting to treat of a matter hardly touched upon by intelligent harmonic theorists, and not, like his opponent, of a matter *nota lippis atque tonsoribus* [familiar to the blear-eyed and to barbers].

Nevertheless I wrote a reply to let it be known that I do not do things by chance,

---

della lettera posta ne' *Scherzi Musicali del Sig. Claudio Monteverdi* (Venice, 1608; facs., Milan, 1924). It has been suggested that Braccino is Artusi himself.

2. *Epistles,* 1.18.39: "Praise not your own studies; blame not those of others."

My brother says that he does not compose his works by chance because, in this kind of music, it has been his intention to make the words the mistress of the harmony and not the servant, and because it is in this manner that his work is to be judged in the composition of the "melody." Of this Plato speaks *melodiam ex tribus constare oratione, harmonia, rithmo* [The "melody" is composed of three things: the words, the harmony, and the rhythm], and, a little further on, *Quin etiam consonum ipsum et dissonum eodem modo, quando-quidem rithmus et harmonia orationem sequitur non ipsa oratio rithmum et harmoniam sequitur.* [And so of the apt and the unapt, if the rhythm and the harmony follow the words, and not the words these.][3] Then, to give greater force to the words, he continues *quid vero loquendi modus ipsaque oratio non ne animi affectionem sequitur?* [Do not the manner of the diction and the words follow and conform to the disposition of the soul?] and then *orationen [sic] vero cetera quoq[ue] sequuntur* [indeed, all the rest follows and conforms to the words].

But in this case, Artusi takes certain portions, or, as he calls them, "passages," from my brother's madrigal "Cruda Amarilli," paying no attention to the words, but neglecting them as though they had nothing to do with the music, later showing the said "passages" deprived of their words, of all their harmony, and of their rhythm. But if, in the "passages" noted by him as false, he had shown the words that went with them, then the world would have known without fail where his judgment had gone astray, and he would not have said that they were chimeras and castles in the air for not entirely following the rules of the First Practice. But it would truly have been a beautiful demonstration if he had also done the same with Cipriano's madrigals "Dalle belle contrade," "Se ben il duol," "Et se pur mi mantieni, Amor," "Poiche m'invita amore," "Crudel acerba," "Un' altra volta,"[4] and, to conclude, with others whose harmony obeys their words exactly and which would indeed be left bodies without soul if they were left without this most important and principal part of music. By passing judgment on these "passages" without the words, his opponent implies that all excellence and beauty consist in the exact observance of the aforesaid rules of the First Practice, which make the harmony mistress of the words. This my brother will make apparent, knowing for certain that in a kind of composition such as this one of his, music turns on the perfection of the "melody," considered from which point of view the harmony, from being the mistress becomes the servant of the words, and the words the mistress of the harmony. This is the way of thinking to which the Second Practice, or modern usage, tends. On such a true basis, he promises to show, in refutation of his opponent, that the harmony of the madrigal "Cruda Amarilli" is not composed by chance, but with beautiful art and excellent study that is not understood by his adversary and unknown to him.

3. *Republic* 398d. Monteverdi quotes Plato in the Latin translation of Marsilio Ficino.
4. Madrigals from Rore's *Fifth Book of Madrigals a 5* (1566), *Fourth Book a 5* (1557), *Le vive fiamme* (1565), and *Second Book a 4* (1557).

And since my brother promises, in refutation of his opponent, to show in writing that with respect to the perfection of the "melody" the writings of his adversary are not based upon the truth of art, let his opponent, in refutation of my brother's madrigal, show the errors of others through the medium of the press with a comparable practical performance—with harmony observing the rules of the First Practice, that is, disregarding the perfection of the melody; considered from which point of view the harmony, from being servant, becomes mistress. For *purpura juxta purpuram dijudicanda* [purple ought to be judged with purple]. Using only words to oppose the deeds of another *nil agit exemplum litem quod lite resolvit* [offers the example that settling one dispute by another accomplishes nothing].[5]

Then let him allow the world to be the judge, and if he brings forward no deeds, but only words, deeds being what commend the master, my brother will again find himself meriting the praise, and not he. For as the sick man does not pronounce the physician intelligent from hearing him prate of Hippocrates and Galen, but does so when he recovers health by means of the diagnosis, so the world does not pronounce the musician intelligent from hearing him ply his tongue in telling of the honored theorists of harmony. For it was not in this way that Timotheus incited Alexander to war, but by singing. To such practical performance my brother invites his opponent, and not others, for he yields to them all, and honors and reveres them all. He invites his opponent once and for all, because he wishes to devote himself to music and not to writing, except as promised on this one occasion, and, following the divine Cipriano de Rore, the Prince of Venosa, Emilio del Cavaliere, Count Alfonso Fontanella, the Count of the Camerata, the Cavalier Turchi, Pecci, and other gentlemen of that heroic school, and wishes to pay no attention to nonsense and chimeras.[6]

and as soon as it is rewritten it will see the light under the title *Second Practice*

Because his opponent seeks to attack the modern music and to defend the old. These are indeed different from one another (in their manner of employing the consonances and dissonances, as my brother will make apparent). And since this difference is unknown to the opponent, let everyone understand what the one is and what the other, in order that the truth of the matter may be more clear. Both are honored, revered, and commended by my brother. To the old he has given the name of First Practice from its being the first practical usage, and the modern music he has called Second Practice from its being the second practical usage.

By First Practice he understands the one that turns on the perfection of the harmony, that is, the one that considers the harmony not commanded, but

5. Horace, *Satires* 2.3.103.
6. Venosa is Carlo del Gesualdo; also named are Giovanni de' Bardi, Giovanni del Turco, and Tomaso Pecci.

commanding, and not the servant, but the mistress of the words. This was begun by those first men who composed music in our notation for more than one voice, followed then and amplified by Ockeghem, Josquin Desprez, Pierre de la Rue, Jean Mouton, Crequillon, Clemens non Papa, Gombert, and others of those times, and was finally perfected by Messer Adriano [Willaert] in actual composition and by the most excellent Zarlino with most judicious rules.

By Second Practice—which was first renewed in our notation by Cipriano de Rore (as my brother will make apparent) and was followed and amplified not only by the gentlemen already mentioned, by Ingegneri, Marenzio, Giaches de Wert, Luzzasco, and likewise by Jacopo Peri, Giulio Caccini, and finally by loftier spirits with a better understanding of true art—he understands the one that turns on the perfection of the "melody," that is, the one that considers harmony commanded, not commanding and makes the words the mistress of the harmony. For such reasons, he has called it "second" and not "new," and he has called it "practice" and not "theory," because he understands its explanation to turn on the manner of employing the consonances and dissonances in actual composition. He has not called it "Melodic Institutions" because he confesses that he is not one to undertake so great an enterprise, and he leaves the composition of such noble writings to the Cavalier Ercole Bottrigari and to the Reverend Zarlino. Zarlino used the title *Harmonic Institutions*[7] because he wished to teach the laws and rules of harmony; my brother has used the title "Second Practice," that is, second practical usage, because he wishes to make use of the considerations of that usage, that is, of melodic considerations and their explanations, employing only so many of them as concern his defense against his opponent.

or, the Perfections of Modern Music.

He will call it "Perfections of Modern Music" on the authority of Plato, who says, *Non ne et musica circa perfectionem melodiae versatur?*[8]

Some will wonder at this, not believing that there is any other practice than that taught by Zarlino.

He has said "some" and not "all," to indicate only the opponent and his followers. He has said "they will wonder" because he knows for certain that these men are wanting not only in understanding of the Second Practice, but (as he will make apparent) to a considerable extent, in that of the First also. They do not believe that there is any practice other than that of Messer Adriano, for the Reverend Zarlino did not intend to treat of any other practice, as he indeed declares, saying, "It never was nor is it my intention to treat of the usage of practice according to the manner of the ancients, either Greeks or Latins, even if at times I touch upon it. My intention is solely to describe the

---

7. Venice, 1558.
8. *Gorgias* 449d: "Does not music also turn on the perfection of the melody?"

method of those who have discovered our way of causing several parts to sound together with various modulations and various melodies, especially according to the way and manner observed by Messer Adriano."[9] Thus the Reverend Zarlino concedes that the practice taught by him is not the one and only truth. For this reason my brother intends to make use of the principles taught by Plato and practiced by the divine Cipriano and by modern usage, principles different from those taught and established by the Reverend Zarlino and practiced by Messer Adriano.

But let them be assured concerning consonances and dissonances

But let the opponent and his followers be assured that "with regard to the consonances and dissonances" [means] "with regard to the manner of employing the consonances and dissonances."

that there is a different way of considering them from that already determined,

By the "determined" way of considering the consonances and dissonances, which turns on the manner of their employment, my brother understands those rules of the Reverend Zarlino that are to be found in the third book of his *Institutions,* which tend to show the practical perfection of the harmony, not of the melody, as is clearly revealed by the musical examples he gives there. Showing in actual music the meaning of his precepts and laws, these [examples] are seen without regard for the words. Therefore they show the harmony to be the mistress and not the servant. For this reason, my brother will prove to the opponent and his followers that, when the harmony is the servant of the words, the manner of employing the consonances and dissonances is not determined in the abovementioned way. Therefore the one harmony differs from the other in this respect.

one that defends the modern manner of composition with the assent of reason and of the senses.

"With the assent of the reason" because he will take his stand upon the consonances and dissonances approved by mathematics (for he has said "with regard to the manner of employing them") and because he will likewise take his stand upon the command of the words, the chief mistress of the art considered from the point of view of the perfection of the melody, as Plato affirms in the third book of his *Republic*[10] (for he has said "Second Practice").

"With assent of the senses" because the combination of words commanding with rhythm and harmony obedient to them (and I say "obedient" because the combination in itself is not enough to perfect the melody) affects the disposition of mind. Here is what Plato says: *Sola enim melodia ab omnibus quotcunque distrahunt animum retrahens contrahit in se ipsum* [For only melody,

9. *Sopplimenti musicali,* bk. 1, chap. 1, p. 9.
10. *Republic* 398d (*SR* 1).

turning the mind away from all things whatsoever that distract, reduces the mind to itself].[11]

And not harmony alone, be it ever so perfect, as the Reverend Zarlino concedes in these words, "If we take harmony absolutely, without adding to it anything else, it will have no power to produce any extrinsic effect." He adds a little further on, "In a certain way, it intrinsically prepares for and disposes to joy or sadness, but it does not on this account lead to the expression of any extrinsic effect."[12]

I wanted to say this both so that the expression "second practice" would not be appropriated by others

My brother has made known to the world that this expression is assuredly his, in order that it may be known and concluded that when his adversary said in the second part of L'Artusi,[13] p. 33: "This Second Practice, which may in all truth be said to be the dregs of the First . . . ," he spoke as he did to speak evil of my brother's works. This was in the year 1603, when my brother had first decided to begin writing his defense of himself against his opponent and when the expression "Second Practice" had barely passed his lips, a sure indication that his adversary was desirous of defaming in the same vein my brother's words and his music as well. And for what reason? Let him say it who knows; let him see it who can find it in writing! But why does the adversary show so much astonishment in that discourse of his, saying further, "You show yourself as jealous of that expression as though you feared that someone would rob you of it," as though he meant to say, in his language, "You should not fear such a theft, for you are not worth imitating, let alone robbing"? I inform him that, if the matter has to be considered in this light, my brother will have not a few arguments in his favor, in particular for the *canto alla francese* [melody in the French style] in this modern manner, which has been a matter of marvel for the three or four years since it was published and which he has applied now to motets, now to madrigals, now to canzonets and airs. Who before him brought it to Italy, until he returned from the baths of Spa[14] in the year 1599? Who before him began to apply it to Latin and Italian words in our tongue? Has he not then composed these *Scherzi?* There would be much to say of this to his advantage, and still more (if I wished) of other things, but I pass over them in silence since, as I have said, the matter does not need to be considered in this light. He will call it "Second Practice" with regard to the manner of its employment; with regard to its origin it might be called "First."

and so that man of intellect might meanwhile consider other second thoughts concerning harmony.

11. Marsilio Ficino, *Compendium in Timaeum*, chap. 30. Compare Plato, *Timaeus* 47d.
12. *Istituzioni armoniche*, pt. 2, chap. 7, p. 84.
13. Venice, 1603.
14. Belgian town southeast of Liège.

"Other thoughts," that is, not clinging obstinately to the belief that the whole requirement of art cannot be found elsewhere than in the rules of the First Practice on the ground that, in all varieties of composition, the harmony is always the same thing, being pre-determined and thus incapable of obeying the words perfectly. "Secondary thoughts," that is, concerning the Second Practice, or the perfection of the melody. "Concerning harmony," that is, concerning not merely the portions or "passages" of a composition, but its fruit. For if the opponent had considered the harmony of my brother's madrigal "O Mirtillo"[15] in this light, he would not, in that discourse of his, have uttered such extravagances with regard to its mode, although he appears to be speaking in general when he says this. L'Artusi has likewise explained and demonstrated the confusion introduced into composition by those who begin in one mode, follow this with another, and end with one wholly unrelated to the first and second ideas, which is like hearing the talk of a madman, who, as the saying goes, runs with the hare and hunts with the hounds. Poor fellow, he does not perceive that, while he is posing before the world as preceptor ordinary, he falls into the error of denying the mixed modes. If these did not exist, would not the Hymn of the Apostles,[16] which begins in the sixth mode and ends in the fourth, be running with the hare and hunting with the hounds? And likewise the Introit "Spiritus Domini replevit orbem terrarum" and especially the "Te Deum laudamus"? Would not Josquin be an ignoramus for having begun his mass on "Faisant regrets"[17] in the sixth mode and finished it in the second? The "Nasce la pena mia" of the excellent Striggio,[18] the harmony of which composition (from the point of view of the first practice) may well be called divine—would it not be a chimera, being built upon a mode consisting of the first, eight, eleventh, and fourth? The madrigal "Quando, signor, lasciaste" of the divine Cipriano de Rore[19] which begins in the eleventh mode, passes into the second and tenth in the middle, and ends in the first [mode], and the second part in the eighth—would not this thing of Cipriano's be a truly trifling vanity? And what would Messer Adriano be called for having begun in the first mode in "Ne projicias nos in tempore senectutis" (a motet for five voices to be found at the end of his first book),[20] making the middle in the second mode and the end in the fourth? But let the opponent read chapter 14 ["On the common or mixed modes"] of the fourth book of the Reverend Zarlino's *Institutions,* and he will learn.

And have faith that the modern composer builds on foundations of truth and you will fare well.

---

15. The madrigal from Monteverdi's *Madrigals, Book 5* that follows "Cruda Amarilli."
16. "Exsultet coelum laudibus" from the Roman Antiphonary, *Hymni antiqui,* p. 33
17. His *Masses,* Book III (Venice, 1514).
18. Alessandro Striggio, *Madrigals a 6* (1560).
19. His *Madrigals,* Book IV a 5 (1557).
20. Adrian Willaert, *Motecta a 5,* Book I (1539).

My brother has said this, finally, knowing that because of the command of the words, modern composition does not and cannot observe the rules of [the first] practice, and that only a method of composition that takes account of this command will be so accepted by the world that it may justly be called a usage. Therefore he cannot believe and never will believe—even if his own arguments are insufficient to sustain the truth of such a usage—that the world will be deceived, even if his opponent is. And farewell.

4 Pietro della Valle

The Roman nobleman Pietro della Valle (1586–1652) is best known for his travels—first throughout Italy, then on the sea fighting pirates—as a pilgrim to the Holy Land and as an observant sojourner in the Middle East, Persia, Turkey, and India. He left Rome before 1609 and returned in 1626 with his second wife, a Persian, and the remains of his first wife, a Georgian. He also brought back a memoir of his travels (published 1650–63), a grammar of the Turkish language, decipherments of cuneiform writing, notes on Eastern astrology, and a wealth of other exotica. He quickly reentered the world of the gentlemen's academies, which included musical performances at their meetings in his own palace. As a youth he had studied harpsichord, gamba, theorbo, counterpoint, and dancing, and had developed an ear that would prompt his studies of Neapolitan and Sicilian song, as well as music of the East. He wrote two librettos for music (in 1606 and 1629) and maintained an intense correspondence with the music antiquarian, Giovanni Battista Doni, proposing instruments that would execute all kinds of ancient and exotic modes. He and Doni had instruments built with multiple keyboards and fingerboards in order to play diatonic, chromatic, and enharmonic *genera* and transpositions of the modes. Della Valle composed four dialogues using these instruments, two of which received public performance at the oratory of San Marcello in 1641.

None of Della Valle's more uncommon interests diminished his appreciation of the public and private music that he heard around him, of which his 1640 discourse in favor of contemporary music bears vivid and concrete testimony. He begins with well-known arguments about compositional style itself—polyphony versus audibility of the text, and consistent imitative texture versus a variety of textures. He also provides a description of the newest musical genres, including the oratorio. But it is as a listener that Della Valle offers valuable comparisons of past and present performance and performers, describing the delight of improvised embellishment in sensitive ensemble playing, praising the greater variety of expressive devices used by modern singers, and extolling the abilities of the castrati and a new cohort of women singers.

FROM Of the Music of Our Time

Which Is Not At All Inferior but Rather Is Better than That of the Past Age

DISCOURSE TO LELIO GUIDICCIONI
(1640)

The other evening Your Lordship said that in the last fifty years music had lost much, and that today there weren't good men in this profession similar to those of the past age. I, who seemed in great measure to disagree, had many things to say to Your Lordship about this. But because we went on to other discussions, and then it came time to take leave of each other, I did not have the opportunity to offer Your Lordship my reasons, which I have decided to send to you written down, hoping that you would favor me by listening to them and would better consider them all together.

I say therefore, that in the first place we must distinguish things in order not to speak confusedly, because counterpoint is one thing, sound is another, melody another—all parts of music; and finally, music in an absolute sense is yet another. Music is a general name that comprises all the things mentioned above that are parts of it, and there are other parts besides. But let it suffice that we speak only of what I have named, to which the other things can easily be reduced. And speaking thus absolutely about music does not at all verify Your Lordship's proposition (pardon me for speaking freely, because it is allowed in differences of opinion and cannot be avoided) on the basis of what are, so to speak, the parts of it, which, I hope, will be proved to Your Lordship in full.

Counterpoint, that part of music most necessary to make good use of every other part, has for its aim not only the foundations of music, but perhaps even more, artifice and the most detailed subtleties of this art. These are fugues forwards and backwards, simple or double, imitations,[1] canons, and *perfidie*[2] and other elegances made like these, which, if used at the right time and place, adorn music marvelously. They are not however to be used continuously, neither always all of them nor always the same ones, but only those which are appropriate, whenever they are appropriate: now these, now those, and often

---

TEXT: "Della musica dell'età nostra, che non è punto inferiore, anzi è migliore di quella dell'età passata," in *De' trattati di musica di Gio. Batista Doni*, ed. Anton Francesco Gori, vol. 2 (Florence, 1763; facs. Bologna, 1974), pp. 249–64, repr. Angelo Solerti, *L'origine del melodramma* (Turin, 1903; facs. Bologna, [1969], pp. 148–79). Translation, by Margaret Murata, is from pp. 148–50, 156–57, 159–66. Guidiccioni (1582–1643), a classical scholar, poet, and literary critic, also wrote a "Discorso sopra la musica," which argues that music teaches virtue (ms. dated 1632).

1. Echoes or antiphonal effects.
2. Counterpoints built on ostinato basses. Zarlino called them *pertinacia*.

enough when they are not needed, none. And experience teaches us that the frequent use of these musical artifices is much more suited to instrumental music than to vocal, and especially when an instrument plays solo. From this I concede to Your Lordship that organs played with so much mastery by those good men that you named for me must have certainly carried people away. But in vocal music these refinements of artifice, although they work very well when made use of sparingly in suitable places (as one sees in many madrigals of the old masters and particularly in the famous "Vestiva i colli" by Palestrina), for the most part, nonetheless, they do not succeed, whether because in solo singing, which nowadays is much heard and is what pleases many people more, there is little place for them; whether, further, because in ensemble singing they create very bad effects, which composers of that time, begging Your Lordship's indulgence, hardly took into consideration, but effects which composers of today have known to anticipate with greater accuracy.[3]

• • • • •

Instrumental music should be considered differently according to the diverse ways in which it is used, because it is one thing to play alone, another to play in the company of other instruments, or of voices, or of voices and instruments together, and another to play in support of a choir.

In playing alone, more than in other forms, all the major artifices of counterpoint work well. But I remind Your Lordship that solo playing, no matter how well done, when it goes on for a long time becomes boring. It has often happened to different organists—and the best ones that, when overly enamored of their counterpoints, they made certain *ricercate*[4] too long, the little bell had to be rung to make them stop. Such a thing does not happen to those that sing; people are sorry when they finish and always want them to go on longer than they have. Under this subject of solo performance I also recognize as extremely great experts those that Your Lordship named, Claudio da Correggio in Parma, Luzzasco in Ferrara, Annibale Padovano, Andrea and Giovanni Gabrieli in Venice, Giovanni Macque in Naples, the Cavalier del Leuto[5] in Rome, and others like them, although they are known to me only by reputation. I am astonished, nonetheless, at what Your Lordship told me about Luzzasco: that

3. Della Valle continues by listing those "bad effects" of the contrapuntal style: the confusion of words and of fugal subjects, and the dominance of melodic and textural effects over what the words are saying.
4. To be understood here as "improvisations."
5. Claudio Merulo (1533–1604), organist at the cathedrals in Brescia, Venice, and then Parma, where he also served as organist to the Duke and the Company of the Steccata. Luzzasco Luzzaschi (d. 1607), organist to the Duke of Ferrara from 1564. Padovano (1527–1575), organist at San Marco, Venice and at the Austrian imperial court in Graz, where he became director of music. Andrea Gabrieli (1533–1585), organist at San Marco, Venice from 1566 until his death. His nephew Giovanni (1557–1612) succeeded him. Jean de Macque (d. 1614) lived in Rome from 1574, then served the viceregal chapel in Naples from 1599. The Cavaliere del Leuto (d. 1608) has not been identified; he was attached to the household of the Cardinal Montalto in Rome from before 1589 until his death.

he did not know how to make a trill, and that he would play the most refined details of his counterpoints so roughly, like a journeyman without any touch of gracefulness. I call this kind of performance bland, because it is just like a special dish, flavored with the best ingredients, but without any salt, or like statues that are roughed out with excellent design but are not finished or smooth or, like others of metal, which likewise of good design are only cast roughly and then neither touched up nor polished.

•   •   •   •   •

Playing in ensemble with other instruments does not demand so much the artifices of counterpoint as it does the art of embellishment; because if the player is good, he does not have to care so much about showing off his skills as a soloist as much as he must make adjustments to all the others. The same can be said of singers, since I don't consider a good singer one who, for example, having an excellent vocal ability always wants to be the one to do all the *passaggi*,[6] without giving time to the others to make some. Or if the others do execute them, he overpowers them with his own. Those that sing and play well in an ensemble must give time to each other; and they should play with the lightness of exchanges rather than with too many subtle contrapuntal artifices. They will demonstrate their skill in knowing how to restate well and promptly that which another has just done; in giving space to others and opportune occasions to restate that which they have done; and thus they will make their ability known to others with a different and not less skillful style, although not as difficult nor of such profound learning. Today not only the most excellent but also the ordinary instrumentalists do this, and they know far better than I think anyone that I heard from those past times could have done. When you play together with voices, the same holds true and more, as what I have said about instruments, because the instruments, serving the voices as the principals in the music, have no other aim than to accompany them well, a thing that I see the instrumentalists of today do with great judgment, so that I do not know how they could have ever done more in other times in this kind of playing. . . .

In singing, then, the only thing about which it is left to for us to speak, there are also several things to consider, because in addition to the differences in solo singing or in ensembles, one must further consider the goodness of the voices, the skill of the person singing, and finally the beauty of the works that are chosen to be sung. Solo singing demands either sweetness of voice or exquisite skill; but one or the other used with judgment, because otherwise you have nothing. Your Lordship praised Lodovico, a falsetto from the past known also to me (although when I was a boy),[7] saying that one long note well sung by him, as almost always he used to do, pleased you more than all the *passaggi* of the moderns. I answered you that Lodovico sang with judgment, because, since

6. A general term for ornamental, melismatic divisions of moderate to extensive duration; they were often improvised. See also the Glossary of Foreign Performance Terms (pp. 223–26).
7. Probably Lodovico Gualtero.

he had the sweet voice of the falsetto but did not have much technique, he hardly ever used either *passaggi* or the other graces when he sang, except only a good vocal placement and graceful finishes with those long notes of his, which pleased very much because of the sweetness of his voice. At the same time, however, or a little later, the tenor Giuseppino flourished,[8] who did exactly the opposite for the same reason, recognizing his talent and availing himself of it. Giuseppino's voice was not good, but he had very great agility. He did not have the most artistry in the world, but his *passaggi* were natural. He sang moreover with judgment as far as his self was concerned, because he made use of his special talent. You hardly ever heard a long note from him without a trembling trill; his singing was all *passaggi*. But with respect to others he did not sing with judgment,[9] because most of the time he added *passaggi* where they should not have gone. You never knew whether his singing was happy or sad, because it was always of one kind. Or, to say it better, his singing was always happy in every thing, whether that was appropriate or inappropriate, due to the quickness of the notes that he continually spewed out, without his knowing, I believe, what notes they were. I remember also from those times, but more graciously, Melchior the bass,[10] who had my favor. And beyond his excellent ability, he also had methods that after him remained for basses as standards in elegant singing. I remember Giovanni Luca the falsetto, a great singer of *gorge*[11] and *passaggi,* who sang as high as the stars; Orazietto, the best singer in falsetto or in tenor; of Ottaviuccio and Del Verovio, famous tenors, and all three of the last named sang in my *Carro.*[12] All these men, however, from their trills and on to their *passaggi,* and with their good vocal placement, hardly had other skills: of singing soft and loud, of increasing the voice little by little, of diminishing it with grace, of expressing the affections, of following the words and their meanings with judgment; of making the voice joyful or melancholy, of making it plaintive or ardent when necessary, and similar other elegances that singers of today do excellently well. In those times you heard no talk of these nor, in Rome at least, did you ever know anything new, until in the last years it was brought to us from the good school of Florence by Signor Emilio de' Cavalieri who, above all, gave Rome a good taste in a little play in the

8. Giuseppino Cenci (d. 1616). Vincenzo Giustiniani considered him, along with Giulio Caccini, a major influence in establishing the monodic style.

9. When he sang with others.

10. Melchior Palentrotti (d. c. 1618), a Neapolitan bass who worked in Rome and Ferrara, and was associated with the Cardinal Montalto. He entered the Sistine Chapel choir in 1597 and sang the role of Pluto in the Florentine *Euridice* of Peri. For an aria with *passaggi* as he sang it, see Caccini's *Le nuove musiche* no. 13-b, "Muove sì dolce, e sì soave guerra."

11. A type of embellishment; see Glossary.

12. Most likely Giovanni Luca Conforti (ca. 1560–1608), author of a tutor for learning how to embellish vocal and instrumental music, as well as three volumes of embellished psalm settings; and Sistine Chapel singer Orazio Griffi. Ottavio Durante and Simone del Verovio were known as tenors and falsettists. The score to Della Valle's *Carro di fedeltà d'amore,* set to music by Paolo Quagliati, was published in 1611 (modern ed. by V. Gotwals and O. Keppler, Northampton: 1957, Smith College Music Archives no. 13).

Oratorio of the Chiesa Nuova,[13] at which I was present when quite young. Since that time in which that good style was introduced also among us, a different, more refined manner than sung by their predecessors, we now hear the Nicolinis, the Bianchis, the Giovanninis, the Lorenzinis, the Marios and so many others[14] who equal these already, and without doubt do better than they, if not in other ways, at least in knowing how to sing with more judgment, whether in ensemble or alone. This aspect is the most important of all in our day: using judgment in an art that has become as perfected as I have described.

But leaving aside some other voices in order to say something about sopranos, who are the major ornament of music, Your Lordship wants to compare the falsettists of those times with the natural sopranos of the *castrati* that today we have in such abundance. Whoever in those days sang like a Guidobaldo, a Cavalier Loreto, a Gregorio, an Angeluccio, a Marc'Antonio[15] and so many others that I could name? The most that one could do then was to have a good boy [soprano]; but just when they began to understand a few things, they lost their voices. And while they had them, like persons who have no judgment because of their age, they also sang without taste and without style, exactly like things that are learned by rote, so that sometimes to hear them grated on my nerves unbearably. The sopranos of today, persons of judgment, of some age, with feelings, and of expertise in their exquisite art, sing with grace, with taste, with true refinement. Dressing themselves in the affections, they carry you away when you hear them. Of such sopranos in persons of judgment, the past age had only a Padre Soto and after that Padre Girolamo[16] who could more readily be included in our age than in the past one. We today have plenty of them in all the courts, all the chapels.

And beyond the castrati, where in the long gone days were so many of those women singers that today we have with singular excellence? In the days of our fathers, one Giulia—or Lulla, as we call her (whom even I came to know but not in her best years)—because she was pretty and could sort of improvise some villanella to a standard tune[17] at the harpsichord—or what do I know?—persuaded a duke to steal her, which resulted in great commotion. Vittoria,[18]

---

13. *La rappresentatione di anima, et di corpo* (Rome, 1600; repr. Farnborough, England, 1967).

14. Singers such as Sistine Chapel bass Bartolomeo Nicolini, tenor Francesco Bianchi, alto Lorenzo Sances, and soprano Mario Savioni.

15. Guidobaldo Boretti, Cavaliere Loreto Vittori, Gregorio Lazzarini, Angelo Ferrotti, and Marc'Antonio Pasqualini were all Sistine Chapel singers who also performed in the chamber and in operas.

16. Francisco Soto de Langa (d. 1619), Spanish soprano in the Sistine Chapel choir from 1562, priest of the Congregation of the Oratory, and composer of polyphonic *laude*. Girolamo Rosini (1581–1644), a virtuoso soprano much patronized by Cardinal Pietro Aldobrandini, had the distinction of being expelled from the Sistine Chapel choir; he later became prefect of music at the Chiesa Nuova from 1623 to his death.

17. "Cantava un poco ad aria," that is, sang strophes to a standard melodic formula.

18. Vittoria Archilei (1550–after 1620) known as "La Romanina," sang at the Medici court from 1588. Peri, Caccini, and Sigismondo d'India, among others, praised her subtle and virtuosic improvisatory style.

her friend, even though she wasn't pretty, was kept in the service of the Grand Dukes of Tuscany because she sang well with art and had a good voice, and was treated very well as long as she lived. But Hippolita[19] of Cardinal Montalto, more recent and who I believe is still living, won the battle at the wedding of Grand Duke Cosimo,[20] for in the concerts the best singers of all Italy competed together.

Today in Rome alone how many women do we have? how many did we have a few years ago? Who isn't beside himself when he hears Signora Leonora sing, with her archlute touched so freely and imaginatively? Who can pass sentence on who is the better of the two, Signora Leonora or Signora Caterina, her sister? Whoever has heard and seen Signora Adriana[21] their mother, as I have, in her more youthful years, and with that beauty that the world knows, on the sea in a galley boat at Posillipo with her gilt harp in hand, well needs to confess that in our times sirens are still to be found on those shores, but sirens who are benevolent and adorned as much with beauty as with *virtù*, not like those murderous evildoers of antiquity. And Signora Maddalena with her sister [Eleonora], whom we call the Lolli, and were the first that I heard sing well in Rome, after my return from the Levant. And Signora Sofonisba, whom an envious distance has stolen from us and to whom a few years ago Rome gave such grand accolades, more than were ever granted to any of the ancients in the Theater of Marcellus.[22] Who was there ever in the present age who could compare with her? Perhaps Cammilluccia,[23] who with so many of her sisters and daughters made her house seem like a Mount Parnassus with all its Muses? But these have also been of our day, and similarly, the Signora Lucrezia Moretti, of Cardinal Borghese, today alive and well, and "la Laudomia" of the Muti family, who died recently. Also flourishing today more than ever are the Campanas, the Valerias,[24] and so many others famous for singing, among whom the contralto Signora Santa, whom I heard three or four years ago, was most refined. I could speak of one other also of great repute about whom I remain silent because to celebrate her only as a good singer, for her qualities, would seem to do her wrong. I remain silent similarly about the sister of Signora Adriana [Basile] whom I do not know, but understand she is in Germany where

19. Hippolita Recupito (d. 1650) and her husband Cesare Marotta (d.1630) both served Cardinal Montalto.
20. Cosimo II de' Medici (1590–1621) married Maria Maddalena, Archduchess of Austria in 1608. Recupito and Archilei performed together, along with the Caccini daughters, on several occasions during the wedding festivities.
21. Adriana Basile (ca. 1580–ca. 1641) and her daughters Caterina (1624–after 1670) and Leonora (1611–70) led celebrated lives as chamber musicians in Mantua, Rome and Naples. The women had as patrons the Gonzaga, the Barberini, the Rospigliosi, and Cardinal Mazarin.
22. The amphitheater by the Tiber completed in 13 B.C.E., dedicated to Marcellus, the nephew and son-in-law of Caesar Augustus.
23. Many of the women mentioned here have yet to be identified.
24. Anna di Valeria caught the French Ambassador's eye in 1635 in Rome. She appeared on the Venetian stage in the role of Poppea in the 1643 opera by Monteverdi.

she was called to serve the Emperor and does great honor to our age;[25] and thus also about Signora Francesca Caccini, young daughter of our [Giulio] Romano, who in Tuscany is called "la Cecchina," whom I also heard in Florence in my youth, and has been greatly admired for many years for her music, as much in singing as in composition, and for poetry, in Latin as well as in Tuscan. I remain silent because my intention here, as I have said, is to mention only those not only heard by me, but who have also flourished or are flourishing in Rome, since to search for all the others in the other cities and countries would be too much to do.

But where have I left the nuns, whom I should have named first, out of honor to them? La Verovia at Spirito Santo has stupefied the world for several years, nor have many years passed since that other nun and that lady, both students of hers I think, both sang with excellent charm in that same convent. Everyone knows how much fame the nun of Santa Lucia in Selce has.[26] Formerly people went out of wonderment to hear those of San Silvestro, now those of Monte Magnanapoli, those of Santa Chiara. The past era was never so rich, either in so many subjects, or such good ones at one time.

25. Margherita Basile (d. after 1636?) received an appointment at the imperial court in Vienna in 1631.
26. Anna Maria Cesi, who became a nun sometime between 1614, the year of her marriage to Prince Michele Peretti, and 1617, when a volume of spiritual monodies was dedicated to her.

5 Pierfrancesco Tosi

Pierfrancesco Tosi (1654–1732), a castrato, began his singing career in Italy and had moved by 1693 to London, where he sang public concerts and taught music. His volume on "ancient" and modern singers appeared in Italy just before he returned to London, having been on the road for twenty-three years as a political agent for the imperial court of the Hapsburgs. The treatise is often consulted for its explanations of appoggiaturas, trills, *passaggi,* the *messa di voce,* and other tools of the singer's trade, but all of Tosi's opinions are arguments against their abuse by younger singers and their teachers in contradistinction to the training and style that his generation represented. He decries the loss of lyric, *cantabile* singing to the virtuosity of modern, eighteenth-century pyrotechnics and the encroachments of the orchestra. Thus Tosi is an "ancient," trying to warn against what he hears as the excesses and imperfections of a new practice.

FROM *Observations on the Florid Song*
(1723)

Besides the errors in keeping time, there are other reasons, why a student should not imitate the modern gentlemen in singing arias, since it plainly appears that all their application now is to divide and subdivide in such a manner, that it is impossible to understand either words, thoughts, or modulation,[1] or to distinguish one aria from another, they singing them all so much alike, that, in hearing of one, you hear a thousand. —And must the *mode*[2] triumph? It was thought, not many years since, that in an opera, one rumbling aria full of divisions was sufficient for the most gurgling singer to spend his fire;[3] but the singers of the present time are not of that mind, but rather, as if they were not satisfied with transforming them all with a horrible metamorphosis into so many divisions, they, like racers, run full speed, with redoubled violence to their final cadences, to make reparation for the time they think they have lost during the course of the aria. . . .

I cannot positively tell, who that modern composer, or that ungrateful singer was, that had the heart to banish the delightful, soothing *pathetick*[4] from arias, as if no longer worthy of their commands, after having done them so long and pleasing service. Whoever he was, it is certain, he has deprived the profession of its most valuable excellence. Ask all the musicians in general, what their thoughts are of the *pathetick*, they all agree in the same opinion (a thing that seldom happens) and answer, that the *pathetick* is what is most delicious to the ear, what most sweetly affects the soul, and is the strongest basis of harmony. And must we be deprived of these charms, without knowing the reason why? Oh! I understand you: I ought not to ask the masters, but the audience, those capricious protectors of the *mode,* that cannot endure this; and herein lies my mistake. Alas! the mode and the multitude flow like torrents, which when at their height, having spent their violence, quickly disappear. The mischief is in the spring[5] itself; the fault is in the singers. They praise the *pathetick*, yet sing the *allegro*. He must want common sense who does not see through them. They know the first to be the most excellent, but they lay it aside, knowing it to be the most difficult.

TEXT: *Opinioni de' cantori antichi, e moderni o sieno osservazioni sopra il canto figurato* (Bologna, 1723; facs. ed. New York, 1968), from chap. 7, pp. 67–73, trans. [J. E.] Galliard, *Observations on the Florid Song; or, Sentiments on the Ancient and Modern Singers* (London, 1743; facs. Geneva, 1978), pp. 105–10; 112–17. Capitalization has been modernized. Some Italian words, such as *aria*, as well as some phrases that Galliard omitted, have been restored.

1. Nuances of phrasing and expression are more likely meant here, not "changes of key."
2. The word "mode" means "fashion" consistently, except at p. 46 below.
3. Those tremendous airs are called in Italian, *un' aria di bravura*, which cannot perhaps be better translated into English, than a *hectoring* song [Tr.].
4. Tosi's phrase is "l'amoroso patetico."
5. That is, the spring, or source of the water.

In former times divers arias were heard in the theatre in this delightful manner, preceded and accompanied with harmonious and well-modulated instruments, that ravished the senses of those who comprehended the contrivance and the melody; and if sung by one of those five or six eminent persons above-mentioned,[6] it was then impossible for a human soul not to melt into tenderness and tears from the violent motion of the affections. Oh! powerful proof to confound the idoliz'd *mode!* Are there in these times any, who are moved with tenderness, or sorrow? —No, (say all the auditors) no; for, the continual singing of the moderns in the *allegro* style, though when in perfection that deserves admiration, yet touches very slightly one that hath a delicate ear. The taste of those called the ancients was a mixture of the lively and the *cantabile,* the variety of which could not fail giving delight; but the moderns are so pre-possessed with taste in *mode,* that, rather than comply with the former, they are contented to lose the greatest part of its beauty. The study of the *pathetick* was the darling of the former; and application to the most difficult divisions is the only drift of the latter. Those perform'd with more judgment; and these execute with greater boldness. But since I have presum'd to compare the most celebrated singers in both styles, pardon me if I conclude with saying, that the moderns are arrived at the highest degree of perfection in singing to the ear; and that the ancients are inimitable in singing to the heart.

•   •   •   •   •

Gentlemen composers, (I do not speak to the eminent, but with all due respect) musick in my time has chang'd its style three times: the first which pleased on the stage, and in the chamber, was that of Pier. Simone, and of Stradella;[7] the second is of the best that are now living;[8] and I leave others to judge whether they be young and modern. But of your style, which is not quite established yet in Italy, and which has yet gained no credit at all beyond the Alps, those that come after us will soon give their opinion; for *modes* last not

6. Galliard, pp. 100–104, provides short biographical notices for Antonio Rivani, or Ciecolino; Francesco Pistocchi; "Sifacio," or Giovanni Francesco Grossi; Giovanni Buzzolini; Francesca Vanini, wife of bass Giuseppe Boschi; "La Santini," that is, Santa Stella, wife of composer Antonio Lotti; and the singer "Luigino," whose surname remains unknown.

7. Piersimone Agostini [d. 1680] lived about threescore years ago. Several cantatas of his composition are extant, some of them very difficult, not from the number of divisions in the vocal part, but from the expression, and the surprising incidents, and also the execution of the basses. He seems to be the first that put basses with so much vivacity; for Carissimi before him composed with more simplicity.[Tr.]

   Alessandro Stradella [1644–1682] lived about Piersimone's time, or very little after. He was a most excellent composer, superior in all respects to the foregoing, and endowed with distinguishing personal qualifications. It is reported that his favourite instrument was the harp, with which he sometimes accompanied his voice, which was agreeable. To hear such a composer play on the harp must have been what we can have no notion of, by what we now hear. [Tr.]

8. When Tosi writ this, the composers in vogue were [Alessandro] Scarlatti, [Giovanni] Bononcini, [Francesco] Gasparini, [Luigi] Mancini, &c. The last and modern stile has pretty well spread itself all over Italy, and begins to have a great tendency to the fame beyond the Alps, as he calls it. [Tr.]

long. But if the profession is to continue, and end with the world, either you yourselves will see your mistake, or your successors will reform it. Would you know how? By banishing the abuses, and recalling the first, second, and third mode,[9] to relieve the fifth, sixth, and eighth, which are quite jaded. They will revive the fourth and seventh now dead to you, and buried in churches, for the final closes. To oblige the taste of the singers and the hearers, the *allegro* will now and then be mixed with the *pathetick*. The arias will not always be drowned with the indiscretion of the instruments, that hide the artful delicacy of the *piano,* and the soft voices, nay, even all voices which will not bawl. They will no longer bear being teased with unisons,[10] the invention of ignorance, to hide from the vulgar the insufficiency and inability of many men and women singers. They will recover the instrumental harmony now lost. They will compose more for the voice than the instruments. The part for the voice will no more have the mortification to resign its place to the violins. The soprano's and contr'alto's will no more sing the arias in the manner of the bass, in spight of a thousand octaves; and finally, their arias will be more affecting, and less alike, more natural and more lyric, more studied, and less painful to the singer; and so much the more grand, as they are remote from the vulgar. But, methinks, I hear it said, that the theatrical licence is great, and that the *mode* pleases, and that I grow too bold. And may I not reply, that the abuse is even greater, that the invention is pernicious, and that my opinion is not singular?

9. The *modes* here spoken of, our author has not well explained. The foundation he goes upon are the eight Church modes. But his meaning and complaint is, that commonly the compositions are in C, or in A, with their transpositions, and that the others are not used or known. [Tr.]. Galliard's original term for "mode" is the English "Mood." He correctly recognizes Tosi's complaint that modern music uses only the major and minor modes. Tosi suggests the revival of the Dorian and Phrygian.

10. The arias, sung in unison with the instruments, were invented in the Venetian operas to please the *barcaroles* [gondoliers], who are their watermen; and very often their applause supports an opera. The Roman School always distinguished itself and required compositions of study and care. How it is now at Rome is doubtful; but we do not hear that there are any Corellis. [Tr.] On the gondoliers, see the account of St. Didier in No. 11, p. 69.

II

THE PROFESSION AND ITS INSTITUTIONS

6 Heinrich Schütz

Heinrich Schütz (1585–1672) published three volumes of *Symphoniae sacrae* in 1629, 1647 and 1650. With the presentation of the last volume to his patron and employer of thirty-six years, Johann Georg I, Elector of Saxony, he also requested that he either be allowed to retire from his position as director of music or be given an assistant to help him in his duties. This request of early 1651 shows the conventional outline of Schütz's career, from chorister to service through the Thirty Years' War for the same ruling prince. It also documents the composer's atypical university education, his musical studies in Venice, Schütz's humanist view of his "profession and position," and finally, his desire to complete the publication of his musical works. His request to retire was not granted. Upon the death of the Elector in 1656 the direction of music at Dresden was divided among three masters of the chapel, Schütz, Giovanni Andrea Bontempi, and Vincenzo Albrici, portending the domination by professional Italians that was to come.

Memorandum to the Elector of Saxony
(1651)

Most Illustrious, Noble Elector, Most Gracious Lord,

With the present most humble offering of my little work,[1] which has just appeared under Your Electoral Highness's exalted name, I am at the same time moved to touch somewhat briefly on the course of my rather troubled life from youth to the present, begging in deep devotion that Your Electoral Highness receive it graciously and, if you are not opposed, to examine it at your leisure. Namely: that (after I was born into this world on St. Burkhard's Day, 1585) not very long thereafter but as early as my thirteenth year of age, I left my late parents' house in Weissenfels, and from that time on always lived abroad, and at first in fact I served as a choirboy for several years in the court ensemble of my lord the Landgrave Moritz in Cassel, but I both lived and was educated in school, and learned Latin and other languages in addition to music.

And as it was never my late parents' wish that I should now or ever make a profession of music, after I lost my soprano voice, on their advice I betook myself to the University of Marburg (in the company of my second brother, who thereafter became a Doctor of Law and who died a few years ago in

TEXT: Gina Spagnoli, *Letters and Documents of Heinrich Schütz, 1656–1672: An Annotated Translation* (Ann Arbor, 1990; reissued Rochester: University of Rochester Press, 1994), pp. 119–31, which gives the original German and this translation by Spagnoli, reprinted here by courtesy of the University of Rochester Press. The autograph manuscript (facs. Leipzig, 1972) is in the Dresden State Archives.

1. His *Symphoniae sacrae*, op. 12.

Leipzig as a member of the Supreme Court of the Judicature and in Your Electoral Highness's employ). There I intended to pursue the studies I had extensively undertaken elsewhere outside of music to choose a reliable profession and therein attain an honorable station. However, my plan was soon altered for me (undoubtedly by the will of God), namely in that my lord the Landgrave Moritz came to Marburg one day (who may perhaps have observed at the time when I was allowed to serve as a choirboy at his court that in some respects I was musically gifted by nature) and made me the following proposal: Because at that time a truly celebrated but quite old musician and composer was still living in Italy, I should not miss the opportunity to hear him and to learn something from him, and the aforementioned His noble Grace generously offered me at the time a stipend of 200 talers[2] yearly to carry out such a journey, which proposal I thereupon accepted most willingly with humble thanks (as a youth eager to see the world), and in 1609 departed for Venice, contrary, however, to my parents' wishes. Upon my arrival (after I had spent a little time with my master), I soon realized the importance and difficulty of the study of composition which I had undertaken and what an unfounded and poor beginning I had made in it so far, and therefore I regretted very much having turned away from those studies which were customary at German universities and in which I had already become rather advanced. I nonetheless patiently submitted and had to apply myself to that which had brought me there. So from that time on, all my previous studies laid aside, I began to deal only with the study of music with the greatest of all possible diligence to see how I would succeed. Then, with divine help, I progressed so far, without boasting, that after three years (and one year before I returned from Italy) I had published there my first little musical work in the Italian language,[3] with superior praise from the most distinguished musicians then in Venice, whence I sent it to my lord the Landgrave Moritz (to whom I dedicated it with humble acknowledgment). After the publication of my first little work, mentioned above, I was urged and encouraged not only by my teacher, Giovanni Gabrieli, but also by the Capellmeister and other distinguished musicians there that I should persist in the study of music and that I should anticipate every auspicious success therein.

And after I remained there another year (although at the expense of my parents) to learn yet something further from my studies, it happened that my aforementioned teacher died in Venice, whom I also accompanied to his final resting place. On his deathbed, he also bequeathed to me out of special affection, in his blessed memory, one of his rings he left behind which was

---

2. One Hessian *taler* was worth 32 *albus*, while the florin was worth 26 *albus*. In 1605 another young musician was given four taler by Moritz to go to the Frankfurt fair. In the first half of the century, organists in the region received salaries from about 30 to 60 florins annually (see Klaus Steinhaüser, *Die Musik an den Hessen-Darmstädtischen Lateinschulen im 16. und 17. Jahrhundert* [Giessen, 1936], p. 36). A cow could cost about ten florins.

3. His *Primo libro de Madrigali* (Venice, 1611).

presented and delivered after his death by his father confessor, an Augustinian monk (from the cloister where Dr. Luther once stayed). Thus the aforesaid premonition of my lord the Landgrave Moritz in Marburg proved true, that whoever wished to learn something from this certainly very highly talented man need remain absent no longer than I.

When I then returned to Germany from Italy for the first time in 1613, I indeed resolved to keep to myself my musical foundations, by now well established for some years, and to keep them hidden until I had developed them somewhat further and thereupon could distinguish myself with the publication of a worthy piece of work. And also at that time, I was not lacking advice and incentive from my parents and relatives, whose opinion was, in short, that I should make use of my other truly modest abilities and strive for advancement, and should treat music, however, as an avocation. As a result of their repeated unremitting admonition, I was finally persuaded and was about to seek out my books which I had previously laid aside when God Almighty (who no doubt had singled me out in the womb for the profession of music) ordained that in 1614 I be called to service in Dresden for the then impending royal christening of my lord the Duke August, now administrator of the archbishopric of Magdeburg (I do not know whether perhaps through the advice of Christoph von Loss, then privy councillor, or of Chamber Counselor Wolffersdorff, also designated commander of Weissenfels). After my arrival and passing an audition, the directorship of your music was soon thereafter graciously offered to me in Your Electoral Highness's name, from which then my parents and relatives as well as I obviously perceived the immutable will of God regarding my person, and hereby a goal was set for my vacillating plans, and I was persuaded not to refuse the honored position offered me, but to accept with humble thanks and to vow to fulfill it with my best efforts.

I hope Your Electoral Highness will to some extent remember my truly insignificant duties, indeed performed not without difficulty since the year 1615 (the year in which I personally assumed this post, and, as long as it pleases God and Your Electoral Highness, I shall hold in the future) until now, and thus over thirty-five years.

And if I may go so far as to praise the charity and favor granted to me by God (over such a long time), along with my private studies and the publication of various works, I have most humbly served Your Electoral Highness at many past diverse festivities which occured during this time, at imperial, royal, electoral, and princely gatherings, in this country and abroad, but particularly at each and every one of your own royal children's weddings, not less, too, at the receiving of their sacred christenings (except for my lady, now the Landgravine of Darmstadt, and my lord the Duke Johann Georg, the elector apparent). From the beginning of my directorship of Your Electoral Highness's court ensemble, I have also always endeavored to spread its fame above all others in Germany to the best of my ability, and, I hope, have always devoted myself to help uphold its praise and fame in some measure even up to the present.

Now I would indeed gladly and sincerely hope that the course of Your Electoral Highness's court ensemble which I have tended up until now could be directed by me in the future; however, not only due to my ceaseless study, travel, writing, and other constant work, which has been, without boasting, continuous since my youth (which my arduous profession and position unavoidably require, the smallest difficulties and hardships of which, then, in my opinion, even our own scholars themselves are in fact unable to judge, because at our German universities such studies are not pursued) but also due to my now advancing old age, diminishing eyesight, and spent vitality, I am now unable to serve it suitably any longer, nor uphold my good name, which I gained to some extent in my youth. I in no way dare continue, nor can I attempt, unless I want to endanger my health and collapse ere long, the constant studying, writing, and contemplation, [from which,] according to the physician's advice, I must henceforth refrain and forbear as much as possible. Therefore, Your Electoral Highness, I hereby submit this for your gracious consideration with due humility, and moreover in most humble devotion I respectfully entreat you, may it please Your Grace (not only because of the reasons I have already cited, but also in consideration of the fact that Your Electoral Highness's most beloved royal children are now all married) to remove me in future to a somewhat calmer situation, and (in order that I might again collect and complete my musical works, begun in my youth, and have them published in my memory) to free me from steady service, and to the extent that pleases Your Electoral Highness, to have me recognized and declared, as it were, a pensioner, in which case I must perhaps accept the situation if Your Electoral Highness were to modify somewhat my present wages, if it please Your Grace.

Nevertheless, I am as willing as I am indebted (in that Your Electoral Highness is unwilling to spare me from your chapel and to employ another Capellmeister at this time, but will continue to be satisfied with the poor service which I will be able to offer in my daily waning strength), yet to persevere in being of all possible aid and to devote myself further to serving the title of [Capellmeister] (of Your Electoral Highness's honored house) and I would hope finally to take [that title] with me to my grave, only if in future (especially since all those old musicians with whom I first began my directorship thirty-five years ago are now all dead and the very few remaining, owing to physical infirmity and old age, are not particularly suited to further service) another qualified person may be allied with me to relieve me in my work, who could daily manage the young people now thriving in the electoral ensemble, continuing the necessary rehearsals, frequently organize the music, and conduct.

Whereas with the imminent waning of my strength yet further (if God should allow me to live still longer) it is perhaps possible that I will experience (if Your Electoral Highness will graciously pardon me for bringing this up) what has happened to one not poorly qualified old cantor, who lives in a noteworthy place and whom I know well, who for some time has written to me and complained bitterly that his young town councillors are quite dissatisfied with his old-fashioned music and therefore would like very much to be rid of him, saying intentionally to his face in the town hall that a tailor of thirty years and a cantor of thirty years are of no use to anyone. And although I am certain that the fact that the young world soon becomes weary of the old customs and ways and changes them is not without its advantages, and though to be sure I anticipate none of this from my lords the sons of Your Electoral Highness (as my gracious lords have treated me kindly), I could encounter it from some other newly arrived young musicians who, with the rejection of the old, usually give preference to all of their new ways, although for poor reasons.

And since my lord the Duke Johann Georg the elector apparent's Italian eunuch, [Giovanni] Andrea Bontempi,[4] has many times made it known that especially since his youth he has been more devoted to composition than to singing and he has volunteered out of his own free will that at my request he would always willingly serve in my place and direct the ensemble, I therefore wish at the conclusion of this writing of mine to Your Electoral Highness to discover and moreover to learn your most gracious opinion in this matter: Namely, whether I may, with your most gracious consent, offer and employ the aforementioned Andrea Bontempi and allow him frequently to direct the ensemble in my place? This, in my modest judgment, Your Electoral Highness (indeed subject to correction) should allow immediately, and could observe and listen awhile for a trial period, so to speak, since he does not seek a salary increase or a change of title for his service, but is willing to be as content one way as the other with the support ordered by his most gracious lord the elector apparent. This young man is thus willing and very well qualified for such work. He has also acquired satisfactory recommendations in Venice (he remained there for eight years) where for several holiday celebrations he often took the Capellmeister's place in publicly directing the music in their churches. Therefore there is little to doubt regarding his qualifications; besides, he seems then to be, in his other transactions, a discreet, polite, good-natured, fine young man. Regarding Your Electoral Highness's most gracious will in this matter, I request a most gracious report, since without Your Electoral Highness's prior knowledge, it would not be proper for me to make constant use of the services of such a person.

Commending you hereupon to the powerful protection of the Almighty for prolonged [and] complete bodily health, long life, blissful reign, and your every other hope for the well-being of body and soul, while [commending] myself to the constant electoral grace most humbly and obediently. Dated Dresden on the fourteenth day of January. In the year of Christ our only Redeemer and Savior, 1651.

> Your Electoral Highness's most
> humble duty-bound old servant,
> Heinrich Schütz, Capellmeister
> In his own hand

4. Giovanni Andrea Bontempi (1625–1705), was a castrato singer from the area of Perugia. Trained in Italy, he began his service in Dresden in 1651.

7 Francesco Coli

Francesco Coli, a priest from Lucca and censor for the Venetian Inquisition, began a series of monthly publications in 1687 titled *Pallade veneta,* a "collection of flowery and novel gallantries from the gardens of the Adriatic." It reported military news, especially of the war with the Turks, but also included essays, poetry, and news of social events and affairs. Its first year included musical scores of arias from current operas. Coli addressed his reports to people outside of the Veneto in the form of letters. Those from 1687 chosen here were addressed to a young lady, Angela Caterina Lupori, of Lucca. They vividly describe musical performances by the poor or orphaned young women living in the Venetian institutions known as *ospedali,* in terms that attempt to conflate virtuosity and virtue and define morally acceptable vehicles of esthetic pleasure.

FROM *Pallade veneta*

(1687)

[MAY 1687]

Since it is not ever my intention to recount the separate details about these sacred choirs of chaste maidens,[1] lack of time not permitting it, I will only tell you that at sung Vespers on the solemn feast of Pentecost at the Mendicanti, which was a banquet of delights for the ear, one tasted, among other savory compositions, a solo *Laudate pueri* delivered by Signora Tonina, one of the singing girls of this learned choir, who is called this out of endearment. It was accompanied by an ensemble of instruments and by a basso continuo and was so well counterpointed and diverse, that Apollo himself in Parnassus neither enjoys a more pleasing voice among his Muses nor hears, moreover, any plectrum more sweet than did those who enjoyed the excellent music in that church. This *virtuosa* has a voice that is a gift from nature and is so unaffected, mellifluous, artful, and expressive of the *affetti,* adorned with so much grace, and of a bearing so elegant, that she has no equal. Her *passaggi* are so skillful,

TEXT: Eleanor Selfridge-Field, ed., *Pallade Veneta: Writings on Music in Venetian Society. 1650–1750* (Venice: Edizioni Fondazione Levi, 1985), nos. 27, 35, 45; pp. 171–72; 175–78; 183–85. Translation by Margaret Murata.

1. The four charity *ospedali* of Venice, those of the Mendicanti, the Derelitti, the Pietà, and the Incurabili, stressed musical education for their female charges to the extent of becoming famous as conservatories. The singers and instrumentalists performed regularly for liturgical services and in public concerts, typically hidden from public view.

she descends, rises, turns, and soars over the grille with such command over the scales, that the birds themselves, who are lighter and poised on wings, are not such absolute masters of the air as she, when she passes through the musical skies without fear. When we got to those words of the psalm, *Matrem filiorum laetantem,*[2] she opened the richest musical treasures, dispersed the most prized goods of her art, and created a majestic display of as much as could be shown in this plentiful gallery of song. Now I see that in describing the stylish manner of this lady, I have tried Your Ladyship's patience, and instead of bringing you delight, I may have put you in despair. Let's then break off this talk, and I'll hold off to another letter describing the lascivious siren, who takes fresh air in the evening by the sea that laps beneath our balconies and lets loose the voices of Paradise, even though they come from the mouth of hell, for she is an angel in her voice and a fury in her ways.

• • •

[JULY 1687]

In this seminary of melodious angels[3] are around forty girls who are trained for use in the choir, some of whom sing and play every kind of musical instrument with such sweetness that they have no equal among the laity. The Apollo of this Parnassus of virtuosos is the most excellent Dr. Domenico Partenio,[4] vice–chapel master of the ducal chapel of San Marco, whose compositions are so attractive that, coupled with the sweetness of those voices from Paradise, their concerts are like those of seraphim. They sang a solemn Mass in which each of the girls could show her own talents; and to not repeat so many times the well-deserved praises of Signora Tonina, who could never be sufficiently raised to heaven with honors, I will say that we heard a solo motet from Signora Maria Anna Ziani, with those sweet ornaments and pleasing *portamenti* that she can offer to test the art of music. Although she is a woman, she enjoys a naturally masculine voice, but a tender one, full, and of a timbre so suave that she sings baritone with such grace that it carries you away and carries with itself the souls of them who hear it. The whole audience rippled at the falling and rising of her *passaggi*. She comforted us with her gladness and just as she has the ability to sow content in one's breast by trilling or simulating joy, she has equally at hand the keys to open a prison of torments, should she encounter the flat keys, the sharp keys, the short rests.[5] Beyond the particular grace of her singing, this woman also plays the violin with such skill and melody that I dare to say that if Eurydice had possessed even only half as much high

2. "And gladdens her heart with children," the last line of Psalm 112, the fourth psalm for Sunday Vespers.
3. Coli heard the women at the Mendicanti on the feast day of Saint Mary Magdalene.
4. Partenio (before 1650–1701), a singer and composer, wrote his first opera *Genserico* for Venice in 1669. He became vice–chapel master at St. Mark's in 1685 and became its *maestro* in 1692.
5. A general term for all rests shorter than the minim (half note) was "sospiro," or "sigh."

virtù,[6] Orpheus would not have had to go down to free her from the jaws of Hell.

•   •   •

[AUGUST 1687]

My Lady, I have several times described to Your Ladyship the Mendicanti, the [Derelitti] of Santi Giovanni e Paolo, and the Incurabili;[7] but I do not remember, if due to my negligence, whether I have ever mentioned the Pietà, which is not inferior to those that I have named. Here also is nurtured a seminary for girls in the art of music and of playing every desirable instrument, and their students become such vivacious and stylish singers that they astound even their own teachers in the art; nor do I believe that there is any other place better in terms of having a team of instruments more practiced or more learned.

Here on the 28th, the feast of Saint Augustine, they sang an oratorio so much to the people's satisfaction that I imagine it will be necessary to repeat it several times, since one hears that the nobility and the populace want to satisfy their ears. The poetry was by Signor Bernardo Sandrinelli and the music by Signor Don Giacomo Spada, organist at St. Mark's, who has so lively a spirit in his works that he concedes nothing to Cavalli, to Frescobaldi, nor to any among the most original who have united voices with strings. The title of the piece was noted as *St. Mary of Egypt, Penitent.* The characters were these given below:

> Santa Maria Egizziaca, portrayed by signora Lucretia
> First Angel, by signora Prudenza
> Second Angel, by signora Barbara
> Penitence, by signora Paolina
> The Narrator, by signora Lucietta
> Zosima, by signora Francesca

This last one, beyond her ability in singing, possesses superhuman qualities in playing the theorbo, and plays the lute so nobly that, after the first part of the oratorio, she swept the entire audience into ecstasies of admiration with the stylish *ricercate*[8] that she executed on the lute. Their singing was so pleasing, so clean in enunciation, that there was nothing to do but ask for more. The acclaim for their virtuoso style of performance has been so noised about that all the people are awaiting the day it will be repeated. You can tell what kinds of virtuous entertainments these noble lords amuse themselves with, of which, as patrons of the virtuosos, the *literati* have sung the glories in every age.

6. Literally, "virtue," but in classically influenced culture, the word conflates moral character with superior merit and abilities, from which sense "virtuoso" descends.
7. See note 1 above.
8. Improvised music.

8 Johann Sebastian Bach

Johann Sebastian Bach (1685–1750) gained his appointment in 1723 as cantor of the St. Thomas School and director of music in Leipzig. His duties included teaching Latin (for which he hired a deputy), training the four choirs of schoolboys, giving instrumental lessons to the most musical, and providing music for four of the city's churches and for its civic occasions. In a period of transition after the headmaster of the school died in 1729, the town council's accumulated complaints about Bach were aired, as were, in turn, Bach's dissatisfactions with the conditions of his position. After having met his obligations as composer, director, and teacher for seven years, Bach finally stated his requirements for performing contemporary concerted church music in a memorandum to the council, which was, characteristically, ignored.

Short but Most Necessary Draft for a Well-Appointed Church Music
With Certain Modest Reflections on the Decline of the Same (1730)

A well-appointed church music requires vocalists and instrumentalists.

The vocalists in this place are made up of the pupils of the Thomas-Schule, being of four sorts, namely, sopranos [*Discantisten,*] altos, tenors, and basses.

In order that the choruses of church pieces may be performed as is fitting, the vocalists must in turn be divided into 2 sorts, namely, concertists and ripienists.

The concertists are ordinarily 4 in number, sometimes also 5, 6, 7, even 8, that is, if one wishes to perform music for two choirs [*per choros*].

The ripienists, too, must be at least 8, namely, two for each part.

The instrumentalists are also divided into various kinds, namely, violinists [*Violisten*][1] oboists, flutists, trumpeters, and drummers. N.B. The violinists include also those who play the violas, the violoncellos, and the *violones*.

The number of the *Alumni* [resident students] of the St. Thomas School is 55. These 55 are divided into 4 choirs, for the 4 churches in which they must partly perform concerted music with instruments [*musiciren*] partly sing motets, and partly sing chorales. In the 3 churches, St. Thomas's, St. Nicholas's,

---

Text: Hans T. David and Arthur Mendel, eds., *The New Bach Reader: A Life of Johann Sebastian Bach In Letters and Documents*, rev. and enl. by Christoph Wolff (New York: Norton, 1998).

1. That is, string players.

and the New Church, the pupils must all be musical. St. Peter's receives the residue [*Ausschuss*] namely, those who do not understand music and can only just barely sing a chorale.

Every musical choir should contain at least 3 sopranos, 3 altos, 3 tenors, and as many basses, so that even if one happens to fall ill (as very often happens, particularly at this time of year, as the prescriptions written by the school physician for the apothecary must show) at least a double-chorus motet may be sung. (N.B. Though it would be still better if the group were such that one could have 4 subjects on each voice and thus could provide every choir with 16 persons.) Hence, the number of those who must understand music comes to 36 persons.

The *instrumental music* consists of the following parts, namely:

2 or even 3 for the	*violin 1*
2 or 3 for the	*violin 2*
2 for the	*viola 1*
2 for the	*viola 2*
2 for the	*violoncello*
1 for the	*violon[e]*
2, or, if the piece requires, 3, for the	*oboe*
1, or even 2, for the	*bassoon*
3 for the	*trumpets*
1 for the	*kettledrums*

summa 18 persons at least, for the instrumental music

N.B. If it happens that the church piece is composed with flutes also (whether they are recorders [*à bec*] or transverse flutes, [*Traversieri*]), as very often happens for variety's sake, at least 2 more persons are needed, making altogether 20 instrumentalists.

The number of persons appointed to play church music is 8, namely, 4 town pipers [*Stadt Pfeifer*], 3 professional fiddlers [*Kunst Geiger*], and one apprentice. Modesty forbids me to speak at all truthfully of their qualities and musical knowledge. Nevertheless it must be remembered that they are partly *emeriti* and partly not at all in such practice [*exercitio*] as they should be.[2]

This is the plan for them:

Mr. Reiche	for the	1st *trumpet*
Mr. Genssmar	————	2nd *trumpet*
vacant	————	3rd *trumpet*
vacant	————	kettledrums
Mr. Rother	————	1st *violin*
Mr. Beyer	————	2nd *violin*
vacant	————	viola
vacant	————	violoncello
vacant	————	violon[e]

2. Two of the town musicians were past retirement age and were not in such good practice.

Mr. Gleditsch	——	1st *oboe*
Mr. Kornagel	——	2nd *oboe*
vacant	——	3rd *oboe* or *taille*
The Apprentice	——	*bassoon*

Thus there are lacking the following most necessary players, partly to reinforce certain voices, and partly to supply indispensable ones, namely:

2 *violinists* for the 1st *violin*
2 *violinists* for the 2nd *violin*
2 that play the *viola*
2 *violoncellists*
1 *violonist*
2 for the *flutes*

The lack that shows itself here has had to be supplied hitherto partly by the students [*studiosi*],[3] but mostly by the *alumni*.[4] Now, the *studiosi* have shown themselves willing to do this in the hope that one or the other would in time receive some kind of reward and perhaps be favored with a *stipendium* or *honorarium* (as was indeed formerly the custom). But since this has not occurred, but on the contrary, the few slight *beneficia* formerly devoted to the *chorus musicus* have been successively withdrawn, the willingness of the *studiosi,* too, has disappeared; for who will do work or perform services for nothing? Be it furthermore remembered that, since the 2nd *violin* usually, and the *viola, violoncello,* and *violone* always (in the absence of more capable subjects) have had to be played by students, it is easy to estimate how much the chorus has been deprived of in consequence. Thus far only the Sunday music has been touched upon. But if I should mention the music of the Holy Days (on which days I must supply both the principal churches with music), the deficiency of indispensable players will show even more clearly, particularly since I must give up to the other choir all those pupils who play one instrument or another and must get along altogether without their help.

Moreover, it cannot remain unmentioned that the fact that so many poorly equipped boys, and boys not at all talented for music, have been accepted[5] to date has necessarily caused the music to decline and deteriorate. For it is easy to see that a boy who knows nothing of music and who cannot indeed even form a second in his throat can have no natural musical talent, and *consequenter* can never be used for the musical service. And that those who do bring a few precepts with them when they come to school are not ready to be used immediately, as is required. For there is no time to instruct such pupils first for years until they are ready to be used, but on the contrary: as soon as they are accepted they are assigned to the various choirs and they must at least

3. Students of the University of Leipzig. [Tr.]
4. The younger resident pupils of the St. Thomas School.
5. Accepted into the school. [Tr.]

be sure of *measure,* and *pitch* in order to be of use in divine service. Now, if each year some of those who have accomplished something *in musicis* leave the school and their places are taken by others who either are not yet ready to be used or have no ability whatsoever, it is easy to understand that the *chorus musicus* must decline.

For it is notorious that my honored predecessors, Messrs. Schell[e] and Kuhnau, already had to rely on the help of the *studiosi* when they wished to produce a complete and well-sounding music which, indeed, they were enabled to this extent to do, that not only some vocalists, namely, a bass, a tenor, and even an alto, but also instrumentalists, especially two violinists, were favored with separate *stipendia* by A Most Noble and Most Wise Council and thus encouraged to reinforce the musical performances in the churches. Now, however, that the state of music is quite different from what it was, since our artistry has increased very much and the taste [*gusto*] has changed astonishingly, and accordingly the former style of music no longer seems to please our ears, considerable help is therefore all the more needed to choose and appoint such musicians as will satisfy the present musical taste, master the new kinds of music, and thus be in a position to do justice to the composer and his work. Now the few *beneficia,* which should have been increased rather than diminished, have been withdrawn entirely from the *chorus musicus.* It is, anyhow, somewhat strange that German musicians are expected to be capable of performing at once and *ex tempore* all kinds of music, whether it come from Italy or France, England or Poland, just as may be done, say, by those virtuosos for whom the music is written and who have studied it long beforehand, indeed, know it almost by heart, and who—it should be noted—receive good salaries besides, so that their work and industry is thus richly rewarded, while, on the other hand, these things are not taken into consideration, but they[6] are left to look out for their own wants, so that many a one, for worry about his bread, cannot think of improving—let alone distinguishing—himself. To illustrate this statement with an example one need only go to Dresden and see how the musicians there are paid by His Royal Majesty. It cannot fail, since the musicians are relieved of all concern for their living, free from *chagrin* and obliged each to master but a single instrument; it must be something choice and excellent to hear. The conclusion is accordingly easy to draw: that with the stopping of the *beneficia* the powers are taken from me to bring the music into a better state.

In conclusion I find it necessary to append the enumeration of the present *alumni,* to indicate the skill of each *in musicis* and thus to leave it to riper reflection whether in such circumstances the music can continue to be maintained, or whether its still greater decline is to be feared. It is, however, necessary to divide the whole group into three classes.

Accordingly those who are usable are as follows:

6. That is, German musicians. [Tr.]

(1) Pezold, Lange, Stoll, *Praefecti.* Frick, Krause, Kittler, Pohlreüter, Stein, Burckhard, Siegler, Nitzer, Reichhard, Krebs *major* and *minor,* Schöne- mann, Heder, and Dietel.

The names of the motet singers, who must first have further training in order to be used eventually for concerted music [*Figural Musik*], are as follows:

(2) Jänigke, Ludewig *major* and *minor,* Meissner, Neücke *major* and *minor,* Hillmeyer, Steidel, Hesse, Haupt, Suppius, Segnitz, Thieme, Keller, Röder, Ossan, Berger, Lösch, Hauptmann, and Sachse.

Those of the last sort are not *musici* at all, and their names are:

(3) Bauer, Gross, Eberhard, Braune, Seyman, Tietze, Hebenstreit, Wintzer, Össer, Leppert, Haussius, Feller, Crell, Zeymer, Guffer, Eichel, and Zwicker.

Total: 17 usable, 20 not yet usable, and 17 unfit.

Leipzig, August 23, 1730

Joh. Seb. Bach
Director Musices

9 Geronimo Lappoli and Anna Renzi

The institution of the Venetian opera house financed principally by subscribers made possible the new musical profession of the freelance opera singer. The Teatro Novissimo (The Newest Theater) was the first theater in Venice built to be devoted exclusively to opera. Geronimo Lappoli undertook four or five operatic seasons in the leased venue, defaulting on payments for the site in 1645. The Roman soprano Anna Renzi performed there in 1641 and 1642. The following year she sang in two operas at the Teatro Grimani (one role was that of Ottavia in Monteverdi's *Coronation of Poppea*) and returned to the Novissimo in 1644 and 1645. The contract between impresario and singer for Renzi to sing the title role in *Deidamia,* whose score is lost, reveals succinctly the legal expectations and perquisites on both sides. The opera opened less than a month after this contract was signed, on January 5, 1644.

Contract for the 1644 Season at the Teatro Novissimo

(1643)

Thursday, the seventeenth of the month of December 1643, at the residence of the below-mentioned Signora Anna near San Giovanni in Bragora.

The Most Illustrious Signor Geronimo Lappoli having requested the consent of the Most Illustrious Signora Anna Renzi to favor his theater called the Novissimo near SS. Giovanni et Paolo with her merit by performing in the operas, one or more, that will be given in said theater this coming carnival season, and, also due to the mediation of certain gentlemen, to which she has agreed, on the authority of the present instrument said Signora Anna for her part and said Signor Lappoli on the other do declare and agree upon the following, that is:

That said Signora Anna is obligated, as pledged, to perform in one or more operas that will be given in said Teatro Novissimo this coming Carnival, participating in every rehearsal of these very operas, only, however, those done in the theater or in the residence of Signora Anna herself.

Against this said Signor Geronimo promises to give to said Signora Anna 500 silver Venetian *scudi* cash[1] in this manner: that is, 100 *scudi* for all the present month of December, another 150 at the second performance, another 150 after half the performances, and at the next to last performance the remaining 100 *scudi*, without any opposition or delay.

And in case (God forbid) said Signora Anna should take ill after some of the performances have been done, in such case said Signora Anna may not claim other than one half of above-said 500 *scudi;* but if for any other cause or circumstance, nothing [else] excepted, Signor Lappoli should be prevented from presenting the show, he is held in such case to give her the 500 *scudi* in the manner above.

In addition, Signor Lappoli is held in any case to give and consign to her a box for her use for all of Carnival, and further [he must provide] all the costumes that must serve for the performances for said Signora Anna, completely at the expense of Signor Lappoli himself, which costumes will then remain with

---

TEXT: The text of the original document (Venice, Archivio di Stato, Archivio notarile, Acts of Fr. Beatian, *busta* 658, fols. 163v–164v) is given in Beth Glixon, "Private Lives of Public Women: *Prime donne* in Mid-Seventeenth-Century Venice," *Music and Letters* 76 (1995): 509–31, where portions are also given in English. The present translation is by Margaret Murata.

1. One Venetian silver *scudo* was worth 9 *lire* and 6 *soldi* in 1635 (with 20 *soldi* to a *lira*). The large sum of 500 silver *scudi* or 4,650 *lire* promised to Renzi may be compared with the 300 ducats (the equivalent of 1,920 Venetian *lire*) granted in 1643 as annual salary to Monteverdi's successor as chapel master at St. Mark's in Venice.

above-mentioned Signor Lappoli, all for which said Signor Geronimo pledges himself and his goods of all kinds, present and future.

As greater security for Signora Anna, present, with respect to the above-said matters, the excellent Signor Giosef Camis, Jewish physician, also present in person, does constitute himself and his heirs and successors guarantor, fidejussor,[2] and principal payor either for these 500 *scudi* or for that part which might be owed to said Signora Anna as stated above, as well as for every other obligation of said Signor Lappoli included in the present instrument, for which he pledges himself with his goods of all kinds, present and future.

Item, said Signor Geronimo promises to give to the Most Illustrious Signor Filiberto Laurenzi sixty silver *scudi* for which he is obligated to play in the rehearsals as well as in all the operas that will be given in above-said theater in the coming Carnival.

Item, to the same, another 25 *scudi* to teach the musicians, [and for] the prologue, and *intermedi*,[3] as said Signor Filiberto here present promises to perform in said capacities, as it has been agreed to above, etc.

Witnesses: The Most Illustrious Lord Francesco Michiel, son of the late
Most Illustrious Lord Antonio.
Lord Giorgio Giorgi [son of] the late Lord Antonio, Roman

2. In civil law, one who provides surety for another.
3. In other words, as a performer Laurenzi would participate in rehearsals and help prepare performers; as a composer he would provide the music for the prologue and *intermedi* (and earn a total of 85 *scudi*, or 790 *lire*, 10 *soldi*).

10 Evrard Titon du Tillet

In 1697 Evrard Titon du Tillet (1677–1762) purchased the office of first steward in the household of the twelve-year-old Duchess of Burgundy, newly married to the heir presumptive to the throne of his grandfather, the "Sun King" Louis XIV. The duchess became a constant delight of the monarch's last years. In 1708 Titon commissioned a colossal bronze sculpture that honored the great poets and musicians of the reign of the Sun King. A seven-and-one-half-foot model in bronze of the *Parnassus of France* was completed by 1718, though by then the duchess, her husband, and Louis XIV had all died. In hopes of gaining patrons to execute the sixty-foot monument, Titon published a description of the project in 1727 that gives invaluable biographical and bibliographic entries for the multitude of figures and ninety lesser ones to be portrayed in the sculpture. The musician with the highest place in this Parnassus was, of course, Jean-Baptiste Lully (1632–1687).

The final work was never cast, and Titon continued to expand the description of the *Parnassus of France* in book form. The 1732 edition offers 259 entries. His eulogies memorialized many writers and musicians that he knew of or had known personally. A supplementary essay to the 1743 edition, "The Famous Actors and Actresses of the Comedy and Opera, Whom Death Has Taken or Who Have Left the Theater," begins by recounting the life of Marie Le Rochois (c.1658–1728) a soprano whom he had heard perform in his youth. Titon's praise of Le Rochois conveys the expressive intensity he remembered in Lully's operas and indicates the high level of social esteem that a theatrical singer could achieve.

FROM THE First Supplement to *The Parnassus of France*
(1743)

I will begin the illustrious Mademoiselle Marie Rochois,[1] born of a good family of Caen, but little favored by the blessings of fortune, which thus obliged her, having come to Paris, to enter the Opéra in 1678, where Lully admitted her for the beauty of her voice. She began to distinguish herself in the role of Arethuse in the opera *Proserpine*[2] in 1680 and became in short time the greatest performer and the most perfect model for declamation who had appeared on stage. . . . She played heroines' roles and [Lully] often attributed to her the success of his operas. Indeed, beyond all the talents that she had for singing and for declamation, which she possessed in the highest degree, she had a great deal of the wit, knowledge and acuteness of any woman, and excellent and most unerring taste. If she surpassed herself in any one thing, it was, in my opinion, in her acting and in her expressive and striking *tableaux* in the roles she played, with which she delighted all her spectators. Even though she was fairly short, very dark, and looked very ordinary outside of the theater, with eyes close together which were, however, large, full of fire, and capable of expressing all the passions, she effaced all the most beautiful and more attractive actresses when she was on stage. She had the air of a queen and of a divinity, the head nobly placed, an admirable carriage, with all her movements beautiful, appropriate and natural. She understood marvelously well that which is called the *ritournelle*, which is played while the actress enters and presents herself to the audience, as in pantomime; in the silence, all the feelings and passions should be painted on the performer's face and be seen in her move-

---

TEXT: *Le Parnasse françois suivi des Remarques sur la poësie et la musique* (Geneva: Slatkine Reprints, 1971); facs. of eds. 1732–43, pp. 790–95. Translation by Margaret Murata.

1. In modern sources she is also called Marie Le Rochois and, erroneously, Marthe Le Rochois.
2. The ninth opera by Jean-Baptiste Lully; libretto by Philippe Quinault.

ments, something that great actors and actresses have not often understood. When she would become passionate and sing, one would notice only her on the stage. This struck me especially in the opera *Armide*,[3] in which she played the greatest and most powerful role in all our operas. She appeared in its first act between two of the most beautiful and imposing actresses ever seen on the stage, Mesdemoiselles Moreau and Desmatins,[4] who served her as confidantes and who sought to alleviate the sadness in which she appeared to be immersed. They sang to her these verses

> On a day of triumph, and in the midst of pleasure
> who could cause within you such melancholy gloom!
> All glory, greatness, and beauty with youthful bloom
> now fulfill your desires beyond measure.
> . . . .
> In Hell you have come to extend your hand as law;
> defenseless against you is every valiant knight,
> fallen before the force of your might, etc.[5]

At the moment in which Mademoiselle Rochois opened her arms and lifted her head with a majestic air, singing,

> Triumphed I have not o'er the most valorous of all,
> The invincible Renaud by my wrath has yet to fall.

these two confidantes were, in a manner of speaking, eclipsed. We saw only her on the stage and she alone seemed to fill it. And in what rapture we were in the fifth scene of the second act of the same opera, to see the dagger in her hand, ready to pierce the breast of Renaud, as he slept on his bed of grass! Fury animated her face, love seized her heart. Now one, now the other agitated her in turn; pity and tenderness succeeded them in the end, and love finished the victor. What beautiful and true bearing! What movements and different expressions in her eyes and on her face during this monologue of twenty-nine lines, which begins with these two

> Finally he is in my power,
> This mortal enemy, this haughty conqueror.[6]

One may say that this is the greatest piece in all our opera and the most difficult to deliver well, and it was one in which Mademoiselle Rochois shone the most, just as in the one at the end of the same opera where she sang

3. First performed in Paris in 1686, libretto by Quinault with music by Lully.
4. Fanchon Moreau (1668–after 1743); the Christian name of the soprano Desmatins (fl. 1682–c. 1708) is unknown.
5. These are the opening lines of the opera, act 1, scene 1, sung by Phenice, with a later speech sung by Sidonie. Titon's text varies from that in Robert Eitner's musical edition in *Publikation älterer praktischer und theoretischer Musikwerke*, vol. 14 (Leipzig: Breitkopf und Härtel, 1885). Titon's next quotation, of Armide's first words, immediately follows.
6. "Enfin il est en ma puissance," act 2, scene 5; a reprint of Eitner's edition of this scene is available in the *Norton Anthology of Music*, ed. by Claude V. Palisca, 3d ed. (New York, Norton, 1996), vol. 1, pp. 401–7.

The trait'rous Renaud flees from me,[7] etc.

It suffices to cite the opera *Armide* without enlarging upon the other operas of Lully in which she enchanted the spectators in the leading roles that she sang.

This great actress, sensing her voice and her powers diminishing due to the great efforts that she had made in 1697 when she had sung in the opera *Armide,* asked to retire in 1698, after having appeared in the first performance of the ballet *L'Europe galante* with music by Campra. The king granted her a pension of 1500 *livres*[8] from the Opéra, which, when added to a smaller one from the Duke of Sully, made it possible for her to live like a true *philosophe,* passing part of the year in a little country house that she had in Certrouville-sur-Seine, four leagues from Paris. Several great musicians, actors, and actresses, and other individuals of spirit and talent betook themselves to visit her with great pleasure during the time she was in Paris and profited from her amiable society, her knowledge and her good taste. She died there in a small apartment on the rue St. Honoré, near the Palais Royale,[9] on October 9, 1728, at about seventy years of age.

7. Act 5, scene 5, Armide's final soliloquy and the last scene of the opera.
8. In 1700, a standard unit (*voie*) of firewood for heating cost about 10.56 Parisian *livres;* in the year Le Rochois died, it had risen to 14 *livres.*
9. The Opéra was located here.

11 Alexandre-Toussaint Limojon, Sieur de Saint-Didier

The French nobleman Saint-Didier spent the years 1672–74 in Venice. Struck by the uniqueness of Venetian society and government, he began to write a thorough history of the republic and its people. However with the appearance in 1675 of the massive *History of the Government of Venice* by A.-N. Amelot de la Houssaie, a former secretary in the French embassy to Venice, Saint-Didier revised his project. He covered Venetian history and its government in parts 1 and 2, which he followed with observations on "the manner of living and customs of the Venetians." He wrote in his preface (in the language of the 1699 English translation), "I cannot think them less different from the other parts of Europe, than the Kingdom of China is from that part of France." In part 3, his preface continues, he aimed to describe "the conduct of the young nobility, with their particular customs. And the better to shew all the singularities of them, there is the manner of living of almost all the different degrees of people;

. . . [and] an exact description of all the publick diversions of Venice, to shew the mighty difference, between the relish of this people, and those of other nations." Those diversions included the Venetian public opera, which Saint-Didier duly compared with the court operas of Jean-Baptiste Lully.

FROM *The City and Republic of Venice*
(1680)

PART THREE: OF THE CUSTOMS AND MANNER OF LIVING OF THE VENETIAN GENTLEMEN AND LADIES, AS LIKEWISE OF OTHER SECULAR AND REGULAR PERSONS, WITH THE DESCRIPTION OF THE PUBLIC DIVERSIONS OF VENICE

OF THE OPERA

The invention of operas is due to the city of Venice. Although they were formerly particularly fine, yet Paris at present surpasses whatever can be seen here of this nature. It was not at first imagin'd that these compositions could agree with the genius of the French language, which is almost natural to the Italian; and in reality, if it had not been for that able master who first undertook it, who was no less familiar with all the beauties of the Italian musick, than with those delicacies of the French,[1] if it had not been, I say, for his great experience, in making those agreeable compositions which are sung in two such different ways, it may be believed, that this noble and magnificent diversion would not have been attended with that success which it has since had both at court and in town.

At Venice they act in several operas at a time.[2] The theaters are large and stately, the decorations [*décors*] noble and the alterations of them good. But they are very badly illuminated; the machines are sometimes passable and as often ridiculous; the number of actors is very great, they are all very well in clothes, but their actions are most commonly disagreeable.[3] These operas are long, yet they would divert the four hours which they last, if they were compos'd by better poets, that were a little more conversant with the rules of the

---

TEXT: *La Ville et la république de Venise* (Paris: C. Barbin, 1680), pt. 3, pp. 417–23; translation by F. Terne, *The City and Republick of Venice* (London: Char. Brome, 1699), pt. 3, pp. 60–65; capitalization and punctuation have been modernized. For the French text see H. Becker, ed., *Quellentexte zur Konzeption der europäischen Oper im 17. Jahrhundert* (Kassel: Bärenreiter, 1981), pp. 83–85.

1. Lully's name appears in the margin (it is not in the French edition). In 1675 Lully had presented four operas, by 1680, nine.
2. That is, several theaters were offering operas during the same weeks.
3. St. Didier refers to the theaters themselves, the stage sets and set changes, lighting, stage machines, costumes, and, probably, Italian stage gestures.

theater. For in this matter their present compositions are very deficient, inso-much they are frequently not worth the expence that is made upon them. The ballets or dancings between the acts are generally so pittiful, that they would be much better omitted; for one would imagine these dancers wore lead in their shoes. Yet the assembly bestow their applauses on them, which is meerly for want of having seen better.

The charms of their voices do make amends for all imperfections. These men without beards have delicate voices, besides which they are admirably suitable to the greatness of the theater.[4] They commonly have the best women singers of all Italy, for to get a famous girl from Rome or any other place, they do not scruple at giving four or five hundred pistoles,[5] with the charges of the journey, and yet their operas last no longer than the Carnival.[6] Their airs are languishing and touching; the whole composition is mingl'd with agreeable songs, that raise the attention. The symphony is mean,[7] inspiring rather melan-choly than gaiety. It is compos'd of lutes, theorbos and harpsicords, yet they keep time to the voices, with the greatest exactness imaginable.

If the French have at first some difficulty to understand their words, the Italians and all other strangers have much more trouble in France, where they do not only sing lower,[8] but pronounce their words with much less distinction. The great chorus of musick that so often fills the French theater, of which one indeed can hardly distinguish the words, is very disagreeable to the Italians, who say that this is much more proper to the Church than the stage, as likewise that the great number of violins[9] spoils the symphony of the other musick, which they think can be only agreeable to the French, unless it is when they play alone in other occasions.[10] Although they allow the French to succeed very well in their dances, yet they are of the opinion, that there are too many of them in their operas, whose compositions are likewise too short for their fan-cies,[11] which they think are not sufficiently fill'd with intrigues. Their composi-tions are always concluded with the character of an old woman that gives good advice to the young, but falling in love herself without any probability of a return, she runs into the repetition of a great many pleasant fancies.

They that compose the musick of the opera endeavour to conclude the

---

4. The "voix argentines" or "silvered voices" of the castrati were able to fill the theaters with sound.
5. A term used for the French gold *louis*, which as of 1679 were in fact minted from Spanish coins in circulation. At this time its value wavered between ten and eleven Parisian *livres*, but it is unclear whether St. Didier is converting Venetian into French values in his report.
6. The Carnival season, which began sometime after Christmas and ended at Lent.
7. That is, the orchestra is small.
8. More softly.
9. This term includes all the strings.
10. The Italians complain of the French orchestra, except in purely instrumental music because, due to its size, its sound covers the voices.
11. "Compositions" here refers to the parts of the dramatic plot, not to musical numbers. The Italians preferred librettos in which multiple plots are intertwined.

scenes of the principal actors with airs that charm and elevate, that so they may acquire the applause of the audience, which succeeds so well to their intentions, that one hears nothing but a thousand "Benissimos" together. Yet nothing is so remarkable as the pleasant benedictions and the ridiculous wishes of the gondoliers in the pit to the women singers, who cry aloud to them, "Sia tu benedetta, benedetto el padre che te generò."[12] But these acclamations are not always within the bounds of modesty, for those impudent fellows say whatever they please, as being assur'd to make the assembly rather laugh than angry.

Some gentlemen have shewn themselves so transported and out of all bounds by the charming voices of these girls, as to bend themselves out of their boxes crying, "Ah cara! mi butto, mi butto,"[13] expressing after this manner the raptures of pleasure which these divine voices cause to them. I need not omit the priests in this place, for according to the example of Rome, they are no ways scrupulous of appearing upon the stage in all manner of parts, and by acquiring the character of a good actor they commonly get that of an honest man.[14] I remember once, that one of the spectators discerning a priest in the disguise of an old woman, cry'd aloud, "Ecco, Padre Pierro, che fa la vecchia."[15] Nevertheless all things pass with more decency at the opera than at the comedy,[16] as being most commonly frequented by the better sort of people. One pays four *livres* at the door, and two more for a chair in the pitt, which amounts to three shillings and sixpence English,[17] without reckoning the opera-book and the wax-candle every one buys; for without them even those of the country would hardly comprehend any thing of the history,[18] or the subject matter of the composition.

The *gentledonnas* frequent the opera much more than the comedy, by reason the diversions of that place are express'd with more civility than those of the other. As they are at this time allowed to dress with their jewels,[19] so they appear most splendidly by the means of the many lighted tapers which are in those boxes. Here their lovers are employed in the contemplation of their charms, and they on their side, shew by some signs that they are pleas'd with the assiduity of their services. Whenever a new girl appears to sing at the opera, the principal nobles esteem it a point of honour to be master of her, and if she sings well they spare nothing that may accomplish the design of getting her.

12. "Bless you, blessed be the father that conceived you!"
13. "O sweetheart! I'm going to jump, I'm going to jump."
14. Acquiring reputations as good actors gains them respect as men.
15. "Look, Father Peter's playing the old lady!"
16. Than in the spoken theater.
17. Forty-six French *sols*, which in terms of prices in Paris was the average price between 1670 and 1680 for about a hundred eggs.
18. The background events of the plot and the identification of the characters are often provided in librettos.
19. At various times Venetians were subject to sumptuary laws that affected the kinds of luxury items, or the materials of which they were made, that could be worn in public.

One of the Cornaros[20] was upon one of these occasions rival to the Duke of Mantua; they both endeavour'd to exceed each other in their presents, yet the charms of her voice were not accompanied with all those of beauty. The Venetian was successful and got the better of the Duke.

The owners of these admirable female singers print a great many songs[21] in praise of 'em, which are scatter'd up and down the pit and boxes, when any of 'em acquire the general applause of the audience.

20. The Venetian Cornaro (or Corner) family amassed immense wealth in the fourteenth century from their already considerable capital, by establishing sugar plantations on Cyprus, worked by slaves. They continued to hold the highest offices in Venetian government in the seventeenth and eighteenth centuries.
21. Sonnets; for a sampling see Lowell E. Lindgren and Carl B. Schmidt, "A Collection of 137 Broadsides Concerning Theatre in Late Seventeenth-Century Italy: An Annotated Catalogue," *Harvard Library Bulletin* 28 (1980):185–233.

12 "The Truthful Reporter"

The Roman Teatro delle Dame (Theater of the Ladies) opened in 1726 with the first performance in Rome of a libretto by Pietro Metastasio (to music by Leonardo Vinci). Another Roman opera house, the Teatro Argentina, was built in 1731 and is still in use today. In a series of letters, an opera lover who signed himself "Il relator sincero" left firsthand accounts of this flourishing time for new opera. They reveal what was important to a successful production, what strengths and weaknesses were noted in singers, how new music was assessed, and how vital it was to have good orchestral writing. His letters reveal the high expecta-tions of the audience, especially in the Italians' love of complex plots and their demand for the dramatic integration of characterization, dancing, and musical style. In these two letters to an unknown and possibly fictitious "friend," the writer discusses operas by the Neapolitan Gaetano Latilla (1711–1788) and the Venetian Baldassare Galuppi (1706–1785). Then, as now, the opera season began after the Christmas holidays and ran through Carnival, with each theater usually mounting two works.

Two Letters on Opera in Rome

Rome, January 30, 1739

Dearest Friend,

Being obliged to satisfy your desire to know in detail the outcome, happy or unfortunate, of the operas in our theaters, I attended the staging of the second opera in the Teatro Alibert[1] entitled more truthfully, *Romolo,* or otherwise, *The Rape of the Sabine Women;* and telling you the title, I might as well speak of the libretto. It was damned by all. People say it is lacking in intrigue, which is what allows for surprise, and since it has in consequence no tumultuous actions, it cannot arouse the emotions of the people, which is the most necessary part of theater. The roles were not consistent at all; the versification most uneven in style and not lacking in many errors of language and diction.

The music of Signor Latilla[2] in the first act and part of the second is wondrously beautiful, both for its ideas and for the expression of feeling, and also for the impressive and novel harmony. On top of this, it appears competent, but without much flavor, and this, as far as people are saying, is not just because the libretto has become an oratorio and so is unsuitable to fire the inspiration of a composer, who can't extract manna from stones, but it is also because he himself wanted to vary his style and give a sample of himself to the canons of Santa Maria Maggiore where he is the designated maestro. He has written *a cappella,* whereupon begin the yawns in the audience, produced by the boredom that extended up till the chorus. It is said that the disaster of the second and third acts was partly due to the malice of the players; but this doesn't make sense. How could they not affect the opening sinfonia and the first act, but ruin the second and third? It has since revived a bit, since the drama has been fixed by shortening it a lot. On subsequent evenings, with everything in place, the public gave it general applause.

I won't speak to you of the Company. We will have to sigh for one eternally, as long as we are *amateurs* of such a fine art. Giorgi played the part of Tazio with a majesty, an expressiveness that I haven't words to convey to you. Annibali played Romolo with such gentle gravity that you would have believed that he intended to propose himself as our image of the Father of the great Roman Republic—if he weren't a castrato. Lorenzino, called the Bavarian, uttered a recitative in the third act with comic animation that delighted everyone. Porporino gave a demonstration quite different from the one he made in the first

TEXT: Fabrizio della Seta, "Il relator sincero (Cronache teatrali romane, 1739–1756)" in *Studi musicali* 9 (1980): 73–116, letters 1 and 3, pp. 86–88; 90–92. Sixteen of the original letters are in the Borghese Archives in the Vatican. Translation by Margaret Murata.

1. He calls the Teatro delle Dame by its name from 1717 to 1725, the Teatro Alibert.
2. Gaetano Latilla (1711–88) began his career writing comic operas for Naples; his first opera for Rome was a *dramma giocoso* staged in 1737 for the Teatro Tor di Nona; his first serious opera was a setting of Metastasio's *Demofoonte* for Venice in 1738. His collaborator on *Romolo* was Domingo Terradellas.

opera.[3] The *seconda donna* has much grace and has an action aria that was extremely well liked. The costumes of the men were first-rate, those of the women could not have been worse. The sets were mediocre, except for the last, which is a very beautiful creation. This is a sincere review; if you hear something different, it will be out of envy or flattery. Goodbye.

•   •   •

Rome, January 10, 1751

I am relieved, friend, from the regret that I had in sending you the day before yesterday the report about *Merope* at the Argentina,[4] and am feeling quite happy in having to describe to you the fortunate outcome last night of the opera at the Teatro delle Dame about the princess Antigona,[5] daughter of Oedipus and heir to the kingdom of Thebes, of which the author is Signor Gaetano Roccaforte, resident of the Lipari Islands, where instead of making lightning strikes, he has issued forth with his fiery spirit a drama in which he presents a mother who has never been a bride and expresses the feigned role of this princess with such tenderness, that it is necessary to weep at the power of his words.

Rome, dismayed by the unlucky event of the first opera, went to hear the second with suspended hopes, fearing to run into a similar disgrace. But quite soon it was clear that a celebrated *maestro di cappella* is useful to make even a bad actor look good; while in a company in which there is no star, you can still get pleasure and quite complete satisfaction.

This is all due to Signor Baldassare Galuppi, called il Buranello, who has made Rome hear what refined taste he has in musical composition. His great music was free of all exceptions and was applauded by all, because it was full of new ideas, of harmonious arias, of stupendous recitatives and strong scenes. The first act succeeded most beautifully. The second was a little tedious at the beginning, revived later, and finished with a marvelously wrought aria. The third held up because of the action scenes in it, and for a terzetto that is truly the soul of the work.

Lorenzino the Bavarian,[6] who, under the name of Antiope, priestess of a temple and interpreter of the oracles of Apollo, represented Antigona, sang with spirit and would have stood out more if he would rid himself of certain old-fashioned howls, when he wants to move into the high notes. The tenor Basteris,[7] as the figure of Creonte, tyrant and usurper of the Kingdom of Thebes that belonged to Princess Antigona, as much as he has a timbre similar to that of Vittorio Chiccheri and a pronunciation with the open E,[8] contributes nonethe-

---

3. Della Seta has identified these performers as Filippo Giorgi (fl. 1728–1749); alto castrato Domenico Annibali (c. 1705–1779 or later), who sang for Handel; Lorenzo Ghirardi (fl. 1738–44); and castrato soprano Antonio Uberti, known as "Porporino."
4. An earlier letter describes a performance of this score by Matteo Capranica.
5. This was the premier of *Antigona*, Galuppi's forty-sixth operatic score.
6. See note 3 above; for what little is known of the other singers named, see Della Seta, "Il relator sincero."
7. Gaetano Basteris.
8. This vowel sound is represented in the International Phonetic Alphabet as [ɛ].

less in his good way toward maintaining a great part of the reputation of the opera itself. Casimiro Venturini exacted great applause representing Euristeo, believed to be the widower of Antigona and destined by his father Creonte to be the husband of Ermione, since he sang with singular grace, making every effort to imitate the trills of Gizziello.[9] Much, however, is due to the orchestra, which made good for him, since with his thin voice he cannot lead them well in the finale. Giuseppe Belli, called Ermione, unknown daughter of Euristeo and of Antigona, did himself great honor and succeeded almost better than the *prima donna*. If the second tenor, in the person of the shepherd Alceste, believed to be the father of Ermione, had not moved like the marionettes on strings in the Vicolo dei Leutari,[10] he would have also got good marks, because he delivered with spirit. All the others are so well covered by the great sound of the orchestra and by the good music, that their defects do not appear.

The orchestra is memorable, and stands out from the beginning with a marvelous new *sinfonia* that is surprising.

The dances did not find favor, being too serious and long, and because people have seen those of Monsieur Sotter,[11] which have left a very refined taste.

The theater was completely lit up and was properly adorned. There were new costumes of splendid style, and old scenery out of storage, really ordinary and cheaply touched up by a famous painter who did the fireworks displays in Piazza Farnese.

At this unexpected success Rome has returned to nourish its good, old appetite and to declare the intention of taking itself to the Capranica and Valle[12] to amuse itself among the thespians. If, as I hope, this sincere witness of my well-owed attention pleases you, I will give myself the benefit of informing you at the right time about the second operas. Take care of yourself, and remember sometimes the person who doesn't forget You. Addio.

9. Castrato soprano Gioacchino Conti (1714–1761) created roles in Neapolitan operas of the 1730s and later sang for Handel in London and at the court in Lisbon to 1755.
10. "Alley of the lute-makers," a short street in Rome near the Palazzo Farnese.
11. François Sauveterre (d. 1775), who before this date had created ballets for theaters in Venice, Stuttgart, Florence, etc., including Rome in 1749.
12. Two other Roman theaters that presented operas.

13 Guillaume Dumanoir

Guillaume Dumanoir (1615–1697) headed the musicians' guild of France, known as the Confrérie de Saint-Julien-des-Ménétriers, (which maintained its own hospital and chapel). It had governed and protected freelance instrumentalists and dancing masters since 1321. As "King of the Violins" from November

1657, he oversaw the first major revision since 1407 of the articles governing the guild. The changes further institutionalized the profession and defined its jurisdictions clearly, especially with respect to "private" musicians such as those in the household of the King of France, whom Dumanoir also served. The 1658 statutes indicate the new prestige accorded instrumental musicians, though their hegemony was weakened when the dancing masters broke away in 1661 to take advantage of the even higher prestige that dance was gaining at the court of Louis XIV.

FROM Statutes of the Masters of Dance and Players of Instruments
(1658)

1. The masters in Paris and the other cities of this realm will be obliged to bind their apprentices for four full years, without being able to excuse them from said time, anticipate it, or discharge their brevets by more than one year,[1] on pain of a fine against these said masters of 150 *livres*,[2] a third to go to the King, a third to the confraternity of St. Julien,[3] and the other third to the king of the violins; and against said apprentices who wrongfully circumvent or gain said discharge for a longer time, [the penalty is] to be forever inadmissible to the mastership.

2. The above-said masters will be obliged, according to the accustomed manner, to present their apprentices at the time they accept them to the aforementioned king of the violins and have them register their brevets, both in his register and in that of the guild, for which registration said apprentice will pay to said king three *livres* and to the masters of the confraternity 30 *sols*.[4]

3. Said masters may not teach how to play instruments and other things except to those who are bound to them and currently dwell with them as apprentices, on pain of 50 *livres*, applicable as above.

4. When the said apprentices, after their terms of apprenticeship expire, present themselves to be admitted to the mastership, they will be obligated to demonstrate their skill before the said king, who may call twenty masters of his

TEXT: René Lespinasse, *Histoire générale de Paris: Les Métiers et corporations de la ville de Paris,* vol. 3 (Paris: Imprimerie National, 1897), pp. 587–89. The manuscript source from the Collection Lamoignon, tome 13, fol. 900, was first published in 1763. Translation by Margaret Murata.

1. For example, by buying out the contract of apprenticeship.
2. Examples of the value of a *livre*: in 1642 Dumanoir charged a nobleman ten *livres* a month for a period of eighteen months for daily dance lessons in the musician's home; wages for a lutenist of the king's chamber in 1658 were 600 *livres* a year.
3. The document mentions two separate, though overlapping social organizations, the *corporation* or guild and the *confrérie* of St. Julien of the Minstrels (here translated as "confraternity"), a musicians' benevolent society. The statutes are discussed in Catherine Massip, *La Vie des musiciens de Paris au temps de Mazarin (1643–1661)* (Paris: A. et J. Picard, 1976), pp. 70–86.
4. One *livre* = 20 *sols*. A *sol* would buy about nine eggs at this time.

choice for apprentices, and ten for sons of masters; and if he finds them able, he will deliver to them the patent of mastership.

5. Everyone who aspires to the mastership, whether they be apprentice or son of a master, will be obliged to receive the patents of said king, and will pay to the bursary of said guild for his right of reception and entry: if he is the son of a master, the sum of 25 *livres* only, and if he is an apprentice, the sum of 60 *livres*.

6. The husband of the daughter of a master, aspiring to the mastership, will enter as the son of a master, and will be received and treated in like manner.

7. The customs observed up to the present time with respect to the violins of the Chamber of His Majesty for the reception into the mastership will be continued, and they will be received on the basis of their brevet of retainership,[5] and upon payment by each for his right of reception the sum of 50 *livres* to the coffer of said corporation.

8. No person, royal subject or foreign, may conduct a school, teach dancing or the playing of high or low instruments privately, gather an ensemble night or day in order to give serenades or play said instruments in any weddings or assemblies public or private, nor anywhere else, nor in general do anything else concerning the exercise of said science, if he is not an admitted master or approved by said king or his lieutenants, upon pain of a fine of 100 *livres* for the first offense for each of the violations [and] seizure and sale of the instruments, all divisible a third to the confraternity of St. Julien and the remainder to above-said king of the violins or his lieutenants, and upon pain of corporal punishment for the second [offense].

9. The judgment of the Prefect of Paris of March 2, 1644, and the decree of Parliament of July 11, 1648, which confirmed it will be executed according to their form and terms, and in conformance with them, it is not permitted that masters or any other persons play instruments in cabarets and places of ill repute; and in case of violation, the instruments of the offenders will be broken and destroyed on the spot, without a formal trial, by the first commissioner or sergeant called upon by said king or one of the masters of the confraternity, and the offenders imprisoned for the payment of said fine, which cannot be waived or reduced for any reason, nor may the offenders be set free until the fines are paid.

10. The master of the fauxbourgs and of subordinate districts may not undertake any performing in the cities, neither make any oath nor mastership to the prejudice of said king, on pain of a fine of 100 *livres*, applicable as above.

11. The violins licensed to the Court may not gather any ensemble to play serenades nor play instruments, nor do any thing concerning said mastership, in the absence of His Majesty in this City of Paris.

12. Should any apprentice, during the time of his apprenticeship or after its expiration, go to play in cabarets or places of ill repute or other public places such as wedding halls, he may never aspire to the mastership; on the contrary he will be excluded forever.

5. That is, the terms of appointment to the royal household.

13. The masters may not encroach upon each other, nor present themselves before those [musicians] who would have need of them, nor take other than their companions to play with them; and when they are hired to someone for one or more days, neither the one who made the agreement nor the associates he chose [to play] with him, may excuse themselves for any cause from the service which they have promised, hiring other associates[6] in said time or contracting several jobs at the same time, upon pain of a fine of 30 *livres* for each offense, applicable as above.

14. No master may either associate or arrange to play in any place whatsoever with anyone who is licensed to the Court, or is an apprentice, or with anyone else who is not a master. And in case of a violation, any master who is found guilty will pay a sum of 10 *livres,* and anyone who is not a master, one half less.

15. Each of the said masters will be obliged to pay 30 *sols* a year as dues to the confraternity of St. Julien, and the revenues deriving from said dues and the fines applicable to said confraternity will be used to maintain the said chapel of St. Julien, and the dues to the coffer be used for the necessities of said corporation.

16. The masters of the confraternity who will be elected each year will be obliged to account for the proceeds of all said dues in the presence of said King of the Violins and the masters of the hall;[7] in the account he will give over the remainder, if there is any, into the hands of the one who takes his place.

·   ·   ·   ·   ·

20. The custom immemorial for admitting masters of the confraternity and masters of the hall will be continued, and in so doing, no one may be admitted as master of the confraternity who is not a master of the hall without the consent of said king and the other masters of the confraternity and of the hall, on any day other than that of St. Thomas. And for the admittance of a said master of the hall, each of those about to be admitted will pay to the coffer for the fees of entrance, 10 *livres.*

21. And because the king of the violins cannot be present in all the cities of this realm, he will be permitted to name lieutenants in each town, to have the present statutes and ordinances observed, to admit and approve masters; to which lieutenants all the necessary patents will be sent upon the nomination and presentation to said king and who will share in all instances half of the dues owed to abovesaid king in each admission of an apprentice and master.

Louis, by the grace of God, King of France and of Navarre . . . Given at Paris in the month of October, the year of grace 1658 and of our reign the sixteenth.

Registered in Paris, in Parliament, August 22, 1659; obtained and procured by Guillaume Dumanoir, king and master of all the master players of instruments and masters of dance, for all the realm of France.

6. Substitutes.
7. Dancing masters.

14 Roger North

Roger North (c. 1651–1734), the sixth son in a noble family from Cambridgeshire, England, grew up in a musical household (see No. 17 below). He trained in law and served the royal family in various legal offices but retired early from public life after the Glorious Revolution of 1688. He left copious writings on music, of which the latest appears to be his "Memoires of Musick, being some Historico-Critticall Collections of that Subject." His manuscript is dated 1728, but the work draws in part on his own earlier writing. The "Memoires" were first published in 1846 by Edward F. Rimbault for the Council of the Musical Antiquarian Society. In the extracts below, North reports on the lively concert life of late seventeenth-century London and on the first series of public instrumental concerts established there. Notices of the Banister concerts at White Friars that are mentioned by North appeared in the *London Gazette* between 1672 and 1678. Those held in York Buildings received notices until 1710. Later, occasional concerts were given there, such as a performance of Handel's *Esther* in 1732.

FROM *Memoirs of Music*
(1728)

THE RESTAURATION, AND THE STYLE OF BABTIST

But now to observe the stepps of the grand metamorforsis of musick, whereby it hath mounted into those altitudes of esteem it now enjoys: I must remember that upon the Restauration of King Charles,[1] the old way of consorts were layd aside at Court, and the King made an establishment, after a French model, of 24 violins, and the style of the musick was accordingly.[2] So that became the ordinary musick of the Court, Theaters, and such as courted the violin.

●　　●　　●　　●　　●

During the first years of Charles II all musick affected by the *beau-mond* run into the French way; and the rather, because at that time the master of the

TEXT: *Roger North on Music, Being a Selection of his Essays written during the years c. 1695–1728*, ed. John Wilson (London: Novello, 1959), pp. 349–53. Reproduced by permission of Novello and Co., Ltd. Further detailed annotations are in Mary Chan and Jamie C. Kassler, eds., *Roger North's* The Musicall Grammarian 1728 (Cambridge: Cambridge University Press, 1990), pp. 261–66.

1. Charles II returned from exile in France in 1660.
2. The *24 violons* of Louis XIV were distributed six, four, four, four, and six instruments to five parts.

Court musick in France, whose name was Babtista (an Itallian frenchifyed)[3] had influenced the French style by infusing a great portion of the Italian harmony into it; whereby the Ayre was exceedingly improved. The manner was theatricall, and the setts of lessons composed, called *Branles* (as I take it) or Braules; that is, beginning with an Entry, and then *Courants,* &c. And the Entrys of Babtist ever were, and will be valued as most stately and compleat harmony; and all the compositions of the towne were strained to imitate Babtist's vein; and none came so neer it as the hon[ble] and worthy *vertuoso* M[r] Francis Roberts.[4] But the whole tendency of the ayre had more regard to the foot, than the ear, and no one could hear an *Entree* with its starts, and *saults,*[5] but must expect a dance to follow, so lively may human actions be pictured by musick.

●   ●   ●   ●   ●

This French manner of instrumentall musick did not gather so fast as to make a revolution all at once, but during the greatest part of that King's reigne, the old musick was used in the countrys, and in many meetings and societys in London; but the treble violl was discarded, and the violin took its place. In some familyes organs were used to accompany consorts, but the old masters would not allow the liberty of playing from a thro-base figured, as harpsicords of late have universally practised, but they formed the organ part express;[6] because the holding out the sound required exact concord, else the consort would suffer; or perhaps the organists had not then the skill as since, for now they desire onely figures. There were also divers societys of a politer sort, who were inquisitive after forrein consorts, and procured divers, as from Itally Cazzati and Vitali; and one from Sweeden by Becker[7] composed for from 2 to 6 parts, which was too good to be neglected and lost, as it is at present. And however England came to have the credit of musicall lovers, I know not, but am sure that there was a great flocking hither of forrein masters, as from Germany, Sheiffar, Vuoglesank, and others; and from France, Porter and Farinell, these latter for the violin. And they found here good encouragement, so that the nation (as I may terme it) of Musick was very well prepared for a revolution.

3. Jean-Baptiste Lully, dominant composer at the French court. North here describes as "sets of lessons" those varied movements that can make up an instrumental suite.
4. Or Robartes (d. 1718), a prominent lawyer and gentleman scientist and musician.
5. Leaps.
6. That is, they made their own short or reduced scores.
7. "Diverse" ensemble music ("consorts") from composers like Maurizio Cazzati (d. 1677), chapel master of the principal church in Bologna from 1657 to 1671, composer of vocal music as well as canzonas, trio and solo sonatas for violins and for trumpet; Giovanni Battista Vitali (1632–1692) of Bologna published twelve volumes of instrumental music, including the first Italian sonatas to include French dance movements; Dietrich Becker (1623–1679) was active in Hamburg from 1662 and influential in transforming the multipartite sonata into the suite.

THE PUBLICK MUSICK-MEETINGS

A great means of bringing that foreward was the humour[8] of following publick consorts, and it will not be out of the way to deduce them from the beginning. The first of those was in a lane behind Paul's,[9] where there was a chamber
organ that one Phillips played upon, and some shopkeepers and foremen came
weekly to sing in consort, and to hear, and injoy ale and tobacco; and after some
time the audience grew strong, and one Ben. Wallington got the reputation of
[a] notable base voice, who also set up for a composer, and hath some songs in
print, but of a very low sence; and their musick was cheifly out of Playford's
Catch Book. But this shewed an inclination of the citisens to follow musick.
And the same was confirmed by many litle enterteinements the masters voluntarily made for their scollars, for being knowne they were always crowded.

The next essay was of the elder Banister,[10] who had a good theatricall vein,
and in composition had a lively style peculiar to himself. He procured a large
room in Whitefryars, neer the Temple back gate,[11] and made a large raised box
for the musitians, whose modesty required curtaines. The room was rounded
with seats and small tables alehouse fashion. One s[hilling] was the price and
call for what you pleased. There was very good musick, for Banister found
means to procure the best hands in towne, and some voices to come and per-
forme there, and there wanted no variety of humour,[12] for Banister himself
(*inter alia*) did wonders upon a flageolett to a thro-base, and the severall masters had their solos. This continued full one winter, and more I remember not.

There was a society of Gentlemen of good esteem, whom I shall not name
for some of them as I hear are still living, that used to meet often for consort
after Babtist's manner; and falling into a weekly course, and performing
exceeding well, with bass violins (a course instrument[13] as it was then, which
they used to hire), their freinds and acquaintance were admitted, and by
degrees as the fame of their meeting spread, so many auditors came that their
room was crowded; and to prevent that inconvenience, they took a room in a
taverne in Fleet Street, and the taverner pretended to make formall seats, and
to take mony; and then the society disbanded.[14] But the taverner, finding the
sweet of vending wine and taking mony, hired masters to play, and made a

8. Inclination or tendency.
9. The cathedral of St. Paul in London.
10. John Banister (d. 1679), a royal violinist and composer.
11. East of the Inns of Court and formerly the site of a Carmelite foundation.
12. That is, variety of styles. The four liquid humors of ancient and medieval physiology—blood,
    bile, phlegm, and choler—were thought to determine temperament. Music reflective of differ-
    ent moods, therefore, portrayed different "humors."
13. This "coarse" instrument is to be identified as the violoncello.
14. Castle Tavern in Fleet Street. Gentlemen, whether they performed for listeners or not, would
    not have done so for gain. When the taverner elected to sell places at the concerts, thereby
    turning it into a commercial enterprise, the original performers disbanded. They were replaced
    by professionals.

pecuniary consort of it, to which for the reputation of the musick, numbers of people of good fashion and quallity repaired.

The Masters of Musick finding that mony was to be got this way, determined to take the buissness into their owne hands; and it proceeded so farr, that in York Buildings a fabrick[15] was reared and furnished on purpose for publik musick. And there was nothing of musick valued in towne, but was to be heard there. It was called the Musick Meeting; and all the Quallity and *beau mond* repaired to it. But the plan of this project was not so well layd as ought to have bin, for the time of their beginning was inconsistent with the park and the playhouses, which had a stronger attraction. And what was worse, the masters undertakers[16] were a rope of sand, not under the rule or order of any person, and every one foreward to advance his owne talents, and spightfull to each other, and out of emulation[17] substracting their skill in performing, all which together scandalized the company, and poysoned the enterteinement. Besides the whole was without designe or order; for one master brings a consort with fuges, anothers shews his guifts in a solo upon the violin, another sings, and then a famous lutinist comes foreward, and in this manner changes followed each other, with a full cessation of the musick between every one, and a gab-[b]le and bustle while they changed places; whereas all enterteinements of this kind ought to be projected as a drama, so as all the members shall uninterrupt-edly follow in order, and having a true connexion, set off each other. It is no wonder that the playhouses got ground, and as they ordered the matter, soon routed this musick meeting.

15. Building.
16. Entrepreneurs or agents.
17. Envy.

15 Roger North

In his 1695 autobiography *Notes of Me* (see also No. 18, below), North offered one of the earliest opinions regarding the order in which listeners experienced music, that is, the matter of programming, just discussed. The planning of esthetic experience—the manipulation of expectation and surprise on the part of the artist—was a major concern of the Baroque, whether in architecture, city planning, rhetoric, painting, or drama. The selection that follows not only describes an instrumental concert in more detail, but it also presents quite modern notions of a composition as a coherent development and of music as an art for listeners.

FROM *Notes of Me*

(c. 1695)

There is the same rule to be observed in all sorts of composed delights, formed for the regaling of mankind, whether it be fireworks, comedy, or musick. As for eating, I know not what rule to propose because all depends on appetite, which being sharp or cloyed, beginns and ends the matter, so let that pass. But to instance first in fireworks, the master must contrive that the beginning be moderate, for the least thing at first serves, and then other parts enter, with a noise and fire perpetually increasing, and the greatest fury must be the last, and then all expire at once. This draws the spectators from one degree of amazement to another, without any relapse or flagging, till it arives to the ackme, and then to cease; for the least pause, or abatement, nay non-progression, spoyles all. The like as to comedy, which is introduc't with slow, easy, and clear parts, and in the progress grows buisy, perplext, and at last dissolves in peace all at once—*Mercurio vindice*[1] Tragedy is the same; for that, in the way of sorrow and calamity, grows up gradually into a catastrofe of woe, ending as misery itself ends, in mortality.

So for a musicall enterteinement; if there be not a continuall procession of it, with increase of force, and intermixt with variety of measure and parts, to sett off and give lustre to each other, as light and darkness; but [instead] to stopp, and so the measure cease, and incoherent peices added, without designe, perhaps the severall parts and passages may be good in their kind, but the whole taken together cannot be a good enterteinement. As a comedy may have good scenes and be a very ill play. A song, a fuge, a solo, or any single peice (and so all the rest) may be very good in their severall kinds, but for want of a due coherence of the whole, the company not be pleased. And thus it is with the musick exhibited in London publiquely for 1/2 crownes.[2] A combination of masters agree to make a consort as they call it, but doe not submitt to the governement of any one, as should be done, to accomplish their designe. And in the performance, each takes his parts according as his opinion is of his owne excellence. The master violin must have its solo, then joyned with a lute, then a fuge, or sonnata, then a song, then the trumpet and haut-bois, and so other variety, as it happens. And upon every peice ended, the masters shift

TEXT: *Roger North on Music*, pp. 12–14. Reproduced by permission of Novello and Co., Ltd.

1. "With Mercury as deliverer."
2. A crown equalled five shillings. In 1675 three shillings would buy a pound of tobacco.

their places to make way for the next, the thro-base ceaseth, and the company know not whether all is ended, or any thing more to come, and what. Which pauses, and difforme[3] accidentall species of music presented one after the other, without judgment or designe, are so defective, as justly to be compared to a ballad singer, who having done one ballad, begins another to a pleasant new tune.

But this combination regulated, might exhibit very good musick; for the pert forewardness of some, or rather of all the masters, would be restrained, and they oblidged to take the parts designed and to stick to them, without perching forewards to shew their parts, and please themselves in being admired. And the thro-base should never cease but play continually, for that holds the audience in attention, and with the instruments (as some must be always) accompan[y]ing, will be no ill musick, wherein the master hath a latitude to bring in some caprice, or extravagance of measure or humour, conformeable to the musick past or next following. And then any single parts of voice, violin, lute, hautboys, trumpetts, or mixtures of them, may be introduc't, orderly and with coherence; so as the cessation of them before, was not a lacune or rupture, but a pause, as for breath; and when returned are a *denouement* of the enterteinement, so much prized in stage plays. And in short the whole is of a peice, and all the process of it considered and put together with skill and designe to give advantage to each part, and never lett the audience cease attention, but continually improve and raise it 'till the end, when the greatest force ceasing, speaks, there is no more. Such an enterteinement I never heard composed for an hour's passtime, which is enough, but my knowledge of the art tells me it should be so. But for smaller time it is common, as in the Itallian *sonnatas,* French *branles,* and English *fancys,* which well done are a specimen or model of what should be in greater designes. This is my apprehension, and censure,[4] touching these recreations, wherein the hearers are onely considered, and therefore fitt onely for great cittys full of idle people.

3. Not uniform, diverse.
4. "Understanding and criticism."

III

$\mathcal{D}$OMESTIC MUSIC

16 Grazioso Uberti

A jurist from the Italian town of Cesena, Grazioso Uberti (c. 1574–1650) served as a lawyer to the Papal Curia in Rome. He published both juridical treatises and, as befitted a gentleman of letters at the time, Latin poetry. The *Contrasto musico* or "Musical Disagreement," subtitled "an amusing piece," offers a music lover's view of the major criticisms and defenses of the different kinds of music that could be encountered in Rome around 1630. The two speakers are Severo, who is irritated by the noisy school of music that his neighbor runs, and Giocondo, who has several musician friends. The book is divided into seven sections, each representing a different place in which music is made: the music school for boys, private homes, princes' palaces, churches, the Oratorio, the outdoors, and, finally, the houses of composers. Excerpted here from the section on music in private houses is a discussion of women and music. Uberti's use of ancient authors to lend authority to a point or opinion reveals the author's academic training.

FROM *The Musical Disagreement*
(1630)

GIOCONDO: . . . If you like, let us leave these private houses now.

SEVERO: Wait. There are still the ladies—the women singers, the spinsters who learn to sing, the ladies who entertain people in social gatherings with song.

GIOCONDO: If you think that this is not honest entertainment, let's just go.

SEVERO: Many say that nothing should be appreciated in women but honesty, that women should rather avoid dealing with men, than hold them in conversation and charm them with song.

GIOCONDO: The purpose of woman is to give birth to and to raise children, as Claudian said in *Against Eutropius*, Book 1:

A woman is born to bear children and perpetuate the human race.[1]

Furthermore she should know how to manage a household and entertain herself with the distaff and needle, as Virgil said in the *Aeneid*, book 8:

> The housewife, her first task to sustain life
> by weaving and Minerva's humble arts,
> awakes the embers and the sleeping fires,
> as she adds on the night to her day's work

TEXT: *Il contrasto musico, opera dilettevole*, pt. 2 (Rome: L. Grignani, 1630). Repr. Lucca: Libreria Musicale Italiana, 1991), with an introduction by Giancarlo Rostirolla, pp. 67–73. Translation by Margaret Murata.

1. Loeb Classical Library, trans. M. Platnauer (Cambridge, Mass., 1922/1956), line 331; p. 163.

> and keeps her housemaids toiling on at some
> long chore by lamplight, that her husband's bed
> be chaste, and that she raise her children well.[2]

And one shouldn't cause women to be seen, and gazed upon in case there should follow prejudice against their modesty, as Ovid says in book 1 of the *Art of Loving:*

> They come to see, they come that they may be seen:
> to chastity that place is fatal.[3]

This is all true. One shouldn't, however, keep women closed up as if in a dungeon to keep them from talking and being seen; because in this way you offend their wisdom, and you place their chastity in doubt. Those women are called wise who, being able to do something, do not do it. . . . The women are also chaste who guard themselves and have no need for a guardian husband, about which Ovid spoke well in the *Amores,* book 3, elegy 4:

> Hard husband, by setting a keeper over your tender wife you nothing gain; 'tis her own nature must be each woman's guard. If she is pure when freed from every fear, then first is she pure; she who sins not because she may not—she sins! Grant you have guarded well the body, the mind is untrue; and no watch can be set o'er a woman's will. Nor can you guard her [mind], though you shut every door; with all shut out, a traitor will be within. She to whom erring is free, errs less; [the] very power makes less quick the seeds of sin.[4]

SEVERO: One should remove the opportunities to sin; and it seems that this music, this singing, invites a woman to social affairs; it exposes her to admiring gazes, to the desire of each person.

GIOCONDO: The opportunity for every evil is in leisure; about which Ovid says in book 1 of the *Remedies for Love:*

> Toss your leisure away and you've broken the arrows of Cupid;
> Toss your leisure away, his torch is extinguished and scorned.
>
> • • • • •
>
> Why did Aegisthus succumb to that adulterous passion?
> That is no trouble at all—he had nothing to do.[5]

Therefore, one should ensure that women are not idle; when they are occupied in virtuous activities, there is no danger that they could be taken over by dishonest desires. In his *Dialogues,* the Greek author Lucian presents Venus screaming at her son Cupid, scolding him about why he had failed to wound Pallas, and has Cupid answer: because he never found her idle. If a woman be tired of sewing, of spinning, of household duties, what can she do for a little recreation? If she goes to the window to see who's passing by, she's a flirt. If she goes to the balcony

---

2. Uberti quotes lines 408–13; this trans. by A. Mandelbaum (New York, 1971), lines 533–42. Minerva was the Roman goddess of wisdom, of wool working, and of arts and crafts.
3. Loeb Classical Library, trans. J. H. Mozley (Cambridge, Mass., 1920/1962), lines 99–100; p. 19.
4. Loeb Classical Library, G. Showerman trans., rev. by G. P. Goold (Cambridge, Mass., 1977), lines 1–10.
5. Lines 139–40; 162–63 as trans. in *The Art of Love,* trans. R. Humphries (Indiana University Press, 1957), pp. 185–86.

to chat with her neighbor, she's a gossip; if she converse with men, she's a fuse near a fire; but if she sing and play, she is a *virtuosa* in no danger of stepping over any line. Father returns home burdened with household affairs: it quiets him a little. The mother, tired from caring for the family, nears her daughter at the instrument and sends forth her measured voice—oh what pleasure! oh what sweetness for the parents! On certain days the female relatives visit, the spinster friends, the neighbors; a young hand touches the harpsichord, imitating the garrulous bird with melodious voice—oh what sweetness, oh what melody! oh what gentle recreation for lady relatives, friends, neighbors!

SEVERO: Some think that singing is not appropriate to the female sex.

GIOCONDO: To these one can say that the Muses invented by the poets are not male, and that *music*, according to many, comes from the word "muse." One could also add that that concert which is born from music one calls *harmony*, a name which some say is derived from a woman named Harmony, who was the wife of Cadmus, who knew well how to play and sing; and to finish, I will cite Athenaeus on the ancient singers in book 1, chapter 7:

> Singers are to be honored, for the goddesses delight in the songs that the Muses have taught them.[6]

SEVERO: There remain certain others, who say that music from dishonest women should be condemned, because they should be avoided. With their singing and playing they mostly charm men just as bird hunters deceive birds by whistling.

GIOCONDO: It's true that one should shun wanton women. *Remove thy way from the evil woman and come not nigh the door of her house*, we are taught in Proverbs, chapter 5.[7] But it does not say that one ought to flee in order not to hear their singing, but rather in order not to desire their beauty and to not give in to their desires. Thus you read in the same Proverbs, chapter 6: *To keep thee from the prostitute, lust not after her beauty in thine heart; neither let her take thee with her eyelids.*[8] Or rather, music in regard to women like this is like an overcoat that covers every shame. Those women are named and praised for their music, for playing and singing, who are far from any trace of lascivious habits, which otherwise would render them odious and abominable. It seems to me that Isaiah said this in chapter 24 [i.e., 23]:

> Take a harp, go about the city, thou harlot that hast been forgotten; make sweet melody, sing many songs, that thou mayest be remembered.[9]

SEVERO: We have really swept these houses; let's go into the palaces in the courts.

GIOCONDO: I'm with you.

6. Uberti cites a Latin translation of *The Deipnosophists* by the late-classical Greek writer Athenaeus, bk. 1, chap. 24, lines 15–18 (Kaibel; Loeb I. 14c). The passage itself is a quotation from Homer's *Odyssey* (bk. 8, line 480), hence is about "ancient singers" of the archaic age.
7. Prov. 5:8.
8. Prov. 6:24–25.
9. Isa. 23:16.

17 Jean Loret

As a journalist, Jean Loret's distinction was to have disseminated the weekly news of Parisian society between 1650 and 1665 in verse, in what he termed a "gazette burlesque." The poems, appropriately written in doggerel meter and rhyme (reproduced here), were originally addressed to Marie d'Orléans, Mlle de Longueville. They were collected and published in three volumes in 1650, 1660, and 1665 under the title *La Muse historique*. After Loret's death in 1665, several writers continued the tradition to nearly the end of the century. Though each account may seem slight by itself, Loret took note of dance, domestic music making, and everyday performances in church—the kinds of occasions that typically pass without historical record.

FROM *The Historical Muse*
(1654)

I heard such melodies of sound
('twould make the gods to gather round)
from a guitar, and even more
the marvels were from a mandore:[1]
these gave my heart such cheer to see
in the home of Monsieur Sifrédy.[2]
And what's more, his charming niece
played for us many an excellent piece
on the viol and, more disarming,
upon her harpsichord so charming.
All that we've heard of Orpheus' glories
amounts to naught but fairy stories
compared to those celestial chords
a manner rare and fine affords
as we heard there the sound uncurl
from out the fingers of this girl:
the pretty airs she animated
left the listeners charmed and sated.

TEXT: In Yolande de Brossard, "La Vie musicale en France d'après Loret et ses continuateurs, 1650–1688," *Recherches sur la musique française classique* 10 (1970): 117–93; this poem for August 15, 1654, pp. 157–58. Translation by Margaret Murata.

1. A plucked string instrument with a rounded body, a cittern or cittern-like instrument.
2. The gentleman is unknown; a Sifrédy served as a steward in the queen's household, 1652–58, according to Brossard, "La Vie musicale en France," p. 192.

18 Roger North

Sometime after Roger North retired from the law (see No. 14 above) in 1688, he wrote his autobiography, the manuscript of which now rests in the British Library. His recollections of childhood on his grandfather's estate at Kirtling, Cambridgeshire, illustrate the transition from the Elizabethan traditions represented in old Lord North's household to the flourishing musical life in London at the end of the century. During Roger North's youth, regular music making was considered a domestic virtue that contributed to moral education. Occupation in musical performance prevented idleness, as noted by Grazioso Uberti (in No. 15), or less innocuous activities. In the later seventeenth century, the new professionalism in music encouraged music lovers to be passive auditors rather than performers. In North's view, the disappearance of amateur music making—which was due in part to the high level of musical difficulty to which listeners had become accustomed and in part to the attractions of London that had supplanted domestic performances—was a sign of the weakening culture of the landed families. North advises which instruments are best for boys and which for girls and is so sensitive about the moral value of musical instruction in the home that he warns fathers to choose their daughters' music teachers carefully.

FROM *Notes of Me*
(c. 1695)

As to musick, it was my fortune to be descended of a family where it was native. My Grandfather, Dudley the [3rd] Lord North, having travelled in Italy, where that muse is queen, took a liking to it. And when his vanitys, and attendant wants, had driven him into the country, his active spirit found imployment with many airey[1] enterteinements, as poetry, writing essays, building, making mottos and inscriptions. But his poetry call'd him to Musick, for he would have the masters sett his verses, and then his grand-children, my sisters, must sing them. And among others he used to be wonderfully pleas'd with these, being a corus of Diana's nymphs:

> She is chaste, and so are wee;
> Wee may chase, as well as she.

TEXT: From *Roger North on Music*, pp. 9–12 and 15–17 (see also Nos. 14 and 15, above). The dating of the manuscript is John Wilson's, as are all the words in square brackets. Reproduced by permission of Novello and Co., Ltd.

1. Imaginative.

And having a quarrell with an old gentleman, could not hold [from] goding him with poetry and the corus of a song run thus:

> A craven Cock, untry'd will look as brave,
> So will a Curr, a Buzzard, Jade, or knave.

This digression to shew how a retired old fantastik courtier could enterteine himself; . . .

He play'd on that antiquated instrument called the treble viol, now abrogated wholly by the use of the violin; and not onely his eldest son, my father, who for the most part resided with him, play'd, but *his* eldest son Charles, and yonger son [Francis] the Lord Keeper, most exquisitely and judiciously. And he kept an organist in the house, which was seldome without a profes't musick master. And the servants of parade, [such] as gentlemen ushers, and the steward, and clerck of the kitchen also play'd; which with the yong ladys my sisters singing, made a society of musick, such as was well esteemed in those times. And the course of the family was to have solemne musick 3 days in the week, and often every day, as masters supply'd noveltys for the enterteinement of the old lord. And on Sunday night, voices to the organ were a constant practise, and at other times symphonys intermixt with the instruments.

This good old lord took a fancy to a wood he had about a mile from his house, called Bansteads, scituate in a durty soyl, and of ill access. But he cut glades, and made arbours in it, and no name would fit the place but, *Tempe.*[2] Here he would convoque his musicall family, and songs were made and sett for celebrating the joys there, which were performed, and provisions carried up for more important regale of the company. The consorts were usually all viols to the organ or harpsicord.[3] The violin came in late, and imperfectly. When the hands were well supply'd, then a whole chest went to work, that is 6 violls, musick being formed for it; which would seem a strange sort of musick now, being an interwoven hum-drum, compared with the brisk *battuta*[4] derived from the French and Italian. But even that in its kind is well; and I must make a great difference when musick is to fill vacant time, which lyes on hand. Then, that which hath moderate buissness in it, and being harmonious, will lett one sleep or drouse in the hearing of it, without exciting the ball or dance, is well enough. But where heads are brisk and airey hunting of enterteinements, and brought to musick as the best, where it is expected to be accordingly, and the auditors have not leisure or patience to attend moderate things, but must be touched sensibly, brisk, and with *bon goust;*[5] then I confess this sort will not please; but it must come with all the advantages that can be, and even the best

---

2. A classical place name that signifies a pleasant rural setting.
3. The ensembles consisted of a chest, or family, of viols with a keyboard instrument playing either *basso continuo* or *basso seguente.*
4. Beat.
5. Good taste, here with the sense of a taste for the up-to-date.

and most *reliev*[6] harmony will scarce hold out any long time.[7]

And I may justly say, that the late improvements of Musick have bin the ruin, and almost banishment of it from the nation.[8] I shall speak more of this anon; now let me lament the disadvantage this age hath, and posterity will find, in the discontinuance of this enterteinement. And whether the now-reigning humour, of running to London, be more the cause it is discontinued, than the discontinuance of it be the cause (at least in some measure) of that, I will not determine; I am sure both are true *in quanto*.[9] The mischeif is plaine, that is, leaving the country, which I will not demonstrate here, but shew that want of country enterteinement must be a great cause of it. And that is done by observing that vice will start up to fill the vacancy. When wee know not how to pass the time, wee fall to drink. If company is not at home, wee goe out to marketts and meetings to find such as will joyne in debauchery, and the country is dull for want of plentifull and exquisite debauchery. There can scarce be a full family[10] kept, because this humour of drunkening lett in all manner of lewdness. Even father and daughters, with servants and children male and female, goe into promiscuousness. And it is scarce reasonable to expect better unless you can provide diversion, to fill the time of the less imploy'd part of a gentile[11] family, which [diversion] is, and when used heretofore was, of great use towards it. For yong spirits, put in any way, will be very buisy and imploy themselves, but not put into a way, pant after debauchery. Now when Musick was kept in an easy temperate air, practicable to moderate and imperfect hands, who for the most part are more earnest upon it than the most adept, it might be reteined in the country. But since it is arrived to such a pitch of perfection, that even masters, unless of the prime, cannot enterteine us, the plain way becomes contemptible and rediculous, therefore must needs be lay'd aside. By this you may judge what profit the publik hath from the improvement of Musick. I am almost of Plato's opinion, that the state ought to governe the use of it, but not for their reasons, but for the use it may be in diverting noble familys in a generous way of country living.

Nor is this improvement come to that height with us, that it should winn us so to it. I grant in Italy, and the Royall Chappell here, it hath bin extraordinary good. But look out among the celebrated enterteinements that have of late bin

---

6. Vivid or entertaining? Wilson suggests "clearly outlined," p. 11, note 5.

7. North recognizes here that the consort music performed in the 1650s was more "moderate," that is, has less contrast, in its harmony and rhythms and therefore bore sustained performance, unlike the French and Italian instrumental music of the 1690s that was more varied in harmony and derived from dance music, but passed quickly.

8. See No. 14 above; North is thinking of the advanced performance techniques and increased professionalism in music of the 1690s, as well as the establishment of public concerts in London, which he associates with the decline of music making in the home.

9. To a degree.

10. A household.

11. Genteel.

set up in this towne, and wee shall not find any that deserves the caracter of musicall enterteinement.

•   •   •   •   •

It is most certain that gentlemen are not oblidg'd to aime at that [same] perfection, as masters who are to earne their support by pleasing not themselves, for it is their day labour, but others. And therefore audiences are not so well when their owne enterteinement is the buissness,[12] because they indulge their owne defects, and are not distasted or discouraged by stopp, errors, and faults, which an audience would laugh att. But it is so unhappy that gentlemen, seeing and observing the performances of masters, are very desirous to doe the same; and finding the difficulty and the paines that is requisite to acquire it, are discouraged in the whole matter, and lay it aside; which is cheifly to be ascribed to this towne which is the bane of all industry, because many other pleasures stand with open armes to receive them. Whereas in the country, where there are not such variety of gay things to call yong folks away, it is incredible what application and industry will grow up in some active spirits. And this voluntarily, without being incited; as where there is an inlett to Musick, having time and a fancy to it, some will be wonderfully resigned to master a reasonable performance in it. And for want of this or some other vertuous, or at least harmless, imployment within doors, the youth of the country fall to sports, as doggs, horses, hauks and the like abroad, wherein they will become very exquisite artists; which I mention onely to shew how reasonable it is to have in a country family some subject of vertuous pastime, or arts more usefull if not gainefull professions, which may be as food to the industry of youth bred there; who will otherwise, as I noted, fall into sottishness and vice. And nothing, of the unprofitable kind, can be so good as Musick, who is a kind companion and admitts all to her graces, either men by themselves, or men and weomen together, or the latter single, with either instruments and voices, or either alone, as the capacitys are; and [these] fail not to enterteine themselves, and their parents and friends, with pleasures sensible to those that have found the sweets of them. And for this reason I would not have familys discouraged for want of perfection, which, to say truth, is not to be had out[side] of a trade, but to enter their youth, and give them good example, and they will be ambitious enough to improve; and if it be to be had, active spirits will find it. But after all, nothing of musick is so mean and ill performed, which is not comendable and extream usefull in a country family.

This letts me in to speak a litle of Teaching, on which much of this depends. For men the viol, violin, and the thro-base-instruments organ, harpsicord, and double base, are proper; for weomen the espinnett, or harpsicord, lute, and gittarr; for voices both. I cannot but comend the double base, or standing viol, for plaine bases, especially for accompan[y]ing voices, because of its softness

12. When they are performing for themselves, it is not so good for gentlemen to have an audience.

joyned with such a force as helps the voice very much. And the harpsicord for ladys, rather than the lute; one reason is, it keeps their body in a better posture than the other, which tends to make them crooked. The other instruments, and farther of these, I decline to critiscise, because I intend in a discourse apart to doe it fully.

But masters are first to be had, who can reasonably answer for what they undertake, and of those I recommend the elder, rather than the yonger, altho' the latter may be more aggreable for novelty and briskness, which is so in most things, especially Musick. My reason is, that the elder are better artists in teaching the principles of Musick, having more experience; and that is the main designe at first. Elegance of performance is the finishing, which will be look't after in time. First get a teacher who understands, and hath experience in teaching, which is a distinct art from playing, and few or scarce any yong men have it. When they teach it is meerly by imitation, and [they] know not the true reason of the excellencys they have, nor can obviate the devious errors of scollars,[13] nor so well judge of the beauty or deformity of habits, but will lett them run on till past cure. I might add other reasons, such as seducing yong people and betraying them to ruin, which they are too apt to doe; but of that I suppose parents are apt enough to take thought, for if not, their children, being fortunes especially daughters, are in much danger from such gamesters. But the ancienter men who have familys of their owne are safe and will be prudent. Their dullness, and perhaps humours, must be borne with, for they trade in air all together, which is a light buissness.

13. Pupils.

IV

$\mathcal{P}$RINCIPLES FOR PERFORMANCE

19 Giulio Caccini

Born in Rome, the tenor Giulio Caccini (1551–1618) performed and taught singing at the court of the grand duke of Tuscany in Florence for most of his professional life. Solo singing to instrumental accompaniment was by no means an
exclusively Florentine practice in the last quarter of the sixteenth century, but in
his personal style Caccini eschewed the extravagant improvisation prized at the
time in both vocal and instrumental performance. Under the influence of scholars of the ancient Greek theater, he had participated in developing a new way
of singing in staged dramas, a manner of "speaking in tones." This new manner
influenced his chamber singing, in that he insisted that the invention and application of ornamental figures should serve to enhance the declamation and the
expressive force of the text. Display of technical virtuosity was to disappear in
favor of a musical representation of speech—but speech in the artfully simple,
yet high literary manner of poets like Ottavio Rinuccini and Gabriele Chiabrera.
This "speaking in tones" also required a flexible instrumental accompaniment,
because word accents in Italian poetic lines do not make regular patterns of
stress. The Florentine solution—in the form of the figured bass—was presented
to the world in both of Caccini's landmark publications, the score to his opera
Euridice and his collection of monodies called *Le nuove musiche* (*The New
Music*). His bass lines, which prescribed more for the player than did guitar tablature, were still far from the complete scores given in lute or keyboard notation.
Caccini's dedication to the opera briefly introduces both this new notation for
the performers of the basso continuo and his new manner of singing.

Dedication to *Euridice*
(1600)

To the most illustrious lord, Signor Giovanni Bardi, Count of Vernio,[1] Lieuten-
ant-General of both Companies of the Guard of Our Most Holy Father.

After composing the fable of Eurydice in music in *stile rappresentativo* and
having it printed, I felt it to be part of my duty to dedicate it to Your Illustrious
Lordship, whose especial servant I have always been and to whom I find myself
under innumerable obligations. In it Your Lordship will recognize that style
which, as Your Lordship knows, I used on other occasions, many years ago, in
the eclogue of Sannazaro, "Itene all'ombra degli ameni faggi,"[2] and in other

---

TEXT: *L'Euridice composta in musica in stile rappresentativo* (Florence: Giorgio Marescotti, 1600;
facs. Bologna, 1976), pp. [i–ii].; translation by Oliver Strunk. The Italian text is also available in A.
Solerti, *Le origini del melodramma* (Turin, 1903; repr. Bologna [1969]), pp. 50–52 and in T. Carter
and Z. Szweykowski, eds., *Composing Opera* (Cracow, 1994), also trans. into English.

1. For Bardi, see No. 1 above.
2. From the *Arcadia* of Jacopo Sannazaro. The line given is the beginning of the monologue of
   Montano in terza rima, following the "Prosa seconda." Caccini's music seems not to have been
   preserved.

madrigals of mine from that time. "Perfidissimo volto," "Vedrò il mio sol," "Dovrò dunque morire,"[3] and the like. This is likewise the manner which Your Lordship, in the years when Your Lordship's *camerata* was flourishing in Florence, discussing it in company with many other noble virtuosi, declared to be that used by the ancient Greeks when introducing song into the presentations of their tragedies and other fables.

Thus the harmony of the parts reciting in the present *Euridice* is supported above a *basso continuato*.[4] In this I have indicated the most necessary fourths, sixths, and sevenths, and major and minor thirds, for the rest leaving it to the judgment and art of the player to adapt the inner parts in their places. The notes of the bass I have sometimes tied in order that, in the passing of the many dissonances that occur, the note may not be struck again and the ear offended. In this manner of singing, I have used a certain *sprezzatura* which I deem to have an element of nobility, believing that with it I have approached that much nearer to ordinary speech. Further, when two sopranos are making *passaggi*, singing with the inner parts, I have not avoided the succession of two octaves or two fifths, thinking thereby, with their beauty and novelty, to cause a greater pleasure, especially since without these *passaggi*, all the parts are free from such faults.

I had thought on the present occasion to deliver a discourse to my readers upon the noble manner of singing, in my judgment the best one, so that others could practice it, along with some curious points relating to it, and with the new style of *passaggi* and *raddoppiate*[5] invented by me, which Vittoria Archilei, a singer of that excellence to which her resounding fame bears witness,[6] has long employed in singing my works. But since this has not at present seemed best to some of my friends (to whom I cannot and must not be disloyal), I have reserved this for another occasion,[7] enjoying, for the time being, this single satisfaction of having been the first to give songs of this kind and their style and manner to the press.[8] This manner appears throughout my other compositions, composed at various times going back more than fifteen years, as I have never used in them any art other than the imitation of the sentiments of the words, touching those notes more or less passionate that I judged most suitable for the grace which is required for good singing, which grace and which manner

---

3. *Le nuove muische*, nos. 6, 7, and 11. "Perfidissimo volto" appears in the *Norton Anthology of Music*, 3d ed., vol. 1, no. 54.

4. For examples of Caccini's *basso continuato*, see No. 20, pp. 103–8.

5. Literally, "redoublings;" but a precise meaning remains unclear; see the Glossary of Foreign Performance Terms.

6. Archilei, who had taken part in the Florentine *intermedi* of 1589, sang the role of Euridice at the first performance of the Peri-Caccini score; see also No. 4, note 18.

7. The promised discourse was subsequently published as the preface to *Le nuove musiche;* see No. 20.

8. Caccini evidently rushed into print in order to anticipate the publication of Peri's score. His claim is that he is the first to have printed songs in the new style. Peri's claim (see No. 27) is that his *Euridice* was performed before Caccini's was composed or printed.

of singing Your Most Illustrious Lordship has many times reported to me to be universally accepted in Rome as good.

Meanwhile I pray Your Lordship to receive with favor the expression of my good will, etc., and to continue to grant me Your Lordship's protection, under which shield I hope ever to be able to take refuge and be defended from the perils that commonly threaten things little used, knowing that Your Lordship will always be able to testify that my compositions are not unpleasing to a great prince who, having occasion to test all the good arts, can judge them supremely well. With which, kissing Your Illustrious Lordship's hand, I pray Our Lord to bestow happiness upon Your Lordship.

Florence, December 20, 1600

Your Illustrious Lordship's most affectionate and beholden servant,

Giulio Caccini

20 Giulio Caccini

Caccini's first publication of solo madrigals and arias included music from his entire active career. The preface addressed to the readers articulates the main principles upon which Caccini based the claim that his musical style was new. Among these were aspects of composition, such as the suppression of counterpoint, which freed the bass from the rhythms of the vocal line, and a free harmonic rhythm that followed the cadences of spoken Italian. Others were aspects of performance practice, such as his recommendation that ornamental figures should on the whole be of moderate duration and that expressive techniques be reserved for affective texts and be dependent, above all, on the meaning of the words. More particularly, Caccini explained his preferences regarding the special use of crescendos and decrescendos on the part of the singer, and he illustrated the *trillo* on one tone and the *gruppo,* the equivalent of the modern neighbor-note trill. With less comment he offered rhythmic variants of common figures and cadences, followed by examples in which all these devices are applied, including passages to be sung *senza misura,* that is, without strict adherence to the beats within the *tactus.*

FROM THE Preface to *Le nuove musiche*
(1602)

•　　•　　•　　•　　•

At the time that the most excellent *camerata* of the Most Illustrious Signor Giovanni Bardi, Count of Vernio, flourished in Florence, wherein not only a good number of the nobility met, but also the best musicians and clever men, poets, and philosophers of the city. I can truly say, since I attended as well, that I learned more from their learned discussions than I did in more than thirty years of studying counterpoint. This is because these discerning gentlemen always encouraged me and convinced me with the clearest arguments not to value that kind of music which does not allow the words to be understood well and which spoils the meaning and the poetic meter by now lengthening and now cutting the syllables short to fit the counterpoint, and thereby lacerating the poetry. And so I thought to follow that style so praised by Plato and the other philosophers who maintained music to be nothing other than rhythmic speech with pitch added (and not the reverse!), designed to enter into the minds of others and to create those wonderful effects that writers admire, which is something that cannot be achieved with the counterpoint of modern music. In solo singing, especially, with any stringed instrument, the quantity of *passaggi* sung on both long and short syllables meant that not a word could be understood; and in music of every kind, those who provided them would be exalted and praised as great singers by the mob. Seeing, as I am saying, that these kinds of music and musicians were offering no pleasure other than what harmony grants to the ear alone (since the mind cannot be moved by such music without understanding the words), it occurred to me to introduce a kind of music by which anyone could almost speak in music, using (as I have said elsewhere)[1] a certain noble *sprezzatura* in the melody, passing sometimes over some discords while sustaining the pitch of the bass note (except when I wanted to use it in a regular way) and with the middle lines played by the instrument to express some *affetto*,[2] as those lines are not of much other use.

At that time, furthermore, people were beginning to sing this kind of song for solo voice. I thought that they would have more power to delight and move than would several voices together, and so composed the madrigals "Perfidissimo volto," "Vedrò 'l mio sol," "Dovrò dunque morire," and similar pieces,

---

TEXT: *Le nuove musiche* (*The New Music;* Florence, 1602; facs. New York, 1973), pp. ii–x. Translation by Margaret Murata. Musical examples are here given in their original note values. For an extensively annotated translation of the complete preface into English, see H. Wiley Hitchcock, *Le nuove musiche* (Madison: A-R Editions, 1970), pp. 43–56. Hitchcock's example numbering is retained here.

1. See No. 19 above, p. 98.
2. The probable meaning here is of a brief ornament.

and especially an air on the eclogue by Sanazzaro,[3] "Itene a l'ombra de gli ameni faggi," in just that style that I used later for those plays that were staged and sung in Florence.

· · · · ·

In madrigals as in arias I have always achieved the imitation of the ideas of the words, seeking out those notes that are more or less expressive, according to the sentiments of the words. So that they would have especial grace, I concealed as much of the art of counterpoint as I could. I have placed chords on the long syllables and passed over the short ones and also observed this same rule in making *passaggi*. For particular embellishments, however, I have sometimes used a few eighth notes (*crome*) up to the duration of a fourth of a *tactus*[4] or up to a half [of the *tactus*] at the most, largely on short syllables. These can be allowed, because these go by quickly and are not *passaggi* but just an extra graceful touch, and also because good judgment suffers some exception to every rule. But because earlier I have stated that those long turns of the voice are badly used, I must point out that singers do not make *passaggi* because they are necessary to a good singing style, but because, I believe, they titillate the ears of those who understand less well what it means to sing *con affetto*.[5] Because if they knew, then *passaggi* would be abhorred, since nothing is more contrary than they are to expressive singing (which is the reason I have been saying that those long runs are badly used). Therefore, I have introduced them in the kind of music that is less expressive, and used them on long, not short, syllables and in closing cadences.

I have no other technical points concerning vowels with respect to these long runs, except that the vowel "u" is better used in the soprano voice than in the tenor, and that the vowel "i" is better in the tenor than the vowel "u." The rest are all in common use, the open, rather than the closed vowels being much more sonorous,[6] as well as being the most suitable and the easiest with which to practice placement of the voice.

· · · · ·

It remains to say now why the increasing and diminishing of the voice, exclamations, trills, *gruppi*, and the other above-mentioned effects are used indiscriminately, since one can call it indiscriminate use whenever others apply

3. Caccini cited the same four compositions in his preface to *Euridice;* see pp. 97–98 above, notes 2 and 3.
4. The *tactus* was the unit of measure. In duple meter it was usually a semibreve in common time, or a breve in "cut" time. Thus in these embellishments, the number of eighth notes did not last longer than a fourth or half of the prevailing *tactus*. In his edition, Hitchcock has observed (pp. 46–47) that ¢ (*tactus alla breve* or *tempus diminutim*) is the predominant mensuration sign in *Le nuove musiche*. This would allow an embellishment lasting four to eight eighth notes.
5. Expressively, moving the emotions.
6. As represented by the International Phonetic Alphabet, the Italian open vowels are [a], [ɛ], and [ɔ]; the closed vowels are [e], [i], [o] and [u].

these devices as much in canzonettas for dancing as in expressive music. This defect comes about (if I am not mistaken) when a singer does not at first have well in hand that which he wishes to sing. If he did, he would certainly not run into such errors as easily as do those who have been trained in a completely affective style (so to speak)—one that follows the general rule that the foundation of expression lies in the application of crescendos, decrescendos, and exclamations—and who then always make use of them in every kind of music without figuring out whether the words require it. There are [listeners] who well understand the ideas and sentiments of the words. They recognize our defects and know how to distinguish where more and where less of such expressiveness is wanted. In this respect we should strive most to please them and prize their praises more than the applause of any common ignoramus. This art does not suffer mediocrity, and the more exquisite refinements it has, the more effort and diligence we professors of this art ought to exert, with great study and love. This love has moved me (seeing that we obtain the light of every science and art from writings) to bequeath this little glimmer in the following notes and comments, by which I intend to show what befits him who professes to sing solo with chitarrone or other stringed instrument, even though he may already have been introduced to the theory of this music and play well enough. Not that this art cannot be acquired to some extent also by long practice, as one sees that many, both men and women have done—up to a certain point, however. The theoretical in what I write here will take one up to this mark.

In the profession of singer (on its own merits) not only are the details useful, but everything taken together makes it better. To proceed, then, in order, I will say that the first and most important foundations are the intonation of the voice on all pitches:[7] not only that nothing is amiss below or rise too much,[8] but also that one should begin in a stylish manner. Since there are more or less two of these [ways of beginning] in use, we shall see both one and the other, and with my comments below, we will demonstrate which one seems to me more suitable with the other effects, which follows later.

There are, then, some who sing the first note beginning a third lower [than notated] and others who sing this first note at its written tone, always with a crescendo, saying that this is the good way to offer the note with grace. As for the first way, it cannot always be used, because it does not always accord with the harmony; although whenever it is possible to do it, it has now become such a common device, that instead of adding grace, I would say that it is rather

7. Caccini uses the term "intonation" in two contemporary senses here, one referring to being in tune, the other indicating the opening of a musical composition, as in the intonation of a chant. He says little about the first.
8. This odd phrase refers to flatting and sharping. In Caccini's time normal tunings were unequally tempered, requiring a sensitive ear, although plucked string instruments like the lute and chitarrone have their frets placed at spacings that produce equal semitones. A later seventeenth-century translation into English published in John Playford's *Introduction to the Skill of Music* renders this phrase as "and not only that it be neither too high nor too low."

unpleasant to the ear (also because some remain at the lower third for too long a time, whereas it should barely be suggested). Beginners, especially, should use it rarely. Instead of this, I would choose the second way as more attractive, that of increasing the voice. But because I have never been content to stay within ordinary bounds and those observed by others, but have always rather gone in search of the most original possibilities (as long as novelty helps the musician achieve his goal, that is, to delight and move the affections of the soul), I found that a more expressive way to treat the note is to sing the tone in the opposite manner—that is, to sing the first note diminishing it, rather than as an exclamation, even though the exclamation is the principal means of moving the affections. An exclamation proper is nothing other than reinforcing the tone somewhat as you sustain it.[9] Such an increase of the note in a soprano part, especially in falsetto, often becomes harsh and insufferable to the ear, as I've heard on several occasions. Certainly, then, as an expressive device more suitable to move [the affections], diminishing the voice will make a better effect than will increasing it. Nevertheless in the above-mentioned first manner,[10] increasing the voice to make an exclamation, what usually happens is that in sustaining the note, it goes sharp, which is why I have said it appears forced and coarse. A completely opposite effect can be made by diminishing the note. Then while sustaining it, giving it a little extra spirit will always make it more expressive.[11] Beyond this, using sometimes now one, now the other, variety can be achieved, since variety is most necessary in this art, as long as it is directed to the abovesaid goal.

•   •   •   •   •

[Example A]

My heart, pray, do not languish.

What this manner of singing can be then—with greater or lesser grace—can be tried with the music provided with the words "Cor mio, deh, non languire"

9. "Et esclamazione propriamente altro non è, che nel lassare della voce rinforzarla alquanto."
10. Caccini means here the first of the present two alternatives: starting the first note either with a crescendo or with a decrescendo.
11. The main difference between the *esclamazione* and what Caccini is suggesting as an intonation, both of which soften the tone and then make it more intense, is the relative duration of the two changes. In the former, the *crescendo* is longer; in Caccini's intonation, it is the diminishing that is longer.

[see Ex. A],[12] by singing "Cor mio" on the first dotted minim [1], diminishing it little by little, and as the semiminim [2] falls, increasing the voice with a little more spirit. This will produce a very expressive exclamation also on the note that descends by step. But the word "deh" will appear even livelier due to the length of the note (which does not fall by step), and it will seem very smooth after the greater sixth that falls by leap [3]. I wanted to note this in order to show others not only what an exclamation is and whence it originates, but that, furthermore, there can be two kinds, one more expressive than the other, both in terms of the way in which they are notated or sung (in either of the two ways) and of the imitation of the word, when it has significance for the meaning. In addition, exclamations can be sung in all expressive music, according to the general rule of applying them on descending dotted minims and semiminims [𝅗𝅥. 𝅘𝅥.]. They will be very much more expressive as a result of the moving note that follows [the dotted] note, than [exclamations are] with semibreves alone [𝅝]. What will happen more with semibreves is the increasing and decreasing of the voice without making exclamations.[13] It follows that in tuneful music (*musiche ariose*) or dance songs, rather than these affective devices one should use only the liveliness of the song, which is usually conveyed by the melody itself. In these, although sometimes there may be places for a few exclamations, one should keep up the same liveliness and not apply any *affetto* that conveys a sense of languishing. Thus we come to recognize how much it is necessary for the singer to have a certain amount of judgment, which is accustomed to sometimes prevailing over art. We can also recognize from the above-written notes how much more graceful are the first four eighth notes on the second syllable of the word "languire," with the second dotted eighth held back, than are the last four equal ones, marked here "for example."

There are many things employed in a good style of singing, which, in order to find in them a greater elegance, are notated in one way but have a different effect, whence it is said that a person sings with more or less grace.[14] These things force me now to show, first, the way I describe the trill and the *gruppo* and the method I use to teach it to those of my household. Then later, in addition, I will demonstrate all the other more necessary effects, so that no refinement known to me remains without demonstration.

[Example B]

Trill, or plain shake   Gruppo, or double relish

12. The names for Caccini's figures are from the anonymous English translation in John Playford's *Introduction to the Skill of Music*, 4th–12th eds. (1664–94).
13. Hitchcock, *Le nuove musiche*, p. 50, note 29 also points out Caccini's distinction between smooth dynamic increase-and-decrease versus the "exclamation," differences which no doubt involved elements such as the attack on the initial consonant, as well differences in speed and range of dynamic change.
14. In other words, notation can be realized in different ways by different singers.

The trill notated by me on one tone only is not shown in this manner for any other reason than that I have observed no other method in teaching it to my first wife and now to my current wife and my daughters,[15] than this same one that you see written, the one and the other: that is, beginning with the first semiminim [♩] and restriking each note with the throat on the vowel "a" until the last breve, and similarly for the *gruppo* [Ex. B]. And how excellently well this trill and this *gruppo* were learned by my past wife using this model, I will leave to the judgment of whoever heard her sing in her time, just as I leave it to the judgment of others to hear with what refinement it is executed by my current wife. If it is true that experience is the mistress of all things, I can with some assurance state and say that there is no better means for teaching it, nor any better form in which to notate it, than the way it has been expressed [here], both the one and the other. Because this trill and this *gruppo* are a necessary step to many things that are described here (which are effects of that grace that is most sought after in order to sing well, and, as was said above, depending on how they are written, can make the opposite effect from what is wanted), I will show not only how they can be used, but also, all those effects will be notated in two ways, on a note of the same duration. We will realize then, as repeated above several times, that all the refinements of this art can be learned from these writings, taken together with practical study.

[Example C]

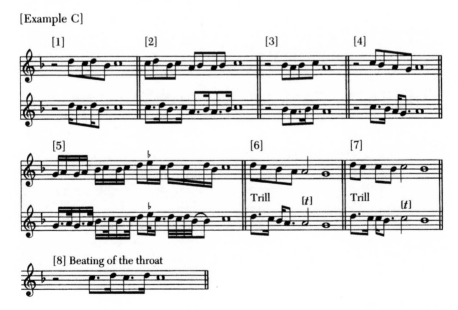

15. Lucia Caccini, mother of musicians Francesca and Settimia, died in 1593. Within two years Giulio married Margherita Benevoli.

In the musical examples [Ex. C] we can see that of the two given, the second instance is more graceful than the first. And so that we can therefore gain better experience, some of them will be notated below with text and a bass line for the chitarrone, along with all the most affective gestures. By practicing these other examples, one will be able to exercise and acquire every greater perfection.

•   •   •   •   •

[Example F]

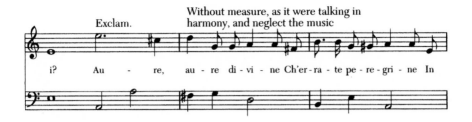

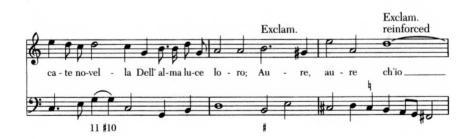

Since in the madrigal "Deh, dove son fuggiti" [see Ex. F] are contained all the best affective devices that could be used with respect to the nobility of this type of song, I wanted to notate it for you, as much to demonstrate where one should increase and diminish the voice—to make exclamations, trills and *gruppi,* and, in short, all the treasures of this art—as well as to not have to illustrate this again for all the compositions that follow. So this will serve as a model to recognize similar places in those pieces where they will be most necessary, according to the affections of the words. I have also come to call the style "noble" that, not subjecting itself to regular meter, often halves the duration of the notes, according to the meaning of the words. From this is born a line with "disregard" *(sprezzatura),* as it is called.

To excel in this art, wherever there are many devices to be applied, it is necessary to have a good voice for them with regard to the breath, in order to be able to execute them in places where they are most necessary. In this regard, it is also advisable that a master of this art, when singing solo with a chitarrone or other stringed instrument and not being forced to adjust to any others, should choose a pitch level at which he can sing with a full, natural voice, in order to avoid going into falsetto.[16] To sing falsetto or at least forced tones, it is necessary to use the breath in order not to expose them much (since they typically offend the ear). And one needs breath in order to give greater animation to the increasing and diminishing of the voice, to exclamations, and to all the other effects we have demonstrated. Be careful not to run out of breath, then, where it is needed. The nobility of good singing, however, cannot come from falsetto; rather it will arise from a natural voice comfortable on all tones, which a person can adjust to his own ability, without relying on the breath for anything other than showing himself to be master of all the best expressive

16. The term "falsetto" appears to have come into use in English only in the late eighteenth century. Today it refers to an entire tessitura. Caccini's phrase in the plural, "le voci finte," refers to those tones on which a singer might or would need to use a "feigned" or "false" voice.

means that are required in this very noble style of singing. Fired in me by natural inclination and by virtue of so many years of study, my love of this way of singing, and of all music in general, will excuse me, if I have let myself get carried beyond what perhaps befits one who esteems not learning less than the communication of what has been learned, and the respect I bear to all masters of the art.

21 Lodovico Viadana

Born in Viadana near Mantua around 1560, Lodovico first appeared in print in 1588 with a set of vesper psalms. A Franciscan, he apparently taught plainsong to the clerics of the cathedral of Mantua before becoming its master of the chapel in the early 1590s. He held similar posts in the cities of Cremona, Reggio Emilia, Concordia (Portogruaro), and Fano. His itinerant life eventually led him back toward Viadana, and he died nearby in 1627 at the newly founded monastery of Sant' Andrea in Gualtieri.

Viadana published a number of volumes of sacred and secular polyphonic music, but his reputation rests chiefly upon the collection of *One Hundred Sacred Concertos,* all but two composed for one to four voices and organ, thought to have been written mostly in Rome around 1596 and published in Venice as op. 12 in 1602. It actually contains more than a hundred works; in addition to eleven solo concertos each for soprano, alto, tenor, and bass with basso continuo it offers twenty duets, seventeen trios, and sixteen concertos for four voices, as well as four psalms, two Magnificats, one instrumental canzona, and nine *falsibordoni.* It was reprinted immediately and repeatedly, appearing in a German edition in 1609 and achieving its eighth edition three years later. Although Viadana's vocal style belongs, not unexpectedly, to the sixteenth century, his practical reduction of the keyboard short score into a basso continuo part exerted a lasting influence on the rapid dissemination and development of sacred music for few voices. The general principles he set out in 1602 for realizing the bass remained valid in keyboard continuo performance long after musical style had changed.

Preface to *One Hundred Sacred Concertos, op. 12*
(1602)

Lodovico Viadana to his kind readers,

There have been many reasons (courteous readers) which have induced me to compose concertos of this kind, among which the following is one of the most important: I saw that singers wishing to sing to the organ, either with three voices, or two, or to a single one by itself, were sometimes forced by the lack of compositions suitable to their purpose to take one, two, or three parts from motets in five, six, seven, or even eight; these owing to the fact that they ought to be heard in conjuction with other parts, as being necessary for the imitations, closes, counterpoints, and other features of the composition as a whole, are full of long and repeated pauses; closes are missing, there is a lack of melody, and, in short, very little continuity or meaning, quite apart from the interruptions of the words, which are sometimes in part omitted and sometimes separated by inconvenient breaks which render the style of performance either imperfect, or wearisome, or ugly, and far from pleasing to the listeners, not to mention the very great difficulty which the singers experience in performance.

Accordingly, having repeatedly given no little thought to these difficulties, I have tried very hard to find a way of remedying to some extent so notable a deficiency, and I believe, thank God, that I have at length found it, having to this end, composed some of these concertos of mine for a single voice (for sopranos, altos, tenors, or basses) and some others for the same parts in a variety of combinations, always making it my aim to give satisfaction thereby to singers of every description, combining the parts in every variety of ways, so that whoever wants a soprano with a tenor, a tenor with an alto, an alto with a cantus, a cantus with a bass, a bass with an alto, two sopranos, two altos, two tenors, or two basses, will find them all, perfectly adapted to his requirements; and whoever wants other combinations of the same parts will also find them in these concertos, now for three, and now for four voices, so that there will be no singer who will not be able to find among them plenty of pieces, perfectly suited to his requirements and in accordance with his taste, wherewith to do himself credit.

You will find some others which I have composed for instruments in various

TEXT: *Cento concerti ecclesiastici a una, a due, a tre, & a quattro voci con il basso continuo per sonar nell'organo* (Venice, 1602). A modern edition of the first part was edited by Claudio Gallico (Kassel: Bärenreiter, 1964), pp. 121–23. This translation, with emendations, from Franck Thomas Arnold, *The Art of Accompaniment from a Thorough-Bass* (London, 1931; repr. New York: Dover, 1965), pp. 2–4, 10–19 (with the Italian text); the last paragraph translated by Oliver Strunk.

ways, which makes the invention more complete and gives the concertos greater adaptability and variety.

Furthermore, I have taken particular care to avoid pauses in them, except so far as is necessitated by the character and form[1] of the melody.

I have, to the very best of my ability, endeavored to achieve an agreeable and graceful tunefulness in all the parts by making them singable and coherent.

I have not failed to introduce, where appropriate, certain figures and cadences, and other convenient opportunities for ornaments and passagework[2] and for giving other proofs of the aptitude and elegant style of the singers, although, for the most part, to facilitate matters, the stock *passaggi* have been used, such as nature itself provides, but more florid.

I have taken pains that the words should be so well disposed beneath the notes that, besides insuring their proper delivery all in complete and logical phrases, it should be possible for them to be clearly understood by the hearers, provided that they are delivered distinctly by the singers.

The other less important reason (in comparison with the one aforesaid) which has also made me hasten to publish this my invention is the following: seeing some of these *Concerti,* which I composed five or six years ago when in Rome (happening then to bethink myself of this new fashion), in such favor with many singers and musicians that they were not only found worthy to be sung again and again in many of the leading places of worship, but that some persons actually took occasion to imitate them very cleverly and to print some of these imitations[3] wherefore, both for the above reason and also to satisfy my friends, by whom I have frequently been most urgently requested and advised to publish my said concertos long before, I have at last made up my mind, after having completed the intended number, to print them, as I am now doing, being convinced that this work need not be altogether displeasing to discerning singers and musicians, and that even though it possess no other merit, a spirit ready and willing to see it done, at least, will not have been lacking, and since it provides, along with its novelty, more than ordinary food for thought, you cannot disdain to read the following instructions, which, in practice, will be of no slight assistance.

First. Concertos of this kind must be sung with refinement, discretion, and grace, using *accenti* with reason and *passaggi* with moderation and in their proper place: above all, not adding anything beyond what is printed in them, inasmuch as there are sometimes certain singers, who, because they are favored by nature with a certain agility of the throat, never sing the songs as they are written, not realizing that nowadays their like are not acceptable, but

---

1. "Il modo e la dispositione del canto." Pauses that Viadana aimed to avoid would occur when singers sang choral parts as solos or performed ensemble works with fewer lines sung than notated (with the organ covering all lines not sung).
2. "Accentuare e passeggiare," see the Glossary of Foreign Performance Terms for *accenti* and *passaggi.*
3. For example, the *Sacri concerti a due voci* of Gabriele Fattorini, published in Venice in 1600.

are, on the contrary, held in very low esteem indeed, particularly in Rome, where the true school of good singing flourishes.

Second. The organist is bound to play the organ part simply, and in particular with the left hand; if, however, he wants to execute some movement with the right hand, as by ornamenting the cadences, or by some appropriate embellishment, he must play in such a manner that the singer or singers are not covered or confused by too much movement.

Third. It will likewise be a good thing that the organist should first cast an eye over the concerto which is to be sung, since, by understanding the nature of the music, he will always execute the accompaniments better.

Fourth. Let the organist be warned always to make the cadences in their proper position: that is to say, if a concerto for one bass voice alone is being sung, to make a bass cadence; if it be for a tenor, to make a tenor cadence; if an alto or soprano, to make it in the places of the one or the other, since it would always have a bad effect if, while the soprano were making its cadence, the organ were to make it in the tenor, or if, while someone were singing the tenor cadence, the organ were to play it in the soprano.[4]

Fifth. When a concerto begins after the manner of a fugue, the organist begins also with a single note, and, on the entry of the several parts, it is at his discretion to accompany them as he pleases.

Sixth. No tablature has been made for these concertos, not in order to escape the trouble, but to make them easier for the organist to play, since as a matter of fact, not every one would play from a tablature at sight, and the majority would play from the *partitura* as being less trouble; organists, however, will be able to make the said tablature at their own convenience, which, to tell the truth, is much better.

Seventh. When passages in full harmony are played on the organ, they are to be played with hands and feet, but without the further addition of stops, because the character of these soft and delicate *concerti* does not bear the great noise of the full organ, besides which, in miniature *concerti*, it has something pedantic about it.

Eighth. Every care has been taken in assigning the accidentals where they occur, and the prudent organist will therefore see that he observes them.

Ninth. The organ part is never under any obligation to avoid two fifths or two octaves, but those parts which are sung by the voices are.

Tenth. If anyone should want to sing this kind of music without organ or

---

4. In the interpretation of this rule, which is a most important one, everything turns upon the exact sense to be attached to the words "in their proper place" (*à i lochi loro*). Do they simply refer to pitch, i.e., to the octave in which the "cadence" (tonic, leading note, tonic) is to be played, or the *part* of the harmony in which it is to appear? . . . [It] seems probable that Viadana's meaning was that, when a bass was singing, the "cadence" should be made in unison with the voice, and that, in the case of the other voices, it was to be in the *part of the harmony* corresponding to the voice in question. Generally speaking (except in the case of a high voice . . .), this would also imply identity of pitch. [Tr.]

clavichord[5] the effect will never be good; on the contrary, for the most part, dissonances will be heard.

Eleventh. In these concertos, falsettos will have a better effect than natural sopranos; because boys, for the most part, sing carelessly, and with little style[6] likewise because we have reckoned on distance to give greater charm; there is, however, no doubt that no money can pay a good natural soprano; but there are few of them.

Twelfth. When one wants to sing a concerto written in four equal voices,[7] the organist must never play up high, and, vice versa, when one wants to sing a concerto of high pitch, the organist must never play down low, unless it be in cadences in the octave, because it then gives charm.

Nor let anyone presume to tell me here that the said concertos are a little too difficult, for my intention has been to make them for those who understand and sing well, and not for those who abuse their craft. And be in good health.

5. "Manacordo"; the clavichord was a standard practice instrument for organists.
6. For the same judgment, see Pietro della Valle in No. 4, p. 41.
7. Strunk's emendation of Arnold's translation, which he explained: Viadana follows the usual practice of his time, which applies the expression *a voci pari* not only to music in a single register, high or low, but also to music in which the overall register is relatively restricted. Then in his "O sacrum convivium" *a voci pari* (Arnold, pp. 31–33) the four clefs are alto, tenor, tenor, and bass.

22 Agostino Agazzari

Agostino Agazzari (c. 1580–1642) and his father were ennobled by the Grand Duke of Tuscany in 1601, having probably resided in the Tuscan city of Siena for some time. Agostino served as organist at the cathedral in Siena from 1597 to 1602. He is best known for his activities during the next five years, which he spent in Rome as director of music at the German-Hungarian College and then at the Roman Seminary. He marked his return to Siena in 1607 with the publication of a little ten-page tutor on the performance of basso continuo lines which reflected his experience with the new styles of sacred and dramatic music in Rome. His precepts were anticipated in a letter of 1606 that was later published in Adriano Banchieri's *Conclusioni del suono dell'organo* (Bologna, 1609). Agazzari discusses the array of instruments that could play basso continuo and notes the distinctive contributions that each could make in an ensemble. What Agazzari does not stipulate are guidelines for choosing continuo instruments to play in different musical styles and genres, presumably because circumstance and taste allowed for a great amount of variety. He served as the master of the chapel at the cathedral of Siena for the rest of his life.

Of Playing upon a Bass with All Instruments and of Their Use in a Consort

(1607)

Having now to speak to you of musical instruments, I must first, for the sake of the order and brevity required in all discussions, classify them according to the needs of my subject and proposed material. I shall therefore divide them into classes, namely, into instruments like a foundation and instruments like ornaments. Like a foundation are those which guide and support the whole body of the voices and instruments of the consort; such are the organ, harpsichord, etc. Like ornaments are those which, in a playful and contrapuntal fashion, make the harmony more agreeable and sonorous, namely, the lute, theorbo, harp, *lirone, cetera,* spinet, *chitarrina,*[1] violin, pandora, and the like.

Further, some are stringed instruments, others wind instruments. Of those of this second group (excepting the organ) I shall say nothing, because they are not used in good and pleasing consorts, because of their insufficient union with the stringed instruments and because of the variation produced in them by the human breath, although they are mixed in great and noisy ones. Sometimes in a small consort, when there are *organetti* at the octave above, the trombone is used as a contrabass, but it must be well and softly played. All this I say in general, for in particular cases these instruments may be played so excellently by a master hand that they adorn and beautify the consort.

In the same way, among the stringed instruments, some have within them a perfect harmony of the parts, such as the organ *[sic]*, harpsichord, lute, double harp, etc.; others have an imperfect one, such as the common cittern, *lirone, chitarrina,* etc.; others have little or none, such as the viol, violin, pandora,[2] etc. For this reason I shall speak in the first place of those instruments of the first class which are the foundation and have perfect harmony and in the second place of those which serve for ornament.

Having made this division and laid down these principles, let us come to the instructions for playing upon a bass. I say, then, that he who wishes to play well

---

TEXT: *Del sonare sopra 'l basso con tutti li stromenti, e dell'uso loro nel conserto* (Siena, 1607; facs. Milan, 1933; Bologna, 1969). Translation by Oliver Strunk, revised by Margaret Murata.

1. The *lirone* is a bass *lira da braccio*, a fretted, bowed instrument with nine to fourteen strings on the fingerboard and two to four drone strings. It typically played sustained chords, and in the seventeenth century was often the instrument of choice to accompany laments. The *cetera* or *cetra* is a six-course, wire-strung cittern, played with a plectrum. The *chitarrina* would be some sort of small guitar.

2. Agazzari appears to refer here to the range of chords or double-stops accessible on the instruments.

should understand three things. First he must know counterpoint (or at least sing with assurance, understand proportions and time,[3] and read in all the clefs) and must know how to resolve dissonances with consonances, how to distinguish the major and minor thirds and sixths, and other similar matters. Second, he must know how to play his instrument well, understanding its tablature or score, and must be very familiar with its keyboard or fingerboard in order not to have to search painfully for the consonances and beats during the music, knowing that his eye is busy watching the parts before him. Third, he must have a good ear in order to perceive the movements of the parts in their relation to one another. Of this I do not speak, for I could not say anything that would make anyone good who was poor in it by nature.

But to come to the point, I conclude that no definite rule can be laid down for playing works where there are no signs of any sort, it being necessary to be guided in these by the intention of the composer, who is free and can, if he sees fit, place on the first half of a note a fifth or sixth, or vice versa, and that a major or a minor one, as seems more suitable to him or as may be necessitated by the words. And even though some writers who treat of counterpoint have defined the order of progression from one consonance to another as though there were but one way, they are in the wrong. They will pardon me for saying this, for they show that they have not understood that the consonances and the harmony as a whole are subject and subordinate to the words, not vice versa, and this I shall defend, if need be, with all the reasons I can. While it is perfectly true that, absolutely and in general, it is possible to lay down definite rules of progression, when there are words they must be clothed with that suitable harmony which arouses or conveys some affect.

As no definite rule can be given, the player must necessarily rely upon his ear and follow the work and its movements. But if you would have an easy way of avoiding these obstacles and of playing the work exactly, take this one, indicating with figures above the notes of the bass[4] the consonances and dissonances placed there by the composer; for example, if on the first half of a note there is a fifth and then a sixth, or vice versa, or a fourth and then a third, as illustrated:

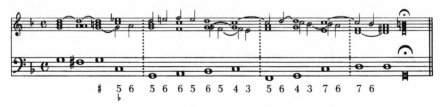

Further, you must know that all consonances are either natural or accidental to the mode. When they are natural, no accidental is written at all; for example,

---

3. Agazzari refers here to musical mensuration—how to perform metric notation and the proportional system of metric modulation.
4. Agazzari's figures have been moved below the continuo line, following modern convention.

when B is natural, the third above G (otherwise B-flat or B-natural) is naturally major. To make it minor, you must write a flat above the note G, in which case the third is accidentally minor. Conversely, when B is flat, to make the third major, you must write a sharp above the note B. I say the same of the sixths, reminding you that an accidental below or near a note refers to the note itself, while one above it refers to the consonance which must be realized, as in the following example:

All cadences, whether medial or final, require the major third, therefore some musicians do not indicate it; to be on the safe side, however, I advise writing the sign, especially in medial cadences.

The instruments being divided into two classes, it follows that they have different functions and are differently used. An instrument that serves as foundation must be played with great judgment and due regard for the size of the chorus; if there are many voices one should play with full harmonies, increasing the registers. While if there are few, one should use few consonances, decreasing the registers and playing the work as purely and exactly as possible, using few runs or divisions, occasionally supporting the voices with some contrabass notes and frequently avoiding the high ones which cover up the voices, especially the sopranos or falsettos. For this reason one should take the greatest possible care to avoid touching or diminishing with a division the note which the soprano sings, in order not to double it or obscure the excellence of the note itself or of the *passaggio* that the good singer improvises on it. For the same reason one does well to play within a rather small compass and in a low register.

I say the same of the lute, harp, theorbo, harpsichord, etc., when they serve as foundation with one or more voices singing above them, for in this case, to support the voice, they must maintain a solid, sonorous, sustained harmony, playing now *piano,* now *forte,* according to the quality and quantity of the voices, the place, and the work, while, to avoid interfering with the singer, they must not restrike the strings too often when the voice improvises a *passaggio* and some embellishment.

Finally, my purpose being to teach how to play upon a bass (not simply how to play, for this must be known beforehand), I take for granted a certain number of principles and terms; for example, that imperfect consonances progress to the nearest perfect ones; that cadences require the major third, as is for the most part true; that dissonances are resolved by the nearest consonance, the seventh by the sixth and the fourth by the third when the part containing the resolution lies above, the opposite when it lies below. But these

matters I shall not discuss at length: he who does not know them must learn
them. At present I shall teach the conduct of the hand on the organ.

The bass proceeds in many ways, namely, by step, by leap, by conjunct divisions,[5] or with disjunct notes of small value. When it ascends by step, the right
hand must descend by step or leap [1]; conversely, when the left hand ascends
or descends by a leap of a third, fourth, or fifth [2], the right hand must proceed
by step, for it is not good for both to ascend or descend together. Not only is
this ugly to see and to hear, but there is in it no variety at all, for it will be all
octaves and fifths. When the bass ascends with a *tirata*, the right hand must
remain stationary [3]. When the progression is disjunct, with notes of small
value, each note must have its own accompaniment [4]. Here is an example of
the whole:

*The parallel octaves are in the original example.

Having now spoken sufficiently of the instruments which serve as a foundation to enable a judicious man to obtain much light from this slender ray (for
saying too much makes for confusion), I shall speak briefly of those which serve
as ornaments.

These instruments, which are combined with the voices in various ways, are
in my opinion so combined for no other purpose than to ornament and beautify, and indeed to season the consort. For this reason, these instruments should
be used in a different way than those of the first class. While those maintained
the tenor and a plain harmony, these must make the melody graceful and let it
flower, each according to its quality, with a variety of beautiful counterpoints.
But in this the one class differs from the other. While the instruments of the
first class, playing the bass before them as it stands, require no great knowledge

---

5. Agazzari's term is "tirata continuata." A *tirata* is a figure of stepwise notes of equal value; see
   Glossary of Foreign Performance Terms.

of counterpoint in the player, those of the second class do require it, for the player must compose new parts above the bass and new and varied *passaggi* and counterpoints.

For this reason, the person who plays the lute (which is the noblest instrument of them all) must play it nobly, with much invention and variety, not as is done by those who, because they have a ready hand, do nothing but play runs and make divisions from beginning to end, especially when playing with other instruments which do the same, in all of which nothing is heard but mess and confusion, displeasing and disagreeable to the listener. Sometimes, therefore, the lutanist must use now gentle strokes and sweet restrikings; now broad *passaggi*, now rapid and repeated ones, sometimes something played on the bass strings, sometimes beautiful exchanges[6] and ostinatos, repeating and bringing out the same fugues at different pitches and in different places. He must, in short, so weave the voices together with long *groppi*, trills, and *accenti*,[7] each in its turn, that he gives grace to the ensemble and enjoyment and delight to the listeners, judiciously preventing these embellishments from conflicting with one another and allowing time to each, especially when instruments are similar, a thing to be avoided, in my opinion, unless they play at some distance from each other or are differently tuned and of different sizes.[8] And what I say of the lute as the principal instrument, I wish understood of the others in their kind, for it would take a long time to discuss them all separately.

But since each instrument has its own peculiar limitations, the player must take advantage of them and be guided by them to produce a good result. Bowed instruments, for example, have a different style than those plucked with a quill or with the finger. The player of the *lirone* must bow with long, clear, sonorous strokes, bringing out the inner parts well, with attention to the major and minor thirds and sixths, a matter difficult but important with that instrument. The violin requires beautiful *passaggi*, distinct and long, with playful figures and little echoes and imitations repeated in several places, expressive *accenti*, *arcate mute*,[9] *groppi*, trills, etc. The *violone*, as the low part, proceeds with gravity, supporting the harmony of the other parts with its sweet resonance, dwelling as much as possible on the heavier strings, frequently touching the lowest ones. The theorbo, with its full and gentle consonances, reinforces the melody greatly, restriking and lightly passing over its bourdon strings, its special excellence, with trills and *accenti muti* played with

6. "Belle gare," literally "contests."
7. These are all melodic ornaments. For *accenti*, see the Glossary of Foreign Performance Terms, p. 223.
8. Agazzari's comments reveal practical experience. Distance diminishes the roughness of unison or same-register playing that is not quite together or in tune. Plucked instruments in different tunings will naturally turn out figures around different pitches, as will instruments of different sizes, which have differences of register.
9. Literally, "mute bow strokes." The exact meaning of this phrase is unknown, but it may refer to playing tones on longer note values without the usual improvising of diminutions, and possibly, in analogy to the *accenti muti* of theorbo playing, some type of movement of the left hand that alters the pitch during a long-held tone. "Mute" may also imply a special kind of sound quality.

the left hand.[10] The double harp, which is everywhere useful, as much so in the soprano as in the bass, explores its entire range with gentle pizzicatos, echoes between the two hands, trills, etc.; in short, it aims at good counterpoint. The cittern, whether the common cittern or the *ceterone*[11] is used with other instruments in a playful way, making counterpoints upon the part. But all this must be done prudently. If the instruments are playing alone in concert, they must do everything and flavor the ensemble. If they play in company, each must regard the other, making space and not conflicting among themselves.[12] If there are many, they must each await their turn and not, chirping all at once like sparrows, try to shout one another down. Let these few remarks serve to give some light to him who seeks to learn. He who relies on his own efforts needs no instruction at all. I do not write for him—I esteem and honor him, but if perchance some wit desires to carry the discussion further, I am at his service.

Finally, one must know how to transpose music from one step to another that has all the consonances natural and proper to the given tone.[13] No other transposition is possible without a very disagreeable sound, for, as I have sometimes observed, in transposing a first or second tone, naturally pleasing because of its many B-flats, to some step whose tone requires B-natural, it will be difficult for the player to be cautious enough and avoid stumbling against some conflicting notes. Thus, with this crudity, the consort is spoiled and the listeners are offended, while the natural character of the given tone does not appear. Most natural and convenient of all is the transposition to the fourth or fifth, sometimes to a step lower or higher; in short, one must see which transposition is most appropriate and suitable to the given tone, not as is done by those who pretend to play every tone on every pitch. For if I could argue at length, I could show these their error and the impropriety of this.

Having treated thus far of playing upon a bass, it seems to me desirable to say something about the bass itself, for it has, I know, been censured by some, ignorant of its purpose or lacking the soul to play it. It is, then, for three reasons that this method has been introduced: first, because of the modern style of composing and singing recitative; second, because of its convenience; third, because of the number and variety of works which are necessary for concerted music.

As to the first reason, I shall say that, since the recent discovery of the true style of expressing the words, namely, the imitation of speech itself in the best possible manner, something which succeeds best with a single voice or with

10. "Accenti muti" are likely quick dissonances played on the fingerboard by the left hand alone after the string has been plucked.
11. A large cittern with one or more unstopped bass strings.
12. Agazzari's distinction here is between an ensemble in which all instruments are realizing a continue bass line that has no composed melody line, which is common in the *sinfonia,* and an ensemble realizing a bass line to another composed part or parts.
13. Equal temperament was still a hundred years away, at least. In unequal temperaments, transposition could be made satisfactorily only to modes in which the sizes of the intervals relative to their scale steps were approximately those of the original mode. For a discussion of this problem see Arthur Mendel, "Pitch in the 16th and Early 17th Centuries," *Musical Quarterly* 34 (1948): 28–45, 199–221, 336–57, 575–93.

few voices, as in the modern airs of certain able men and as is now much practiced at Rome in concerted music, it is no longer necessary to make a score[14] or tablature, but, as we have said above, a bass with its signs suffices. And if anyone objects that a bass will not suffice to play ancient works, full of fugues and counterpoints, I shall reply that music of this kind is no longer in use, both because of the confusion and babel of the words, arising from the long and intricate imitations, and because it has no grace, for, with all the voices singing, one hears neither period nor sense, these being interfered with and covered up by imitations. Indeed, at every moment, each voice has different words, a thing displeasing to men of competence and judgment. And on this account music would have come very near to being banished from Holy Church by a sovereign pontiff had not Giovan Palestrina found the remedy, showing that the fault and error lay, not with music, but with the composers, and composing in confirmation of this the mass entitled *Missa Papae Marcelli*. For this reason, although such compositions are good according to the rules of counterpoint, they are at the same time faulty according to the law of music that is true and good, something which arises from disregarding the aim and function and good precepts of the latter, such composers wishing to stand solely on the observance of canonic treatment and imitation of the notes not on the affect and the resemblance to the words. Indeed, many of them wrote their music first and fitted words to it afterwards. For the moment, let this suffice, for it would not be to the purpose to discuss the matter at length in this place.

The second reason is the great convenience of the method, for with little labor the musician will have a large stock for his needs; apart from this, the learner is free from tablature, a matter difficult and burdensome to many and likewise very liable to error, the eye and mind being wholly occupied with following so many parts, especially when it is necessary to play concerted music on the spur of the moment.

The third and last reason, namely, the number of works which are necessary for concerted music, is alone sufficient ground, it seems to me, for introducing this so convenient method of playing. For if he were to put into tablature or score all the works which are sung in the course of a year in a single church in Rome, wherever the concert music is professional, the organist would need to have a larger library than a Doctor of Laws. There was then abundant reason for the introduction of this kind of bass, with the method described above, on the ground that there is no need for the player to play the parts as written, if he aims to accompany singing and not to play the work as written, a matter foreign to our subject. Accept what I have said in place of all I might have said, my desire being to satisfy in brief your courteous demands, so many times repeated, and not my natural bent, which is rather to learn from others than to teach them. Take it as it is, then, and let the shortness of the time be my excuse.

14. "Spartitura."

23 Anonymous

The unknown Italian author of the twenty-three chapters that make up *Il corago*, a manuscript treatise on the staging of dramatic works, certainly knew ancient and modern poetry and plays and had seen modern theatrical spectacles in Florence, Mantua, and Ferrara. The *choregos* was a wealthy producer in the ancient Greek theater and a kind of stage manager in the Roman whose Baroque-era counterpart could be considered an impresario. Writing sometime within the decade after 1628, the author needed neither to explain nor to justify modern spectacle but aimed, rather, to advise on all the aspects involved in producing and directing a well thought-out and polished court performance, an undertaking that required the supervision and coordination of "carpenters, tailors, builders, scene painters, singers, instrumentalists, dancers, actors, fencers, jousters, tourneymen, inventors of marvelous machines, and poets of the most sublime kind of poetry." Appropriately, the chapters focus on costumes, lighting, stage machines, and building temporary stages and sets, and he discusses practical alternatives for staging dramas, especially the new genre that would become known as opera. Chapters 11 and 12 even advise poets on how to write suitable verse for recitative and composers on how best to express the sense of poetry in their music. The next chapters illustrate considerations in choosing instrumental forces and where to place them, meter in recitative, stage placement and movement of the singers and chorus, theatrical dance, and stage combat. In the concreteness with which everything is discussed, this clearly experienced *corago* reveals a passion for the stage and standards for the ideal theatrical performance.

FROM *The Choragus, or, Some Observations for Staging Dramatic Works Well*

(c. 1630)

CHAPTER 13: WHETHER WINDS OR STRINGS ARE MORE SUITABLE TO ACCOMPANYING SUNG DRAMA

• • • • •

If you use string instruments, make sure that the sound goes upward and not to the near sides, because if the hall is big and it is necessary to play

TEXT: *Il corago, o vero alcune osservazioni per metter bene in scena le composizioni drammatiche*, Paolo Fabbri and Angelo Pompilio, eds. (Florence: L. S. Olschki, 1983), pp. 87–95. The manuscript

somewhat loudly, the important people in the audience who usually are near the stage will be deafened due to the overly robust sound, and they will not hear the singing well. For this reason it helps to make a well-enclosed partition of large boards between the instruments and the listener. String instruments should not be kept behind the scenes,[1] because since there are many of them they naturally block the passageways, bothering the singers. Second, because then the player and singer cannot see each other, and probably will not hear each other; for this reason some have placed the instruments above the houses of the stage between balustrades. But this orientation, aside from being an inconvenience to the sets, does not unite the instrumental sound very well with the voice of the actor. And what is worst is that the harpsichord player, who is used more than anyone, will not see the singer. And if the singer's voice is weak, the harpsichordist will not hear it, so that either someone will have to beat time or there will be the danger of disagreement. Others place said instruments at the threshold of the stage floor, raising a partition and a parapet between it and the listener, as far from the stage as is necessary in order to hold the instruments, but this method carries with it some inconveniences. First, that the players, being lower than the floor of the stage, if they are taller, will have their hair or heads seen, an enormous defect. They cannot see the actors well if they do not come downstage. Secondly, a parapet higher than the end of the stage ruins the borders of the set, and prevents one from seeing the feet and boots of the actors, with which the elegant individual who is fully seen brings about greater delight. Third, it takes the space from the best part of the hall that should belong to the listener and, with its extremely close sound, it offends the prominent people in the audience who might place themselves near the stage.

To escape these inconveniences, others place the players at the sides of the stage, beyond it, taking the place that belongs to the listener at the right and left of the sets, in little boxes at a height equal to the end of the stage. And these boxes, in order to obstruct the space and the view of the spectators less, have the shape of a triangle whose point is in the direction of the listener, that is, from the part farthest away from the set and next to the wall. This method seems most suitable because it leaves the stage free; it lets the principal player at least see and hear the singers, and it takes away less space belonging to the listener; nor will it offend the most important people in the audience, who usually sit in the middle.

source is Modena, Biblioteca Estense, MS. γ.F.6.11 (Campori collection). The editors speculate that the author could have been Pierfrancesco Rinuccini (1592–1657), son of Ottavio. A summary with some extended passages in English, including chapter 15 entire, is in R. Savage and M. Sansone, "Il corago and the Staging of Early Opera: Four Chapters from an Anonymous Treatise circa 1630," Early Music 17 (1989):494–511. Translation by Margaret Murata.

1. Some productions before this time placed the orchestra offstage. The long necks of archlutes easily get in the way, as do harps and harpsichords.

Last, you have to remember that if you want to use string instruments, it is necessary that from the musicians' platform there be a passage that goes backstage, so that any one of them can remove himself to tune his instrument, because that tuning is bothersome, especially if it goes on near the listeners for any length of time.

To remove the problem of the instruments' flatting little by little due to the extreme heat generated by the lights and breathing, it seems that no one before now has sufficiently anticipated keeping duplicate instruments that in due course can come and go. The least damage occurs when all the instruments go flat uniformly; then you do not have discords or notable ugliness. Placing two enclosed organs in these boxes, so that they overwhelm neither the voice of the singer nor the ear of the player so that he cannot hear the person reciting, seems to be the easiest way to hold the pitch, in order that the other instruments can come and tune, adjust, and stay in tune with perpetual diligence, which you cannot do with harpsichords.

CHAPTER 14: WHETHER THE RECITATIVE STYLE SHOULD BE SUNG WITH OR WITHOUT A BEAT

Some think that the recitative style must be used with a musical beat, for many reasons. First, for the greater sureness of the singer who, with the measure visible, is more certain not to err. Secondly, for greater security in keeping with the instrumentalist, who either cannot always see and hear the actor well who is singing or cannot give it much thought; this at least makes it easier for both sides. Thirdly, because in the long course of many works, it is inevitable that now and then passages will occur of very difficult music; also in terms of observing the time. Then it will be not only useful, but necessary, to have the beat.

Nonetheless, the common feeling and practice among those that sing on stage is not to use a beat. First, since the perfection of the recitative style taken to the stage lies in showing and imitating the natural manner of discourse, one must remove everything that demonstrates patent artifice as much as possible, if it is not absolutely necessary. The beat is not necessary; one knows often enough through experience.

Second, if it is necessary to conduct in such a way that the beat is seen by the player as well as the actor, it is inevitable that it will also be visible to the spectator, for whom it is extremely annoying to keep seeing that unseemly up and down for two or three hours.

Third, since the actor must stop to sigh at length as nature tells him and hold on to the same note more or less according to the affect, he should not be tied to any one else's measure, but should freely follow the impulse of feeling, which is of great importance in reciting well. . . .

In difficult passages with respect to rhythm or tempo, the instrumentalist should accommodate the actor, as long as the passage has been rehearsed beforehand several times and it has been determined that there is some aria or passage for many voices in madrigal style that will truly have need of conducting. Then it can be done; but this will happen rarely, and then you would beat for the entirety of that aria or madrigal for chorus, leaving the rest without beating.

CHAPTER 15: OF THE MANNER OF RECITING IN MUSIC

Two sorts of advice are useful to anyone who acts in singing in dramatic works. Some admonitions which are general and common to all actors and are fully part of this discussion, must be taken from what we will say further on about speaking on stage. Others, presupposing the common attributes of a good actor, are special to singers of *stil recitativo,* and these we must discuss briefly in giving the following reminders.

Because declaiming in song[2] goes more slowly than declaiming in speech, it is inevitable that making gestures will also be slower, so that the hand does not finish before the voice does. Therefore it will be necessary to move it very slowly right from the start, and the gesture ought to be broad. You should not sing continuously, even if there is no pause in the musical part; but at the end of each thought, the singer should stop a bit. Also the instrumentalist can sometimes stop, sometimes temporize on the same pitch, other times play special and different music, as long as they have rehearsed it well together beforehand.

If in ordinary acting one avoids walking while speaking, especially walking quickly, so much more should it be avoided during songs, which are noticeably altered and ruined by motion. It cannot be denied, however, that sometimes you will want to move while singing, when the affect and the narrative have been designed to show motion such as assault, flight, and other events, because then the song affected by movement will better express what is wanted. Walking about ought to be done from time to time in the midst of a song, during which there should be played either a ritornello made expressly, or other music, or at least arpeggios played gracefully on the same [bass] note. One could also improvise, because this variety can bring delight.[3] One should not always stop in the middle [of the stage] to sing, but now here, now there—naturally, however, and with a plan, especially if others are supposed to follow and move with you.

When the chorus performs roles, they will use both gestures and motions that are more natural and usual than when they imitate those who sing [solo]. And it will lend not a little grace, if persons who sing together with the same sentiment and feeling also have similar gestures, because in this manner we will see harmony in the gestures, too, which can look quite special. But how

2. "Recitar cantando."
3. That is, the instrumentalist may improvise a ritornello or interlude, if it is decided that the singer should move about during a song.

the chorus should conduct itself when they only sing, following the rhythm and harmony, will be treated below.[4]

•   •   •   •   •

Above all, to be a good singing actor it would be necessary to be also a good speaking actor, as we have seen that some who have had special grace in acting have done marvels when they have known how to sing as well. . . . In the meantime, since the musician must cast the parts suitably and use everyone in the best way, he will try as much as possible to limit the singers who are excellent but bloodless and old to acting in roles that are not very active and that use stage devices, as in clouds and other machines in the air, where not much motion is required, nor the expressiveness of stage gestures.[5] . . . The musician must accompany his song with gesture according to the variety of affects, in the same way that the speaking actor does, as we will discuss next, observing, however, all that was said above of the differences that singing demands.

CHAPTER 16: OF THE MANNER OF SIMPLE DECLAMATION

The manner of reciting is of great importance, because something said by a person who knows how to deliver it well and accompany it with gesture will make a much greater impression on the spirits of the listeners and will more easily stir in them the affections of anger, of hatred, of passion, of happiness, and the like. This will not happen when it is simply narrated by someone without gesture or modulation of the voice. . . .

It falls to the choragus to impart what and how the gestures should be, according to the different aspect of the person that is being represented on stage, because sometimes a contrary gesture will serve well, [or] a discordant voice will please the listeners, when [for example] a servant is brought on stage who is pretending to be a prince, a woman, a lover, or the like, as we see every day.

•   •   •   •   •

Because the affections are different that one reveals with words, so must the gestures be with which they are accompanied. The act of praying goes well with the gesture made with both hands, which at the start are moved a little from within the arms; these, barely open, are then smoothly broadened outward. Nor would I be against inclining one's head a little to the side now and then at the same time. The act of praying or petitioning a god or deity, as happens in sacrifices, wants to be done with great submission and reverence. So it is useful at times to curve the chest and motion with a hand, or two, by bringing them up close to it, as it is also useful to kneel. This is always better

4. Chapter 17 is devoted to the chorus, chapter 18 to dances.
5. The next paragraph warns that stage machines that bear singers must also move slowly in order to avoid shaking and disturbing the singer.

done on one knee rather than two, taking care always to place on the ground that knee that is on the side of the spectators, in order to keep your face turned toward them as much as possible. In the act of anger, the gesture wants to be fierce and agitated, moving the hand with more or less fury according to the words. This gesture wants to be made for the most part by moving the hand towards the person and releasing it with force outward at the close of the sentences; furthermore it is better done with one hand, instead of two together.

The movements of grief want to be accompanied with a gesture made now with two hands, now with one. And it seems that this gesture is really a raising of the hand and leaving it—as if the words had become lost—not to say also to let that raised hand fall sometimes, striking lightly. But raising it upward is done very slowly and with great sensitivity. And because it is usual for a narration to occur here that tells the reason for the grief, let us see the gestures one should look for. Because a narration includes many and different actions, then so many and different ought to be the gestures that go with it. Sometimes one relates a duel or a battle, which should be indicated by gesturing now with both hands, now with one, now with the other separately, only in such a case will it be necessary to gesture with the left.[6] Sometimes one happens to narrate the death of some hero and the manner of the death itself, in which case it will be necessary to represent the gestures of the person whose death is being described. Another time it will be required to tell about something happy, which should be accompanied by a gesture of happiness. This is done by holding the arms a little arched, and from the middle where you should slowly approach, throwing them open with moderate quickness, turning your eyes now and then toward the sky and all around to signify your happiness, and pleading in a certain way with a movement of the head, as an invitation for all things to rejoice with you.

6. "If the person with whom you speak is on your right, you must not gesture with your left hand, which should always be avoided, because it is an ugly thing to see someone gesture with the left hand" (p. 94). In the same passage, we are told that the left hand is allowed to gesture, for example, when the right holds a spear.

24 Christopher Simpson

Christopher Simpson (c. 1605–1669), a well known performer on the viola da gamba, published two instructional books that were inspired by two of his noble students. His *Principles of Practical Musick* (1665/67) was designed for a ten-year-old Sir John St. Barbe to whom Simpson willed his music books. The more famous of the two books, *The Division-Violist* was first published in 1659. John, the son of Simpson's patron, Sir Robert Bolles, became an accomplished player under Simpson's tutelage. Dedicating the second edition to the younger Bolles, the author notes, not immodestly, "As it was made for You, so it has made You (by your ingenuity) not only the greatest Artist, but also the ablest Judge of it, that (I think) is this day in Europe; (I mean) of a Gentleman, and no Professor of the Science." The viol tutor offers elementary instruction in bowing, tuning, ornamenting, and recognizing intervals of pitch. The heart of the book is part 3, which treats of improvising florid counterpoint over a bass. The sections given here, however, demonstrate more than the art of melismatic invention. Simpson discusses ensemble improvisation and instructs players to consider variety, formal coherence, and bringing an improvisation to a satisfying close. These are all aspects that, in the end, determine a good composition, whether it is ever written down or not and whether it has been invented by a Christopher Simpson or a jazz improviser.

FROM *The Division-Viol, or, The Art of Playing* Ex Tempore *upon a Ground*

(1665)

PART III

§12. CONCERNING ORDERING OF DIVISION

When you are to play division to a ground, I would have you, in the first place, to play over the ground itself, plainly and distinctly; for these reasons:

1. That others may hear what notes you divide upon.
2. That your self may be better possessed of the ayre[1] of the ground, in case you know it not before.
3. That he who plays the ground unto you may better perceive the measure of time.

The ground being played over, you may then break it into crochets and quavers;[2] or play some neat piece of slow descant to it, which you please. If your ground consist of two or three strains, you may do by the second or third, as you did by the first. This done, and your ground beginning over again, you may then break it into division of a quicker motion, driving on some point or points as hath been shewed. When you have prosecuted that manner of play so long as you think fitting, and shewed some command of hand; you may then fall off to slower descant or binding-notes,[3] as you see cause; playing also sometimes

TEXT: *The Division-Viol or The Art of Playing* Ex tempore *upon a Ground*, 2d ed. in Latin and English (London, 1665; facs. London, 1965), pp. 56–61. Capitalization has been modernized.

1. "Air" or melody.
2. Eighth and quarter notes.
3. Suspensions.

loud or soft, to express humour[4] and draw on attention. After this you may begin to play some skipping division; or points, or tripla's, or what your present fancy or invention shall prompt you to, changing still from one variety to another; for variety it is which chiefly pleaseth. The best division in the world, still continued, would become tedious to the hearer; and therefore you must so place and dispose your division, that the change of it from one kind to another may still beget a new attention. And this is generally to be observed, whether your ground consist of one or more strains, or be a continued ground; of which I must also speak a little.

§13. Of a Continued Ground

A continued ground used for playing or making division upon, is (commonly) the through-bass of some motet or madrigal, proposed or selected for that purpose. This, after you have played two or three semibreves of it plain, to let the organist know your measure; you may begin to divide, according to your fancy, or the former instructions, until you come near some cadence or close, where I would have you shew some agility of hand. There, if you please, you may rest a minim [♩], two or three, letting him that plays the ground go on: and then come in with some point: after which you may fall to descant, mixt division, tripla's, or what you please. In this manner, playing sometimes swift notes, sometimes slow; changing from this or that sort of division, as may best produce variety, you may carry on the rest of the ground; and if you have any thing more excellent than other, reserve it for the conclusion.

• • •

§ 15. Of Two Viols Playing Together *Ex tempore* to a Ground

After this discourse of division for one viol,[5] I suppose it will not be unseasonable to speak something to two viols playing together upon a ground; in which kind of musick, I have had some experimental knowledge; and therefore will deliver it in such order and manner as I have known the practice of it; referring the improvement thereof to further experience.

First, let the ground be prick'd down in three several papers;[6] one for him who plays upon the organ or harpsichord: the other two for them that play upon the two viols: which, for order and brevity, we will distinguish by three letters viz. **A.** for organist, **B.** for the first Bass, and **C.** for the second. Each of these having the same ground before him, they may all three begin together; A. and B. playing the ground, and C. descanting to it, in slow notes, or such as may suit the beginning of the music. This done, let C. play the ground, and B.

4. Character or mood.
5. Section 14, "Of composing division for one viol to a ground," is omitted here.
6. Written out in parts for three instruments.

descant to it, as the other had done before, but with some little variation. If the ground consist of two strains, the like may be done in the second [strain]: one viol still playing the ground whilest the other descants or divides upon it.

The ground thus play'd over, C. may begin again and play a strain of quicker division; which ended, let B. answer the same with another something like it, but of a little more lofty ayre. For the better performance whereof, if there be any difference in the hands or inventions, I would have the better invention lead, but the more able hand still follow, that the music may not seem to flac-cess[7] or lessen, but rather increase in the performance.

When the viols have thus (as it were) vied and revied one to the other, A. if he have ability of hand, may, upon a sign given him, put in his strain of division; the two viols playing one of them the ground, and the other slow descant to it. A. having finished his strain, a reply thereto may be made, first by one viol, and then by the other. Having answered one another in that same manner so long as they think fit, the two viols may divide a strain both together. In which doing, let B. break the ground, by moving into the octave upward or downward, and returning from thence either to his own note, or to meet the next note in the unison or octave. By this means, C., knowing B's motion, he knows also how to avoyd running into the same, and therefore will move into the third or fifth, (or sixth where it is required) meeting each succeeding note in some one of the said concords, until he come to the close; where he may (after he has divided the binding) meet the close note in the octave; which directions well observed, two viols may move in extemporary division a whole strain together, without any remarkable clashing in the consecution of fifths or eighths.

When they have proceeded thus far; C. may begin some point of division, of the length of a breve or semibreve, naming the said word, that B. may know his intentions: which ended, let B. answer the same upon the succeeding note or notes to the like quantity of time; taking it in that manner, one after another, so long as they please. This done, they may betake themselves to some other point of a different length, which will produce a new variety.

This contest in breves, semibreves, or minims being ended, they may give the sign to A., if (as I said) he have ability of hand, that he may begin his point as they had done one to another; which point may be answered by the viols, either singly or jointly. If jointly, it must be done according to the former instructions of dividing together; playing still slow notes and soft, whilest the organist divides; for the part which divides should always be heard loudest.

When this is done, both viols may play another strain together, either in quick or slow notes, which they please; and if the musick be not yet spun out to a sufficient length, they may begin to play triplas and proportions,[8] answering each other either in whole strains or parcels; and after that, join together in a thundering strain of quick division; with which they may conclude; or else

7. To become flaccid.
8. Sections in different meters with a common note value between them.

with a strain of slow and sweet notes, according as may best sute the circumstance of time and place.

I have known this kind of extempory musick, sometimes (when it was performed by hands accustomed to play together) pass off with greater applause, than those divisions which had been most studiously composed.

25 Lorenzo Penna

Lorenzo Penna (1613–1693), a Carmelite monk and doctor of theology, held memberships in several academies and was among the founders of the Accademia Filarmonica of Bologna. He composed sacred music, but it was as a music pedagogue that he was most influential in the seventeenth century. He published a tutor for beginners in plainchant, the *Directory of Plainchant, from which to learn how to sing in choir* (1689), and a tutor called *Musical Daybreaks* (1672), which treats of *canto figurato,* that is, of singing countrapuntal music, and teaches the fundamentals of figured bass. The latter book descends from a line of elementary guides for musicians that begins in the Baroque era with the handbooks by church musicians such as Adriano Banchieri. Although their presentation of the elements of music remained fairly standard through the century (echoes of Agostino Agazzari and Lodovico Viadana may be heard in *Musical Daybreaks*), Penna also offers advice that goes beyond rules for reading musical notation and reveals his practical experience in training students of voice who will sing in ensembles and with continuo accompaniment. Above all, Penna tells his students to learn by listening to good performers.

FROM *Musical Daybreaks for Beginners in Measured Music*
(1684)

BOOK I

CHAPTER 21. SOME RULES TO FOLLOW AND SOME THINGS TO AVOID FOR BEGINNERS OF *CANTO FIGURATO*

1. When singing in an ensemble, no one voice should dominate any other; rather one should strive for equality, so that no one is either louder or softer than the others.

TEXT: *Li primi albori musicali per li principianti della musica figurata,* 4th ed. (Bologna, 1684; facs. Bologna, 1969), pp. 49–50; 183–87; 197–98. Translation by Margaret Murata.

2. You should not sing for yourself, being content just to read notes and get the rhythm right; and this is so that you won't sing out of tune.

3. Do not twist or distort your waist, your head, your eyes, your mouth, etc., because it is ugly to see.

4. Do not sing in your nose, or through your teeth, or in your throat.

5. Sing precisely with some mordents, *accenti*,[1] graces, etc., and if your voice has a natural trill or *gorga,* employ it in performance with great modesty, without using it on every note; and if you do not have it naturally, seek to develop one by artifice.

6. Give liveliness to the notes as well as to the words, making them clear and understandable.

7. If two parts have *gorghe* or trills, do them one after the other and not both together, one imitating the other in the exchange (*chiamate*).

8. In order for the five vowels to be sung with the proportionate opening of the mouth, you should know that

for the A, you open the mouth at the maximum a little less than three fingers one above the other;

for the E, at the maximum, a little less than two,

for the I, of one finger,

for the O, of three fingers,

for the U, of one finger only.

9. Do not make *passaggi,* or *movimenti,*[2] on the vowels I and U.

10. Count the beats in your head, or at least softly, so as not to disturb your partner.

11. Follow the words, as discussed in chapter 18. That is, sing happily if the words are happy; if they are lively and spirited, sing with spirit and *vivace;* if they are about grief, pain, torment, etc., sing mournfully and slowly.

12. And lastly go as often as possible to concerts, especially where there are good singers, because you always learn something; and if nothing else, you will learn the style, the sweetness, the *accenti*, the graces, etc. of good singing. This much suffices for beginners in singing figured music.

---

1. Improvised escape tones on or before the beat; see the Glossary of Foreign Performance Terms, p. 223. Caccini's one-note trill was obsolete; the distinction between Penna's trill and the related *gorga* may have been one between trills beginning above the main note and on the main note. The complete text of Penna's chapter 19 "Of Melodic Accidentals" reads: "Because singing the notes and words in rhythm as they are written, without any embellishments would not give pleasure to the ear, one must learn to sing with some graces. Among the other things that give grace to singing are making some mordents and trills on the notes, emitting the voice now with smoothness, now with caprice, now with sweetness, etc., following as much as possible the sense of the words, pronouncing them distinctly to make them understood, etc. But because it is difficult to explain such things with written examples, and because the student is well informed by his maestro, not only about all that I have written here but about many other things that I will let go to avoid tedium, I will not put any more on paper. I only point out that in compositions where a "t" appears with a dot in this manner: **t.**, there a trill must be made."

2. *Movimenti* are illustrated in chapter 20 of book 1, as divisions between semibreves (pp. 46–49); see the Glossary of Foreign Performance Terms, p. 224.

BOOK III

CHAPTER 14. OF ACCOMPANYING COMPOSITIONS FOR SOLO VOICE

In all compositions, whether in two, three, or four voices, etc., the organist must be accurate and ready of hand, eye, and ear, as well as of spirit, in order to accompany the singers' voices on the keyboard. But in compositions for solo voice, it is necessary to be very alert and ready to accompany the voice. And this is true as much in *ariette,* in quick pieces, etc., as well as in expressive and slow ones, etc.

Ordinarily in compositions for solo voice you see the singer's line in score, placed above the organist's line, scored up, although at times (but rarely) you will meet a part without it. In both cases you observe the following rules.

First rule

The organist should keep a quick, open eye not only on his part, but also on the singer's line, placed above, to accompany with the keys that correspond to the voice, for example, for a soprano, play in the soprano register [see Ex. A1]; if contralto, play in the alto register [Ex. A2], striving to be ready to touch the key to give the pitch to the singer.

[Example A1]   [Example A2]

Second rule

When it is not possible to accompany all the notes sung, take only the consonances, or at least the first and last of the downbeat part of the *tactus,* and the first and last of the upbeat part,[3] letting the others go, as in the example, taken from the examples given above. All this holds true even in *ariette.* [Exx. B1 and B2]

---

3. "Levar di mano." In common time, the hand descended at the beginning of a semibreve *tactus,* or whole note, and rose on the second half. In modern terms, the "beat is in two." Penna is thus saying that the organist is to play on whatever begins the *tactus* and on the pickup to the second half of the *tactus;* similarly the continuo sounds the first and last notes of the second half of the *tactus.* If the *tactus* were a semibreve, chords would occur on each quarter-note. The implied falling and rising of the hand have been marked by the editor in the musical example.

[Example B1]   [Example B2]

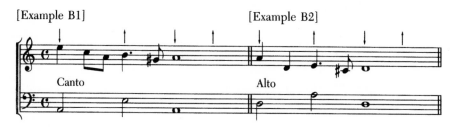

Third rule

In the ritornelli or during rests placed to relieve the singer, the organist should play something improvised, imitating the arietta or something spirited newly invented. This is clear without giving any examples.

Fourth rule

In the recitative style, where there are many expressive devices using dissonances, you must be ready to play them quickly, making the necessary harmony. The most frequent of the dissonant *affetti* are the following five:

• The first is based on the basso continuo which plays a tone of one or one-half measure, or longer, in the same place.

   • The second occurs when the basso continuo leaps down a fourth, or up a fifth.

   • The third, when it falls down a fifth or leaps up a fourth.

   • The fourth, when two successive notes descend by step, making a cadence.

   • The fifth, when the bass makes a suspension of a second, and resolves to a third, making a cadence.

The realizations of all five are in the following rules.

Fifth rule

If the bass remains on the same tone for one or one-half bar or for even more notes, the dissonances, or bad notes as we call them, must be played; which is to say the major 7ths, 9ths, 11ths, and minor 13ths, or their equivalents, all sounded together with the right hand, whether descending [Ex, C1] or ascending [Ex. C2]; and before resolving to the consonances, play the 10th or 12th, as it better.

[Example C1]   [Example C2]

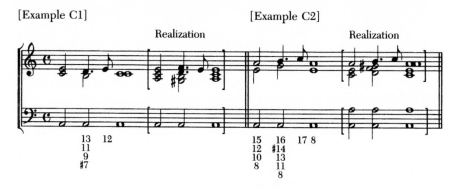

Sixth rule

When the bass leaps a fourth down or a fifth up, accompany the dissonance of the singer with a raised 4th or a raised 6th, the octave and the 10th, and before resolving, touch the 9th. [Exx. D1–2]

[Example D1]   [Example D2]

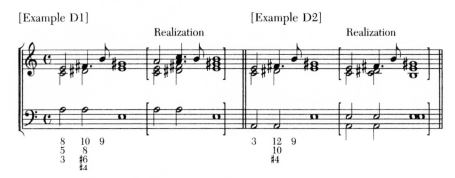

Seventh rule

When the bass leaps a fifth down or a fourth up, make an accompaniment with dissonances of a minor 7th [Ex. E1–2]. The accompaniment for the fourth and fifth *affetti* are demonstrated in chapters 12 and 13 from the present third book. You will find them there [Exx. E3–4].

[Example E1]   [Example E2]

BOOK III

CHAPTER 15. OF PLAYING FUGATO *A CAPPELLA*

In *a cappella* works (whether thin or thick), the fugue begins with one [vocal] line; then the second enters, and afterwards, the third, etc. Therefore the beginner should note that the fugue begins with one finger, playing the same note as the [voice] part that begins the fugue. . . .

BOOK III.

CHAPTER 20. SOME PRINCIPLES TO OBSERVE AND THINGS TO AVOID IN PLAYING ORGAN FROM A PART

1. As soon as you receive a part to play, try to understand its nature [in order] to realize it appropriately.
2. When the right hand rises, the fingers move one after the other, first the third, then the fourth, then the third, and so forth for as long as the line goes on and the fingers are not playing together. But on descending you change to third, second, third, etc. In the left hand you do the opposite. . . .
3. Both the left and right hands should not be held low with the fingers high, but the hands and the fingers should be extended to form a nice hand.

•   •   •   •   •

6. On a [bass] note that receives a 6th, this sixth can be alone without the octave; this will sound better.
7. It is good to play legato all the time, if it does not interfere with the singer's part.

•   •   •   •   •

9. All numbers [of a figured bass] which are above the octave must be played by the right hand, when playing in ensembles.
10. In performing with a soprano or contralto, you must not play above the part that sings, nor add diminutions.
11. With a tenor, you may play above and stay above [the singer's register], but do not play in octaves with the line he sings, nor [add] diminutions [to it].
12. With a bass, you can make a few *movimenti*,[4] but if the bass line has *passaggi*, it is not good to ornament at the same time.
13. When you accompany a solo voice, do not play more than three or (rarely) four notes at the same time;[5] it is not good to sound the octave above.

4. See above, note 2.
5. This is most applicable to the sustained sound of the organ.

14. With two parts, similarly, you should use few keys and avoid the octave.

15. In three and four parts you can fill out the sound a bit more, but rarely double the bass when it is on *mi* or #.[6]

16. In eight voices, in three or four choirs, etc., you fill and double even the doublings, the sharps, and whatever you want, because it will make a good effect with so much variety or sonority.

17. In accompanying instruments, it is good to avoid making *movimenti*, so that the listener can hear their ensemble, the imitations, the exchanges, the answers between them, etc.

18. Practice a lot, exercising yourself for speed, trills, as much with the right as with the left hand, because in this way you break in the hand and gain mastery over the keyboard.

19. Try to arpeggiate in order not to leave the instrument empty.

20. Go often to academies and concerts, noting well the techniques of those who play this instrument, to put them to use.

6. When it is on a note that would be solmized as "mi" or a note accidentally raised by a sharp. Such pitches are often secondary, applied leading tones.

26 Georg Muffat

Like the cosmopolitan Mozart, Georg Muffat (1653–1704) had firsthand opportunities to absorb the varied national styles of his day. Born in Savoy, he studied music in Paris from 1663 to 1669 while hardly out of childhood, then studied and served as a cathedral organist in Alsace, enrolled as a law student in Ingolstadt in 1674, worked in Vienna and Prague, and finally became organist and chamber musician to the Archbishop of Salzburg, all in his first twenty-five years. From 1680/81 to 1682 he was in the Rome of Arcangelo Corelli and Alessandro Scarlatti, and in 1690 he entered permanent employment in Germany with the Bishop of Passau. In addition to the Italianate concertos and French-influenced suites for instrumental ensemble for which he is best known, Muffat composed three operas for Salzburg, solo organ works, and a treatise on continuo practice.

Muffat published his suites and concertos only after he felt that the climate in Germany and Austria was open enough to their foreign-influenced styles. Even then, he provided prefaces in four languages to explain points of performance practice. These prefaces tell us much about violin playing in France and Italy and about what was not common practice in the German-speaking lands. He explained signs for sectional repetitions; the varied relationships between meter signs, tempo, and dance types; the practice of playing unequal notes that are notated with equal values; and differences among the French, Italians, and Germans in their ways of bowing. He touched briefly on his preferences for higher or lower pitches to serve as a reference pitch for tuning. And he illustrated standard melodic ornaments using an idiosyncratic system of signs that was neither French nor Italian and has therefore been avoided here. Muffat gives a view of string playing in the 1660s to 1690s and also heralds the absorption and integration of French and Italian idioms that mark the music of the next generation of German composers.

FROM Prefaces to *Florilegia*

PREFACE TO THE *FIRST FLORILEGIUM*
(1695)

Here you have my pieces, composed in Salzburg before I came to Passau and conforming in the main to the French ballet style, now submitted to you, gracious *amateur*,[1] for your entertainment and approval. Heard with pleasure by several princes and also praised by many of the higher nobility, they are published at the repeated entreaty of good friends and with the approbation of distinguished musicians, both Italian and German. To these requests I have given in the more gladly, observing that here in Germany the French style is gradually coming to the fore and flourishing. When this style was at its height under the celebrated J. Baptiste de Lully, I studied it diligently for the six years I was in Paris, beyond my other musical activities; and returning from France, I was perhaps the first to bring this manner, which is not displeasing to musicians of good taste, into Alsace; and driven from there by the last war, to Vienna in Austria and to Prague, and finally afterwards to Salzburg and Passau. Inasmuch as the ballet compositions of the said Lully, and other things in a similar style, entirely reject—for the sake of flowing and natural movement—all superfluous artifices, such as immoderate divisions as well as frequent and ill-sounding leaps, they had at first the misfortune in these countries to displease many of our musicians, who at that time were more intent on the variety of unusual conceits and artificialities than on grace. For this reason, when occasionally performed by those ignorant of the French manner or envious of foreign art, they came off badly, robbed of their proper tempo and usual ornaments. When, however, they were exhibited with greater perfection, first in Vienna by certain

TEXT: *Suavioris harmoniae instrumentalis hyporchematicae florilegium primum* (Augsburg: J. Koppmayr, 1695) and *Suavioris . . . florilegium secundum* (Passau, 1698). Modern edition in *Denkmäler der Tonkunst in Österreich*, Jg. 1, pt. 2, and Jg. 2, pt. 2, ed. Heinrich Rietsch (Vienna, 1894–95; repr. Graz, 1959). Muffat's prefaces in his Latin, German, Italian, and French versions are also available in Walter Kolneder, *Georg Muffat zur Aufführungspraxis* (Strasbourg: P. Heitz, 1970), pp. 30–37 and 44–98. Portions of the second preface are also in Carol MacClintock, *Readings in the History of Music in Performance* (Bloomington, 1979), pp. 297–303. Translation by Oliver Strunk, revised and expanded by Margaret Murata.

1. Music lover.

foreign violinists and soon after in Bavaria by His Electoral Serenity's excellent musicians, they were more favorably considered, and many began to form a better opinion of them and to accustom themselves to this style and grace, and even to study it, in order to conform to the genius of the princes and lords applauding such music. No doubt they discovered the truth of what an extremely discerning prince once said to me with regard to this style: namely, that what they had learned previously was more difficult than what, to charm the ear, they needed to have learned. Now that the ill-considered contempt for the aforesaid ballet style has gradually fallen off, it has seemed to me that I might the more confidently come forward with my admittedly insignificant pieces, which have as much need of the artistry and favor of our violinists as they appear simple. To give reasons for the names prefixed to each set seems needless, especially since these have been named only to distinguish one from another, either for some cause, or effect, or some event that happened to me, or for some state of mind in which I found myself.[2]

It still remains for me to remind and request such musicians as are as yet unfamiliar with the aforesaid style that, when notes are enclosed in such brackets as these ⌐‾‾‾‾‾┐└‾‾‾‾‾┘, after the first playing of those notes which precede the sign of repetition **.S.** **:‖:**, in the second playing they are to omit them altogether, skipping instead straightway over to those notes which follow immediately after said repetition.[3] In addition, this sign **.S.**, whether placed at the very opening or after the sign of repetition **:‖:**, marks the note from which the repetition should begin, omitting the preceding ones altogether.[4] This is also to be observed, following the most common practice, when it occurs near the middle of the second part or somewhat further from the end.[5] Although I find the practice not displeasing, of some who, having repeated the whole second part, retake this [petite] reprise a third time from said sign **.S.**, this is a matter to be settled by the musicians before the performance.

Beyond this, when the measure of two beats is marked **2** [or] **₵**, it necessarily follows the common rule to go twice as fast as that which goes under the sign **C** divided into four.[6] This assumes that the measure **2** must be quite slow[7] in

---

2. The Latin titles of the seven suites making up the *Florilegium primum* might be translated: I. *Eusebia*—Piety; II. *Sperantis gaudia*—The Joys of the Hopeful; III. *Gratitudo*—Gratitude; IV. *Impatientia*—Impatience; V. *Sollicitudo*—Solicitude; VI. *Blanditiae*—Flatteries; VII. *Constantia*—Constancy.
3. This describes the notational practice of providing a repeated strain with first and second endings.
4. This explains the operation of the *dal segno* mark.
5. A "petite reprise."
6. The four prefaces use different idioms to mean the same thing: *dupplò citius* in Latin for "twice as fast," *noch einmal so geschwind* in German for "once again as fast"; and the Italian and French phrases—*a metà presto* and *la moitie plus vite*—which translate as "faster by half," all double the tempo when the duration of the note values is halved.
7. "Assai adagio o grave; Fort lente; Ziemlich langsam."

the overtures, preludes, and symphonies,[8] a little more gay for the ballets, and for the rest, in my opinion, almost always more moderately than under the ¢, which, however, goes less quickly in the gavottes than in the bourrées.[9] Further, when the measure **2** is performed very slowly and (as said above) in two, the notes have nearly the same value as they have with the Italian under the sign **C** played quickly in four under the additional word "Presto." The difference between the two is simply that in the latter case one must not, as in the former and better, give to successive eighth notes 𝅘𝅥𝅮 𝅘𝅥𝅮 𝅘𝅥𝅮 𝅘𝅥𝅮 a dotted rhythm 𝅘𝅥𝅮. 𝅘𝅥𝅮 𝅘𝅥𝅮. 𝅘𝅥𝅮, but must, on the contrary, play them evenly. The *symphonie* of the fourth set, called *Impatientia*, provides an example of this.[10] As to the other signs, ³⁄₂ requires a very slow movement, ³⁄₄ a gayer one, yet uniformly somewhat slow in the sarabandes and airs; then more lively in the *rondeaux*, and finally the most lively but without haste in menuets, courantes and many other dances, as also in the fugues in the overtures. The remaining pieces, such as are called gigues and canaries, need to be played the fastest of all, no matter how the measure is marked.

Gracious *amateur*, may it please you to accept this my *Florilegium primum*, protecting it from the envious and grudging, and excusing such errors of mine and of the press as may have crept in. Await what is promised at the end of the work.[11] Farewell and favor him who would deserve your favor.

8. "Suonate."
9. For Muffat, then, the slowest tempo for an even meter is indicated by **C** in four, which occurs only once in the *First Florilegium*, in an Allemande with the cautionary word "Largo." Slow duple meters are given under the sign two, faster ones under ¢.

10. In Italian ("the latter") style, eighth notes are not subject to the French practice of performing equally notated subdivisions unequally.

An example of "the former" would be the passage from Muffat's overture to *Eusebia* in note 9, in which he indicated French unequal eighths by notating dotted eighths followed by sixteenths.

11. The afterword to the volume promises that further instructions for performance practice will appear in the second volume, which they did.

FROM PREFACE TO THE *SECOND FLORILEGIUM*
(1698)

FIRST OBSERVATIONS BY THE AUTHOR ON THE PERFORMANCE OF
BALLETS IN THE LULLIAN-FRENCH MANNER

The art of playing ballets on the violin in the manner of the most celebrated
Jean-Baptiste Lully (here understood in all its purity, admired and praised by
the world's most excellent masters) is so ingenious a study that one can scarcely
imagine anything more agreeable or more beautiful. To reveal to you, gracious
reader, its chief secrets, know that it has at one time two aims: namely, to
appeal to the ear in the most agreeable way and to indicate properly the measure of the dance, so that one may recognize at once to what variety each piece
belongs and may feel in one's affections and one's feet, as it were without notic-
ing it at all, an inclination to dance. For this there are, in my opinion, five
considerations necessary.

First, one must, for purity of intonation, stop the strings accurately. Second,
the bow must be drawn in a uniform way by all the players. Third, one must
bear constantly in mind the time signature, or tempo and measure, proper to
each piece. Fourth, one must pay strict attention to the usual signs of repetition
introduced and also to the qualities of the style and of the art of dancing. Fifth,
one must use with discernment certain ornaments making the pieces much
more beautiful and agreeable, lighting them up, as it were, with sparkling precious stones. Of which the following distich:

> Contactus, plectrum, tempus, mos, atque venustas
> Efficient alacrem, dulcisonamque chelyn.[1]

I. CONTACTUS. ON PLAYING IN TUNE.

With regard to correct intonation, there is no difference among the best
masters, no matter what their nations be, whose precepts only weak pupils or
unprofessional ignoramuses fail to observe. Nothing serves better to avoid false
tones than instruction and correction by a good master, from whom one will
have learned the first principles of this art and of which I do not intend to treat
here. I will say only that after good instruction in how to acquire and maintain
a delicate ear, nothing is more helpful than frequent practice with players of
exquisite taste and to avoid playing with those who would corrupt more ears
and fingers than they would improve. Beyond this I have observed that the
defects of the majority who play falsely come from playing the two tones that
make the semitone (for example, *mi* and *fa*; E and F; A and Bb; B♮ and C; or

---

1. "Fingering, bowing, measure, practice, and ornamentation/Will to the viol bring liveliness and
   sweetness of tone." The distich reiterates the five topics Muffat will cover in the subsequent five
   sections.

F♯ and G; C♯ and D; G♯ and A, etc.). They never take the *mi,* or the sharp very high, nor that of the *fa* or the flat very low. They err greatly also against the true proportion of the pitches[2] and the course of the tones or modes, or against the harmonic relation with respect to that which went before or after, whenever they make trills or other embellishments with improper pitches. Finally they offend the ear even when playing in tune, when the strings are not played with enough force or attention; whence one hears a very unpleasant hiss, scrape, or squeaking.

II. PLECTRUM. HOW TO DRAW THE BOW.

Most Germans, in playing the high or middle parts, conform with the Lullistes in their manner of holding the bow, squeezing the hair with the thumb and resting the other fingers on top of it. The French hold it in the same way to play the "violoncino,"[3] The Italians differ with them in the soprano parts— since they do not touch the hair; so also the gambists, as well as others on the bass [part], who place the fingers between the hair and the stick.

Beyond this, although the best masters of all nations agree that inasmuch as a bow stroke is long, firm, equal, and sweet, so much is it to be valued. Nonetheless up to now, neither the Italians nor the Germans have always agreed on how much to draw it down or up; this is not the case with the French, except in rare and scattered cases. With all this it is evident that those who follow the manner of the late Lully, as do the French, the English, Dutch, and Flemings, and many others, all equally observe the same way of drawing the bow on the principal notes of the measure (even if there be a thousand playing together), especially with respect to those notes that begin the measure, those that finish the cadences, and those that most mark the movements of the dance. Since the kind of uniformity so helpful in expressing the rhythms of the dance has not been found in our German players (however expert), many nobles returning from those countries, noting such a great difference in ensemble, have often been amazed and complained of the alteration that the dances suffer. To avoid such inconveniences and the danger of some mix-ups in similar situations, I believed it would be of service to draw up here some of the principal rules of the French way of bowing: in the examples of which this sign **|**, placed above a note indicates a down-bow; and this other, *v,* an up-bow.

I.[4] The first note of each measure that begins without a quarter- or eighth-note rest, should always be a down-bow no matter what its value. This is the principal, general, and almost indispensable rule of the Lullistes, upon which

2. For example, in the era before equal temperament became widespread, semitones were of different sizes (in theory in the ratios of 8:9 and 9:10), and intervals of the perfect fifth and major and minor thirds were variously tempered.
3. The violoncello or bass instrument of the violin family.
4. When Muffat subdivides the five main topics marked I.–V., he again uses Roman numerals for the subdivisions.

nearly all the entire secret of bowing depends and the difference between them and the others, and which all other rules obey. But to know how the other notes are accommodated and played, it is necessary to observe the following rules.

II. In the common ordinary imperfect time of the theorists,[5] among the notes that divide the measure into equal parts, those that are odd are played with a down-bow and those that are even, with an up-bow. The odd are [beats] 1, 3, 5, 7, 9, 11, etc. and the even are 2, 4, 6, 8, 10, 12, etc. See Example A. This rule is also observed in triple meters and in other proportional meters with respect to notes equally subdivided. I am calling "subdivided" those that go more quickly than those that are denominated by the time signature. [Ex. B]. This manner of counting the equal notes remains in effect when quarter- or eighth-note rests take the place of notes. [Ex. C] For the rest, all the best players easily agree with this rule of the French.

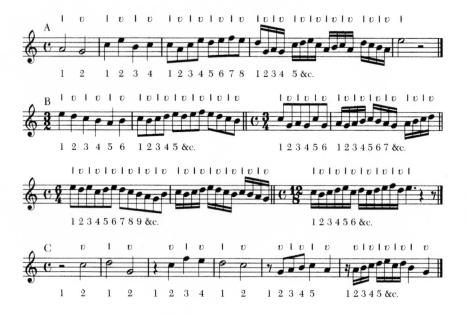

III. Since, according to the first rule, the first note of the measure is a down-bow, of the three equal notes that make up a whole measure in triple time, the second is always an up-bow, and the third is again a down-bow, at least if the tempo is a little slow. This means that with the beginning of the second bar it

---

5. Duple measure indicated by the sign **C**.

is necessary to make two down-bows consecutively [Ex. D]. Most frequently, however, one plays the second as well as the third beats with an up-bow, dividing it distinctly in two (this is called *craquer*[6]), which is much easier, especially in tempos that are somewhat faster [Ex. E].

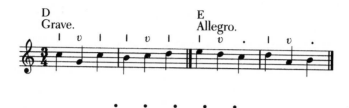

X. The "leftover" note before the beginning of a measure[7] [Ex. Y], or the quick note after a dot, or an eighth rest [Z], or any lesser note that follows a syncopation of greater value [AA], must always be an up-bow. Or if besides these cases an up-bow is required, it will be necessary to divide that up-bow in two, adding to it the succeeding one [Ex. BB].

Sometimes an exception is made of courantes because of the quickness of the notes that begin the second, fourth, sixth or similar even-numbered measures (thinking of them in triple time), which can sometimes be begun with an up-bow when it is more comfortable. Nonetheless those beats that mark the uneven measure and which most strongly mark the rhythm of the dance are always down-bow [CC]. Beside this, the first rule concerning the first note of the measure is rigorously observed. As far as the other beats that begin essential parts are concerned, or as for the rest of the measure, in gigues, canaries and other dances in compound time, it is often necessary to dispense with

6. To "crack" of "snap" implies a push, perhaps by flick of the hand off the wrist. The German text gives "hupfend," or "hopping." See the Glossary of Foreign Performance Terms, p. 224.
7. The "upbeat."

Rules 4, 8, and 10 because of the fast tempo[8] Example DD will show how to bow when there are frequent dotted rhythms mixed among the notes. Similarly because of the quickness of bourées and similar airs, one frequently breaks Rule 8, when (always keeping the validity of the first rule), the others are treated, as can be seen in Example EE. In these last three examples I have marked the licenses with an asterisk ° under the notes. Finally, when two little notes, such as two sixteenths join just as a decoration of some other note, they are sometimes played each with its own bow stroke [FF] and at times for greater sweetness, one runs them into the previous note in one or two strokes [GG].

8. Rule 4 observes the **l v v** bowing for the three-note groups in meters of six, nine, and twelve beats. Rule 8: Of the three notes that make up the essential part of a measure in compound time, if the first is dotted, it should be played with a downbow [Ex. V].

To do otherwise and play any downbeat with an up-bow is an obvious error in this style. This happens often with the Italians and Germans in triple meters, especially when the first note is of a lesser value than the second. From such contrariness of opinion and from the transgression against said first rule comes the very great difference that one finds in bowing, as much with regard to the first notes as to the others following that depend on it. To make it easier to understand this difference I wanted to mark the same succession of several notes played in the two different ways, that is, according to some Italians or Germans [HH], then in the French manner [II]. Furthermore this is contrary to the vivacity of the Lullistes and goes against Rule 7 (which runs the little note after a dot or an eighth rest to the following note in one bow stroke), as Example LL demonstrates. To play the French way, one must play according to Example MM, although the opposite is permitted whenever said little note is joined to the preceding one *en craquent* [NN].

Behold the principal rules of the Lullian method of bowing, which is habitually observed as much for the violins as for the middle lines and even for the bass. The greatest dexterity of the true Lullistes consists of this, that among so many repeated down-bows one never hears anything disagreeable or coarse, but, on the contrary, one finds a marvelous joining of great speed and long bow strokes, an admirable evenness of beat with diversity of rhythm, and a tender sweetness with lively playing.

III. TEMPUS. ABOUT TIME.[9]

•   •   •   •   •

III. Subdivisions of the principal note value—which are sixteenths in common time, eighths in duple or *alla breve* time, those which are twice as fast as the main beats in moderately fast time, and compound meters—are not played equally as notated when given consecutively. They would sound sleepy, coarse, and dull. But these change in the French style by adding a dot to each of those that fall on an odd note, which by becoming longer makes the following one reciprocally shorter. See examples of the different kinds in various meters in Ex. QQ and the way they are usually expressed when the tempo allows in Example RR.

IV. *MOS.* CERTAIN OTHER PRACTICES OF THE LULLISTES RELATED TO OUR SUBJECT

I. One should arrange to tune the instruments well, if it can be done, before

---

9. In this section on meter and rhythm, Muffat refers the reader to his 1695 dances for point I (see above, pp. 138–39). For point II he notes six common rhythmic errors, such as rushing in subdivided passages and not giving the third beat in triple time its full value.

the arrival of the listeners, or it should be done at least as quickly and efficiently as will be possible.

II. One should refrain from making any commotion before playing and from so many confused preludes that at times, by filling the ear and the eye, make as great a nuisance before the overture as what comes after is a delight.

III. The tone to which the French tune [their instruments] is ordinarily one step lower and for operas a step and a half lower[10] than our German *Chor-Ton*. The so-called *Cornet-Ton* seems to them too high, too forced, and too screechy. If it were my choice, and as long as nothing else prevented it, I would always adopt the tone a step lower than what in Germany is called the *Chor-Ton*, with strings a little thicker; this does not lack vivacity along with its sweetness.

IV. One should distribute the parts and, according to the number of musicians, double them with such judgment that one can hear them all distinctly, aggreeably and with the usual ornaments. Nor should one put so many good violins only on the highest line that the middle parts and the bass are deprived of a sufficient number of capable musicians, which would hide one of the greatest ornaments of an ensemble. It displeases me to see this happen often on account of foolish obsessions with status that some have.

V. As for the instruments, the part the Italians call the "violetta" and the French "haute contre" will succeed better if played upon a medium-sized viola on the small side[11] than upon a violin. For the bass one wants what the Italians call a "violoncino" and the Germans a French bass,[12] which cannot be omitted without distorting the balance. One can double according to the number of musicians, which, if it is great and also mixed with a double bass, or the contrabass of the Italians (which is the *Violon* of the Germans), the ensemble will be so much the more majestic, even though up to now the French do not use them in *airs de ballets*.

10. The Paris opera orchestra tuned to an A[4] of c. 410 cycles per second in Lully's time, which seems to have risen to c. 422 cps by 1700. Muffat advocates the "high chamber-pitch" to which German harpsichords and strings tuned, as opposed to the "choir tone" set by the local organs.
11. "A little smaller than the *Taille*."
12. "Une petite Basse à la françoise."

V

IMITATION AND EXPRESSION

27 Jacopo Peri

A singer, organist, and published composer by age 22, Jacopo Peri (1561–1633) played a central role in the formation of Baroque opera. As a singer-composer, he often wrote his own solos for collaborative theatrical projects and at times accompanied himself on the chitarrone. For example, he provided music for sections of the 1589 *intermedi* that were performed in Florence with the play *La pellegrina* and composed his own recitatives for the role of Clori in Marco da Gagliano's opera *La Flora,* staged in Florence in 1628. The most complete surviving theatrical score by Peri, his setting of Ottavio Rinuccini's libretto *Euridice,* was written for performance in Florence in 1600 and published within four months, along with a rival setting by Giulio Caccini. In the preface to his score, Peri explains how he had arrived at a new style of solo theatrical singing in 1597–98 for a staging of the Greek fable of Daphne and Apollo. Although as members of the Florentine Camerata he and Caccini had the same general aim of expressing poetic texts clearly and emotionally, Peri cites his models of verse recitation and describes more precisely how music becomes the elocution of the text. The musical representation of the sound of speech would continue to be a critical issue in vocal music throughout the Baroque era, for example, in the differences over operatic music between Jean Laurent Le Cerf de la Viéville and François Raguenet at the beginning of the next century.

Preface to *The Music for Euridice*
(1601)

Before I offer you (kind readers) this my music, I have judged it appropriate to make known to you what induced me to discover this new manner of song, since reason should be the beginning and fount of all human operations, and he who cannot offer reasons easily gives one to believe that he has acted by chance. Although Signor Emilio Cavaliere, before any other, so far as I know, enabled us with marvelous invention to hear our music on the stage, nonetheless it pleased the Signori Jacopo Corsi and Ottavio Rinuccini (as early as 1594) that I, employing it in another guise, should set to music the tale of Daphne, written by Signor Ottavio, to make a simple trial of what the song of our age could do. Whence, seeing that it was a question of dramatic poetry and that, therefore, one should imitate in song a person speaking (and without a

TEXT: *Le musiche sopra L'Euridice* (Florence, 1600 [i.e., 1601]; facs. New York: Broude Brothers, 1973 and Bologna: Forni Editore, 1973), pp. iii–iv; translation by Tim Carter. The Italian text of this and the front matter to other opera scores, translated into English, also appears in T. Carter and Z. Szweykowski, *Composing Opera: From* Dafne *to* Ulisse Errante (Cracow: Musica Iagellonica, 1994).

doubt, no one ever spoke singing), I judged that the ancient Greeks and Romans (who, according to the opinion of many, sang their tragedies throughout on the stage) used a harmony which, going beyond that of ordinary speech, fell so short of the melody of song that it assumed an intermediate form. And this is the reason why we see in their poetry that the iamb had a place which is not elevated like the hexameter,[1] but yet is said to proceed beyond the confines of everyday speech. And therefore, rejecting every other type of song heard up to now, I set myself to discovering the imitation that is due to these poems. And I considered that that type of voice assigned to singing by the ancients which they called "diastematic" (as it were, sustained and suspended) could at times speed up and take an intermediate path between the suspended and slow movements of song and the fluent, rapid ones of speech, and thus suit my intention (just as they, too, accommodated it in reading their poetry and heroic verse,)[2] approaching the other [species] of speech, which they called "continuous," and which our moderns (although perhaps for another end) have also done in their music. I realized, similarly, that in our speech some words are intoned in such a manner that harmony can be founded upon them, and that while speaking one passes through many other [words] which are not intoned, until one returns to another that can move to a new consonance. And taking note of these manners and those accents that serve us in grief, joy, and in similar states, I made the bass move in time to these, now faster, now slower, according to the emotions; and I held it firm through the dissonances and consonances until the voice of the speaker, passing though various notes, arrived at that which, being intoned in ordinary speech, opens the way to a new harmony. And [I did] this not only so that the flow of the speech would not offend the ear (as if stumbling in encountering the repeated notes of the more frequent consonances), or so that it might not seem in a way to dance to the movement of the bass—particularly in sad or serious subjects, since happier subjects require by their nature more frequent movements—but also because the use of dissonances would either diminish or mask the advantage thereby gained because of the necessity of intoning every note,[3] which the ancient musics had perhaps less need of doing. And so (even though I would not be so bold as to claim that this was the type of song used in Greek and

1. Dactylic hexameters were the poetic meter of ancient epic poetry; iambs were common in ancient drama, especially in dialogue.
2. Renaissance musical theorists inherited from Greek and Latin writers the distinction between the continuous species of voice—the speaking or reading voice—and the diastematic or intervallic one, which was suitable for musical melody. Aristides Quintilianus furthermore recognized an intermediate species—that of poetic recitation, to which Peri's intermediate manner is analogous. See Claude V. Palisca, *Humanism in Renaissance Thought* (New Haven: Yale University Press, 1985), pp. 408–33, esp. pp. 428–30 (see also *SR* 1).
3. Peri is here describing the irregularity of his harmonic rhythm, compared to the regular coordination of chord change and meter in the systematic contrapuntal style. When many vocal tones, which had to be sung, were treated in the new style as passing consonances and dissonances, harmonic change served instead to emphasize the irregular stresses of Italian verse. The problem of harmonization did not apply to Greek and Roman music.

Roman plays) I have thus believed it to be the only type that our music can give us to suit our speech. Whence, having had my opinion heard by these gentlemen, I demonstrated to them this new manner of singing, and it gave the greatest pleasure, not only to Signor Jacopo,[4] who had already composed some most beautiful airs for this tale, but also to Signor Piero Strozzi, to Signor Francesco Cini, and to other most learned gentlemen (for music flourishes today among the nobility) and also to that celebrated lady whom one may call the Euterpe of our age, Signora Vettoria Archilei,[5] who has always made my music worthy of her song, adorning it not only with those *gruppi*[6] and with those long roulades both simple and double which, by the liveliness of her wit, are encountered at every moment—more to obey the practice of our times than because she judges that in them consist the beauty and force of our singing—but also those sorts of delights and graces which cannot be written, and if written cannot be learned from the notation. Messer Giovan Battista Jacomelli[7] heard and commended it,[8] who, most excellent in all the parts of music, has as it were changed his surname to "Violino," on which [instrument] he is marvelous. And for three successive years, when it was performed in Carnival, it was heard with greatest delight and received with universal applause by whomever found himself there. But the present *Euridice* had better fortune, not because those lords and other worthy men that I have mentioned heard it, and also Signor Count Alfonso Fontanella and Signor Orazio Vecchi, most noble witnesses to my thought, but because it was performed before so great a queen[9] and so many famous princes of Italy and France, and was sung by most excellent musicians of our time. Among whom, Signor Francesco Rasi, a nobleman from Arezzo, played Aminta; Signor Antonio Brandi, Arcetro; and Signor Melchior Palantrotti, Pluto. And from behind the stage performed gentlemen distinguished for the nobility of their blood and for the excellence of their music: Signor Jacopo Corsi, whom I have mentioned so often, played the harpsichord, and Signor Don Grazia Montalvo a chitarrone, Messer Giovanbattista dal Violino[10] a large *lira,* and Messer Giovanni Lapi a large lute. And although until then I had done it in the precise way in which it now appears, nonetheless Giulio Caccini (called "Romano"), whose great merit is known to the world, wrote the arias of Euridice and some of those for the shepherd and nymph of the chorus, and the choruses "Al canto, al ballo," "Sospirate," and "Poi che gli eterni imperi"; and this [was done] because they were to be sung by persons

4. Jacopo Corsi (1561–1602), Florentine patron of music from the 1580s. He composed some preliminary music for the opera *Dafne,* which was performed in 1598 with music by Peri.

5. See No. 4 above, p. 41, note 18, and No. 19, page 98, note 6.

6. Trills; see Caccini, No. 20 above.

7. Active in Rome from 1574 to 1583 and a musician of Ferdinando I de' Medici, Jacomelli sang tenor in the Sistine Chapel choir (before being expelled in 1585), and played violin, viola, keyboard, and harp. He went to Florence in 1587, where he died in 1608.

8. The opera *Dafne.*

9. Maria de' Medici, Queen of France and Navarre.

10. That is, Giacomelli, mentioned above.

dependent upon him, the which arias can be seen in his [score], which was composed and printed, however, after mine was performed before Her Most Christian Majesty.[11]

So receive it kindly, courteous Readers, and although I may not have arrived by this means where it seemed I could reach (since concern about novelty has acted as a brake on my course), welcome it nevertheless, and perhaps it will happen that on another occasion I may show you something more perfect than this. Meanwhile, it will seem to me that I have done enough, having opened up the path to the skills of others to progress in my footsteps to glory, where it was not given me to be able to arrive. And I hope that the use of the dissonances, played and sung without fear, with discretion, and accurately (having pleased so many and such worthy men) will not cause you annoyance, especially in the more sad and serious airs of Orfeo, Arcetro, and Dafne, who was played with much grace by Jacopo Giusti, a little boy from Lucca.

And live happily.

Notice

Above the bass part, the sharp next to a 6 indicates a major sixth, and the minor [sixth] is without the sharp, which when it is alone is a sign of the major third or tenth, and the flat the minor third or tenth. And do not ever use it except for that note alone where it is indicated, even though there may be several [notes] on one and the same pitch.

11. Maria de' Medici.

28 Claudio Monteverdi

Although he had become *maestro di cappella* at St. Mark's in Venice in 1613, Claudio Monteverdi did not dissolve his ties with his former ducal patrons, the Gonzagas of Mantua, especially since they offered him continued opportunities to compose theatrical music. In late 1616 plans were begun for a maritime spectacle with music to celebrate the wedding of Ferdinando Gonzaga, the new duke, and Caterina de' Medici, sister of the Grand Duke of Tuscany. Monteverdi received the proposal from Alessandro Striggio (who had written the libretto for Monteverdi's 1607 opera *Orfeo*) with due obsequiousness, but he protested its lack of opportunities to express strong human feelings. The proposed *Marriage of Tethys,* to a libretto by Scipione Agnelli, appears to have been like a set of old-fashioned *intermedio* tableaux, and it was eventually abandoned even though Monteverdi had nearly completed the score.

Letter to Alessandro Striggio
(1616)

My Most Illustrious Lord and most esteemed patron,

I was very happy to receive from Signor Carlo de' Torri the letter from Your Most Illustrious Lordship and the *librettino* containing the *favola marittima* of the *Marriage of Tethys*.[1] Your Most Illustrious Lordship writes that you send it to me so that I should look at it carefully and later tell you what I think of it, since it is to be set to music for the forthcoming wedding of His Most Serene Highness.[2] I, my Most Illustrious Lord, who desire nothing other than to be worthy to serve His Most Serene Highness in something, will say nothing at first other than that I offer myself readily to all that which His Most Serene Highness shall ever deign to command me, and without objection, will always honor and revere all that His Most Serene Highness should command. Thus, if His Most Serene Highness has approved this [story], this would be, then, both very fine and much to my taste. But since you add that I should speak, I am ready to obey Your Most Illustrious Lordship's orders with all respect and promptness, understanding that what I say is trivial, coming from a person who is worth little *in toto* and a person who always honors every *virtuoso*, in particular the present gentleman poet, whose name I do not know, and so much more so since this profession of poetry is not mine.

I shall speak, therefore, with all respect, in obedience to you, since you so command. I shall speak and say first that, in general, music wants to be mistress of the air and not only of the water: I mean, in my language, that the ensembles[3] described in this story are all low and near the earth—a very great defect in making beautiful harmonies, since the harmonies will be given to the largest wind instruments in the stage area, [making the harmonies] difficult to be heard by everyone and coordinated [with the instruments] offstage (and I leave this matter to the judgment of your most refined and intelligent taste), so that with this defect, instead of one chitarrone you will want three of them, in place of one harp three will be needed, and so on; and instead of a delicate singer's voice you will want a forced one. Besides this, the correct imitation of speech would need, in my judgment, to be dependent on wind instruments rather than on delicate strings, since the harmonies of the tritons and other marine gods, I would think, should be with trombones and *cornetti* and not with cetras or harpsichords and harps, because, since this production is to be on water, it has

TEXT: Claudio Monteverdi, *Lettere*, ed. Éva Lax (Florence, 1994), pp. 48–51; translation by Margaret Murata.

1. In Greek mythology, Tethys is a Titanness, daughter of Uranus and Gaia and wife of Oceanus; thus the tale is "maritime."
2. Ferdinando Gonzaga, Duke of Mantua.
3. "Concerti."

to be outside the city[4] Plato teaches that "you should have kitharas in the town and tibias in the fields;"[5] so either the delicate instruments are inappropriate or the appropriate ones are not delicate.

Besides this, I noticed that the interlocutors are winds, cupids, zephyrs, and sirens, and so there will be need of many sopranos; and on top of this, the winds are supposed to sing, that is, the west and the north winds! And how, dear Sir, will I be able to imitate the speech of the winds, if winds don't speak?! How will I be able to move the affections with them? Arianna[6] moved us because she was a woman, and likewise Orfeo moved us because he was a man and not a wind. Harmonies can imitate themselves—and without words;[7] the noise of the winds, the bleating of sheep, the neighing of horses and so forth, but they do not imitate the speech of winds that does not exist!

Next, the dances in the course of this story are few, and they don't have the feet of dances.[8]

Next, the whole story, at least to my not inconsiderable ignorance, does not move me at all, and what is more, it is with difficulty that I understand it; nor do I feel that I am led in a natural progression to a conclusion that moves me: [the story of] Arianna leads me to a proper lament and Orfeo to a perfect prayer; but this story—I don't know to what end. Given this, what does Your Most Illustrious Lordship want the music to do here? Nonetheless, I will always accept everything with all respect and honor, whenever His Most Serene Highness should so command and please, since he is my patron without any question.

And whenever His Most Serene Highness should order that this be set to music, seeing that in it more deities than others speak, whom I like to hear singing in a refined style,[9] I would say that the sirens could be sung by the three sisters, that is Andriana [sic] and the others,[10] who could also write their own parts (likewise Signor Rasi his part, also Signor Don Francesco[11] and so forth for the other men) and here [we would] be copying Signor Cardinal Montalto who presented a comedy[12] in which each person who sang in it wrote his or her own part. For, if it were the case that this story progressed to a single

---

4. The city of Mantua is bordered on the north by three lakes.
5. *Republic* 399d (*SR* 1).
6. The abandonment of Ariadne by Theseus was the subject of Monteverdi's opera *Arianna*, written for Mantua in 1608. His 1607 opera about Orpheus and Eurydice was also commissioned for Mantua.
7. Sounds can imitate other nonverbal sounds.
8. The poetic meters of dance songs.
9. "Di garbo."
10. Adriana, Margherita, and Vittoria Basile; see No. 4 above, p. 42, note 21.
11. Francesco Rasi (1574–1621), a tenor, had sung in Peri's *Euridice* and in Caccini's *Rapimento di Cefalo*, most likely the title role in the 1607 *Orfeo* and probably the part of Theseus in the 1608 *Arianna*, among other productions. He completed an opera *Cibele e Ati* (not performed), for the same Gonzaga wedding for which *Teti* was planned. Francesco Dognazzi, also a tenor, was awarded an annual pension by the Gonzaga in 1616.
12. *L'Amor pudico* (Rome, 1614).

conclusion, like *Arianna* and *Orfeo,* then you would also want a single hand, that is, one that was inclined to speak while singing and not, as in this case, sing while speaking.[13] Also in this regard, I consider the speeches in each part too long from the sirens on, and in certain other short exchanges.

Excuse me, dear Sir, if I have said too much, [it was] not to belittle any thing, but in my desire to obey your orders, so that if I should be so ordered to have to set it in music, Your Most Illustrious Lordship may take my thoughts into consideration. Regard me, I beg you with all affection, a most devoted and most humble servant of His Most Serene Highness, to whom I bow most humbly; and I kiss the hands of Your Most Illustrious Lordship with every affection and pray that God grant you every happiness.

From Venice, December 9, 1616

13. "Al parlar cantando e non . . . al cantar parlando." Monteverdi paraphrases the Florentines' expression for the new monodic style, *recitar cantando.*

29 Claudio Monteverdi

Monteverdi's search for expressive means in music was tantalizingly articulated in 1638, when he published his first serious collection in several years: the *Madrigali guerrieri, et amorosi* (*Madrigals Warlike and Amorous*). The volume, his eighth book of madrigals, also included some small theatrical works; one, the famed *Combat of Tancred and Clorinda,* dated back to 1624. In his preface to the reader, Monteverdi explains how he had discovered new musical styles by searching for *similitudine del affetto,* that is, the "resemblance of emotion."

Preface to *Madrigali guerrieri, et amorosi*
(1638)

I have reflected that the principal passions or affections of our mind are three, namely, anger, moderation, and humility or supplication; so the best philosophers declare, and the very nature of our voice indicates this in having

TEXT: *Madrigali guerrieri, et amorosi . . . Libro ottavo* (Venice, 1638); facs. and an Eng. trans. of preface (New York: Dover, 1991), p. xv. This translation by Oliver Strunk, revised by Margaret Murata.

high, low, and middle registers. The art of music also points clearly to these three in its terms "agitated," "soft," and "moderate."[1] In all the works of former composers I have indeed found examples of the "soft" and the "moderate," but never of the "agitated," a genus nevertheless described by Plato in the third book of his *Rhetoric* in these words: "Take that harmony that would fittingly imitate the utterances and the accents of a brave man who is engaged in warfare."[2] And since I was aware that it is contraries which greatly move our mind, and that this is the purpose which all good music should have—as Boethius asserts, saying, "Music is related to us, and either ennobles or corrupts the character"[3]—for this reason I have applied myself with no small diligence and toil to rediscover this genus.

After reflecting that in the pyrrhic measure the tempo is fast and, according to all the best philosophers, used warlike, agitated leaps, and in the spondaic, the tempo slow and the opposite,[4] I began, therefore, to consider the semibreve [o, which, sounded once, I proposed should correspond to one stroke of a spondaic measure; when this was divided into sixteen *semicrome* [♪] and restruck one after the other and combined with words expressing anger and disdain, I recognized in this brief sample a resemblance to the affect I sought, although the words did not follow in their meter the rapidity of the instrument.

To obtain a better proof, I took the divine Tasso, as a poet who expresses with the greatest propriety and naturalness the qualities which he wishes to describe, and selected his description of the combat of Tancred and Clorinda[5] which gave me two contrary passions to set in song, war—that is, supplication, and death. In the year 1624 it was heard by the best citizens of the noble city of Venice in a noble room of my own patron and special protector Signor Girolamo Mocenigo, a prominent cavalier and among the first commanders of the Most Serene Republic; it was received with much applause and praise.

After the apparent success of my first attempt to depict anger, I proceeded with greater zeal to make a fuller investigation, and composed other works in that kind, both ecclesiastical[6] and for chamber performance. Further, this genus found such favor with the composers of music that they not only praised it by word of mouth, but, to my great pleasure and honor, they showed this by written work in imitation of mine. For this reason I have thought it best to make known that the investigation and the first essay in this genus, so necessary to the art of music, came from me. It may be said with reason that until the present, music has been imperfect, having had only the two *genera*—"soft" and "moderate."

1. "Concitato, molle" and "temprato."
2. *Republic* 399a (*SR* 1).
3. *De institutione musica*, I, i.
4. Plato, *Laws* 816c.
5. *La Gerusalemme liberata*, 12, lines 52–68 by Torquato Tasso (1544–1595), Italian epic poet.
6. An example is Monteverdi's motet "Laudate Dominum in sanctis ejus," published in his *Selva morale et spirituale* (Venice, 1640).

It seemed at first to the musicians, especially to those who were called on to play the basso continuo, more ridiculous than praiseworthy to drum on a single string sixteen times in one *tactus*, and so they reduced this multiplicity to one stroke per *tactus*, sounding the spondaic instead of the pyrrhic foot and destroying the resemblance to agitated speech. Take notice, therefore, that the basso continuo must be played, along with its accompanying parts, in the form and manner of its genus as written. Similarly, you will find all the other directions necessary for performance of the other compositions in the other genus. For the manners of performance must take account of three things: text, harmony, and rhythm.[7]

My discovery of this warlike genus has given me occasion to write certain madrigals which I have called *guerrieri*. And since the music played before great princes at their courts to please their delicate taste is of three kinds, according to the method of performance—theater music, chamber music, and dance music—I have indicated these in my present work with the titles *guerriera, amorosa,* and *rappresentativa*.[8]

I know that this work will be imperfect, for I have but little skill, particularly in the genus *guerriero*, because it is new and *omne principium est debile*.[9] I therefore pray the benevolent reader to accept my good will, which will await from his learned pen a greater perfection in the said genus, because *inventis facile est addere*.[10] Farewell.

7. Plato, *Republic* 398d (see SR 1).
8. This seems to say, but cannot mean, that there is a correspondence between Monteverdi's three methods of performance and his three varieties of madrigal. Among the *Madrigali guerrieri*, for example, some are *teatrali*, some *da camera*, some *da ballo*. To put it differently, *guerriero* and *amoroso* corresponds to kinds of music—*concitato* and *molle*—while *rappresentativo* corresponds to *teatrale*, a method of performance. [Tr.]
9. "Every beginning is feeble."
10. "It is easy to add to inventions."

30 Michel de Pure

The Abbé Michel de Pure (1620–1680) is best known for a work of fiction, *La Prétieuse, or Mystery Down the Lane* (published in four parts, 1656–58). It is, however, neither a novel nor a mystery but an extended dialogue on love, literature, and beauty modeled on the conversations of the consciously cultured salons of Paris, which de Pure knew firsthand. The manners, language, and preoccupations of this intellectual world of women and worldly men gave us the word "preciosity," which suggests their excessive refinement. The death of prime minister Cardinal Jules Mazarin in 1661 reduced de Pure's political standing at court, so he returned to scholarship. Between 1663 and 1666 he published translations into French of Quintilian, histories of the East and West Indies, and of Africa, followed in 1668 by an original work about theatrical and outdoor spectacles, *Aspects of Ancient and Modern Spectacles*. The book describes contemporary jousts, military exercises, and, above all, dance, "one of the principal external ornaments" of a gentleman and "a certain testament of praiseworthy and careful breeding." By placing these activities in the light of Greek and Roman culture, de Pure must have hoped to flatter the King's love of ballet and ingratiate himself back into court circles. Although he thought of the *bourrée* and *menuet* as newfangled inventions of the dancing masters, de Pure clearly regarded dance with its music as a form that at its best revealed the inner passions, apart from any songs, narrative, or poetry that might be included in a ballet. Dance, with its music, was "a mute representation, in which gestures and movements signify what could be expressed in words."

FROM *Aspects of Ancient and Modern Spectacles*
(1668)

CHAPTER 9: OF BALLET

SECTION VIII. DANCING IN BALLET

•   •   •   •   •

Dancing in ballet does not consist simply of subtle movements of the feet or of various turns of the body. It is composed of both and includes all that a nimble and well-instructed body can accomplish in gesture or action in order to express something without speaking. Nevertheless, even though it must be bolder and more vigorous than the common dancing one does at balls and in ordinary and domestic dances, which women as well as men pride themselves on performing well—even though, as I was saying, it must have a quality more lively and gay, it nonetheless has its own rules or laws that render it perfect or defective, according to whether one follows them or ignores them.

The principal and most important rule is to make the dancing expressive, so that the head, the shoulders, the arms, the hands communicate what the dancer does not speak. At the time of Nero, a barbarian king preferred a mime over all the other presents he could hope for from the Emperor, because of the fine talent he had of speaking with his hands while dancing and of representing with his gestures all that he could have stated by means of words. It is

TEXT: *Idée des spectacles anciens et nouveaux* (Paris, 1668; repr. Geneva: Minkoff, 1972). pp. 248–51; 260–65. Carol MacClintock, *Readings in the History of Music in Performance* (Bloomington and London: Indiana University Press, [1979]), offers two additional excerpts from de Pure, pp. 205–8. Translation by Margaret Murata.

easy to see by this that his dancing did not consist solely in the dexterity of his feet, nor in the rightness of his rhythm (for he even wanted to do without all the instruments that were used in those times), but in a certain deliberate manner, modelled on natural movements that pass through the body according to the disquiets and various agitations of the soul, and which signify, against our own will, the interior feelings that we strive to hide and to keep secret. Therein lies the ability of a master dancer: to accord this movement of the dancing with his concept [and] with the rhythm of the music, and to do it so that he does not contradict either the one or the other, [for example,] to give to an enraged character an abrupt and fiery dance from which one can perceive the disorder of the character and his distraction by means of special *temps* or broken *coupés*.[1] Likewise in a lover, in a sick person, in a sad person or in a playful one, he must try to be expressive and to paint well the various alterations that love, infirmity, chagrin, or joy can cause on the face or on other parts that seem the most affected by interior feelings and which by a natural and imperceptible relation become totally charged with them, and despite all our resolve and all our discretion, produce them outwardly. Without this, ballet dancing is nothing but a convulsion of the master[2] and of the dancer, a *bizzarerie* without spirit and without design and, in short, nothing but a defective dance and acrobatic leaping that signify nothing and have no more sense than the one who has done them and made them up.

SECTION X. BALLET MUSIC

•   •   •   •   •

The first and most essential beauty of music for ballet is its seemliness; that is to say, the just relation that the air[3] must have with the thing represented. In an oration one seeks the argument and the conclusion; one criticizes incongruities and digressions. Conversation requires that one speak appropriately: and ballet demands airs that are suitable to its subject. If one is to represent a woman who weeps over the loss of her husband or of her children, one should resort to lugubrious sounds with heavy accents and slow motions. Anyone who then would use a joyous, lively, subtle air would create an incongruity and a discrepancy not only disagreeable but also embarrassing for the spectator and for the subject. For who does not know that grief is the enemy of happy tunes, and who would not be misled to hear a joyous air with sad steps and with drooping gestures?

•   •   •   •   •

This first rule does not, however, exclude several others which are very important and of great beauty. For example, the constraint placed upon the musician in terms of the subject and its individuality does not at all excuse him

1. The *temps* and *pas coupé* were fundamental steps in court dancing, with many variants.
2. The choreographer.
3. "Air" refers to more than the melody; it includes the entire musical composition as performed, which should have the character of its subject.

from making beautiful tunes, maintaining the melody, and caring about the ears of those who listen to it. To succeed in this, one must have more than precepts: only nature may fully inspire his beautiful and happy ideas that charm everyone. For the talent to please is a gift of heaven and the stars, rather than of rules and practice.

•   •   •   •   •

There is, however, generally speaking a certain movement that one is obliged to observe in all the airs for the ballet and in all those of all kinds of dances, and especially French ones. I say French, because I have noted among foreigners movements considerably slower and more lyric. The Italians, who do not ordinarily dance except to guitars, and the Spanish, who use nothing but harps, are astounded by the quickness of our violins and of their melodies, and of their *tirades*[4] at each half-bar or at each semibreve. And far from easily catching on to the rhythms of our dancing, they sweat blood and tears even while singing, in order to give this joyous and sudden movement to their melodies and to execute one of our rhythms. But we will speak of this elsewhere and more amply. It suffices at this point and on this subject to emphasize that music for ballet should be neither held back nor be as languishing as one could make it, if it were just a matter of singing. It is necessary to go yet a little further than with vocal decorations; the ornaments should have a strongly expressed passion or an individual vivacity. The music must always have something of the lofty and bright. It is necessary above all that the air be shorter rather than longer, whether for the convenience of the dancer or whether to liven things up for the sake of the coming break, with the *capriole*[5] or other leap that could be made at the cadence. As far as the length of the two parts of the air are concerned, it makes no difference whether they are equal or not; the musician can do as he likes.

4. Ornamental scale passages; compare the Italian *tirata*. See the Glossary of Foreign Performance Terms, p. 226.
5. A quick beating of the straight legs in a spring.

31 | François Raguenet

As French and Italian music developed along separate lines in the seventeenth century, several French visitors to Italy became strong partisans of Italian music, especially of music for the theater. The Abbé François Raguenet (c. 1660–1722), priest, physician, and historian, had heard the operas of Jean-Baptiste Lully sung in Paris by actresses such as Marie Le Rochois. Visiting the Cardinal de Bouillon in Rome from 1697, Raguenet heard the new works of Arcangelo Corelli and Giovanni Bononcini. He published his enthusiastic opinions of this newest Italian music in a *Paralele des Italiens et des François en ce qui regarde la musique et les opéra.* In this comparison he praised the poetic design, lyricism, costumes, dancing, and bass roles of the Lullian stage but found it all pale next to the sound of the Roman orchestra and the vocal abilities of the castrati. Raguenet, in short, was willing to accept less refinement in poetry, plot, dramaturgy, and instrumental sound in exchange for the Italians' vivid musical means of communicating emotions. His opinions met with some agreement in France, but they also provoked immediate defenders of French music, among them Jean Laurent Le Cerf de la Viéville, whose counter-comparison of the two styles provoked Raguenet to publish a *Défense* in 1705 of his own *Parallele.* The polemic continued back and forth and remained alive in reprints and translations as late as 1759, although the arguments over expressiveness in music persisted even as European musical style changed. Raguenet's strong initial reaction to Italian opera heralds the force of the late Baroque style, with its use of melodic motives for representation, its strongly modulating and tonal harmony, and its more contrapuntal textures. His praise of Italian music also offers rare testimony to a high degree of close listening to those formal aspects of music that indeed contribute to its expressiveness.

FROM *A Comparison between the French and Italian Music and Operas*
(1702)

There are so many things wherein the French musick has the advantage over the Italian, and as many more wherein the Italian is superior to the French, that, without a particular examination into the one, and the other, I think it impossible to draw a just parallel between 'em, or entertain a right judgment of either.

The operas are the compositions that admit of the greatest variety and extent; and they are common both to the Italians and French. 'Tis in these the masters of both nations endeavour, more particularly, to exert themselves, and make their genius shine: and 'tis on these therefore I intend to build my present comparison. But in this there are many things that require a particular distinction, such as the Italian language and the French, of which one may be more favorable than the other for music; the composition of the play that the

TEXT: *Paralele des italiens et des françois, en ce qui regarde la musique et les opéra* (Paris, 1702; facs. ed. Geneva, 1976), pp. 1–60; anonymous English translation as *A Comparison Between the French and Italian Musick and Opera's* (London, 1709; facsim. Farnborough, 1968), pp. 1–29. Only a very few of the original translator's notes are retained here; capitalization has been modernized and minor emendations in light of the French text have been inserted. See also the edition by Oliver Strunk of the London version in the *Musical Quarterly* 32 (1946):411–36.

musicians set to music, the qualifications of the actors; those of the performers; the different sorts of voices; the recitative, the airs, the symphonies, the choruses, the dances, the machines, the decorations, and whatever else is essential to an opera, or serves to make the entertainment compleat and perfect. And these things ought to be particularly inquired into, before we can pretend to determine in favour either of the Italian or French.

Our opera's are writ much better than the Italian; they are regular, coherent designs; and, if repeated without the music,[1] they are as entertaining as any of our other pieces that are purely dramatick. Nothing can be more natural and lively, than their dialogues; the gods are made to speak with a dignity suitable to their character; kings with all the majesty their rank requires; and the nymphs and shepherds with a softness and innocent mirth, peculiar to the plains. Love, jealousie, anger, and the rest of the passions, are touch'd with the greatest art and nicety; and there are few of our tragedies, or comedies, that appear more beautiful than Quinault's opera's.[2]

On the other hand, the Italian opera's are poor, incoherent rapsodies, without any connexion or design; all their pieces, properly speaking, are patched up with thin, insipid scraps; their scenes consist of some trivial dialogues, or soliloquy, at the end of which they foist in one of their best airs, which concludes the scene. These airs are seldom of a piece with the rest of the opera, being usually written by other poets, either occasionally, or in the body of some other work. When the undertaker of an opera has fix'd himself in a town, and got his company together, he makes choice of the subject he likes best, such as Camilla, Themistocles, Xerxes, &c.[3] But this piece, as I just now observ'd, is no better than a patchwork, larded with the best airs his performers are acquainted with, which airs are like saddles, fit for all horses alike; they are declarations of love made on one side, and embraced or rejected on the other; transports of happy lovers, or complaints of the unfortunate; protestations of fidelity, or stings of jealousie; raptures of pleasure, or pangs of sorrow, rage, and despair. And one of these airs you are sure to find at the end of every scene. Now certainly such an opera made of fragments cobbled together and stitched-up patches can never be set in competition with our opera's, which are wrought up with great exactness and marvelous conduct.

Besides, our opera's have a farther advantage over the Italian, in respect of

1. That is, if they are spoken or read.
2. Philippe Quinault (1635–1688), playwright and the principal librettist for Jean-Baptiste Lully, with whom he collaborated on fourteen stage premieres between 1668 and 1686. The two invented the five-act *tragédie en musique*.
3. These are characters in two operas given at the Teatro Capranica that Raguenet attended in Rome in 1698 and to which he refers later: *Rinnovata Camilla, Regina de' Volsci* (libretto by S. Stampiglia, music by Giovanni Bononcini) and *Temistocle in bando* (libretto by A. Morselli, originally for Venice, 1683; music for each act respectively by Giovanni Lulier, M. A. Ziani, and G. Bononcini). Both were designed and produced by Filippo Acciaiuoli.

the voice, and that is the bass,[4] which is so frequent among us, and so rarely to be met with in Italy. For every man, that has an ear, will witness with me, that nothing can be more charming than a good bass; the simple sound of these basses, which sometimes seems to sink into a profound abyss, has something wonderfully charming in it. The air receives a stronger concussion from these deep voices, than it doth from those that are higher, and is consequently fill'd with a more agreeable and extensive harmony. When the persons of gods or kings, a Jupiter, Neptune, Priam or Agamemnon, are brought on the stage, our actors, with their deep voices, give 'em an air of majesty, quite different from that of the falsettists or the feign'd basses among the Italians, which have neither depth nor strength. Besides, the blending of the basses with the upper parts forms an agreeable contrast, and makes us perceive the beauties of the one from the opposition they meet with from the other, a pleasure to which the Italians are perfect strangers, the voices of their singers, who are, for the most part, castrati, being perfectly like those of their women.

Besides the advantages we claim from the beauty of our designs, and the variety of voices, we receive still more from our choruses, dances, and other *divertissements,* in which we infinitely excell the Italians. They, instead of these choruses and *divertissements,* which furnish our opera's with an agreeable variety, and give 'em a peculiar air of grandure and magnificence, have usually nothing but some burlesque scenes of a buffoon; some old woman that's to be in love with a young footman; or a conjurer that shall turn a cat into a bird, a fiddler into an owl, and play a few other tricks of legerdemain, that are only fit to divert the mob. And for their dancers, they are the poorest creatures in the world; they are all of a lump, without arms, legs, a shape or air.

As to the instruments, our masters touch the violin much finer, and with a greater nicety than they do in Italy. All the Italians' bow strokes sound harsh, when they detach them from each other, and when they want to connect the tones, they fiddle in a most disagreeable manner. Moreover, besides all the instruments that are common to us, as well as the Italians, we have the hautbois, which, by their sounds, equally mellow and piercing, have infinitely the advantage of the violins, in all brisk, lively airs; and the flutes, which so many of our great artists[5] have taught to groan after so moving a manner, in our moanful airs, and sigh so amorously in those that are tender.

Finally, we have the advantage of 'em in dress. Our habits[6] infinitely excell

4. "Basses-contres." The translator adds: "I can't think the base-voice more proper for a king, a hero, or any other distinguish'd person, than the counter-tenor, since the difference of the voice in man is meerly accidental. And as the abilities of a man's mind are not measur'd by his stature, so certainly we are not to judge a heroe by his voice. For this reason I can't see why the part of Caesar or Alexander may not properly enough be perform'd by a counter-tenor or tenor, or any other voice, provided the performer, in acting as well as singing, is able to maintain the dignity of the character he represents" (p. 6, note 5).
5. Philbert, Philidor, Descoteaux, & the Hotteterres. [Au.]
6. Costumes.

all we see abroad, both in costliness and fancy. The Italians themselves will own, that no dancers in Europe are equal to ours; the Combatants and Cyclops in *Perseus*, the Tremblers and Smiths in *Isis*, the Unlucky Dreams in *Atys*, and our other ballet *entrées*, are originals in their kind, as well in respect of the airs, compos'd by Lully, as of the steps which Beauchamp has adapted to those airs.[7] The theatre produced nothing like it 'till those two great men appear'd; 'tis an entertainment of which they are the sole inventors, and they have carried it to so high a degree of perfection, that as no person either in Italy or elsewhere, has hitherto rival'd 'em, so, I fear, the world will never produce their equal. No theatre can represent a fight more lively, than we see it sometimes express'd in our dances; and, in a word, ev'ry thing is performed with an unexceptionable nicety; the conduct and economy, through the whole, is so admirable, that no man, of common understanding, will deny, but that the French opera's form a more lively representation than the Italian, and that a meer spectator must be much better pleas'd in France than Italy. This is the sum of what can be offer'd to our advantage, in behalf of our musick and opera's; let us now examine wherein the Italians have the advantage over us in these two points.

The Italian language is much more naturally adapted to musick than ours; their vowels are all sonorous, whereas above half of ours are mute, or at best bear a very small part in pronunciation; so that, in the first place, no cadence, or beautiful passage, can be form'd upon the syllables that consist of those vowels, and, in second place, one cannot hear but half the words, so that we are left to guess at what the French are singing, whereas the Italian is perfectly understood. Besides, though all the Italian vowels are full and open, yet the composers choose out of them such as they judge most proper for their finest divisions. They generally make choice of the vowel *a*, which, being clearer and more distinct than any of the rest, expresses the beauty of the cadences, and divisions, to a better advantage. Whereas we make use of all the vowels indifferently, those that are mute, as well as those that are sonorous; nay, very often we pitch upon a diphthong, as in the words *chaîne* and *gloire*, etc., which syllables, consisting of two vowels join'd together, create a confus'd sound, and want that clearness and beauty that we find in the simple vowels. But this is not the most material part to be consider'd in musick; let us now examine into its essence, and form, that is, the structure of the airs, either distinctly consider'd, or in relation to the different parts, of which the whole composition consists.

The Italians are more bold and hardy in their airs, than the French; they carry their point[8] farther, both in their tender songs and those that are more lively, as well as in their other compositions; nay, they often unite styles, which the French think incompatible. The French, in those compositions that consist

7. Raguenet cites three operas by Quinault and Lully. Pierre Beauchamps (1631–1705) provided the choreography for *Isis* (1677) and *Atys* (1676).
8. "Le caractère."

of many parts, seldom regard more than that which is principal, whereas the Italians usually study to make all the parts equally shining, and beautiful. In short, the invention of the one is inexhaustible, but the genius of the other is narrow and constrain'd; this the reader will fully understand when we descend to particulars.

It is not to be wonder'd that the Italians think our musick dull and stupifying, that, according to their taste, it appears flat and insipid, if we consider the nature of the French airs compar'd to those of the Italian. The French in their airs aim at the soft, the easie, the flowing, and coherent; the whole air is of the same tone, or if sometimes they venture to vary it, they do it with so many preparations, they so qualifie it, that still the air seems to be as natural and consistent as if they had attempted no change at all; there is nothing bold and adventurous in it; it's all equal and of a piece. But the Italians pass boldly, and in an instant from sharps to flats and from flats to sharps;[9] they venture the boldest cadences, and the most irregular dissonances; and their airs are so out of the way that they resemble the compositions of no other nation in the world.

The French would think themselves undone, if they offended in the least against the rules; they flatter, tickle, and court the ear, and are still doubtful of success, tho' ev'ry thing be done with an exact regularity. The more daring Italian changes the tone and the mode without any awe or hesitation; he makes double or treble cadences[10] of seven or eight bars together, upon tones we should think incapable of the least division. He'll make a swelling[11] of so prodigious a length, that they who are unacquainted with it can't chuse but be offended at first to see him so adventurous; but before he has done, they'll think they can't sufficiently admire him. He'll have passages of such an extent, as will perfectly confound his auditors at first, and upon such irregular tones as shall instill a terror as well as surprize into the listener, who will immediately conclude, that the whole concert is degenerating into a dreadful dissonance; and betraying 'em by that means into a concern for the musick, which seems to be upon the brink of ruin, he immediately reconciles 'em by such regular cadences that everyone is surpriz'd to see harmony rising again in a manner out of discord itself, and owing its greatest beauties to those irregularities which seem'd to threaten it with destruction. The Italians venture at ev'ry thing that is harsh, and out of the way, but then they do it like people that have a right to venture, and are sure of success. Under a notion of being the greatest and most absolute masters of musick in the world, like despotic soveraigns,

9. That is, from major to minor and from minor to major. Le Cerf de la Viéville (see No. 32 below) challenged this point by saying, "Can you still find these changes affective, when they are so frequent?" (*Comparison between Italian and French Music,* pt. 1, 2d. ed. [1705], pp. 27–28).

10. "Cadences doublées & redoublées"; see "raddoppiate" in the Glossary of Foreign Performance Terms, p. 225.

11. By the Italians call'd *messe di voce.* [Tr.] The French word here is "tenuës."

they dispense with its rules in hardy but fortunate sallies; they exert themselves above the art, but like masters of that art, whose laws they follow, or transgress at pleasure, they insult the niceness of the ear which others court; they defie and compel it; they master and conquer it with charms, which owe their irresistible force to the boldness of the adventurous composer.

Sometimes we meet with a swelling, to which the first notes of the thorough bass jarr so harshly, as the ear is highly offended with it; but the bass, continuing to play on, returns at last to the swelling with such beautiful intervals, that we quickly discover the composer's design in the choice of those discords, was to give the hearer a more true and perfect relish of the ravishing notes that on a sudden restore the whole harmony.

Let a Frenchman be set to sing one of these dissonances, and he'll want courage enough to support it with that resolution wherewith it must be sustain'd to make it succeed; his ear, being accustom'd to the most soft and natural intervals, is startled at such an irregularity; he trembles and is in a sweat whilst he attempts to sing it; whereas the Italians, who are inur'd from their youth to these dissonances, sing the most irregular notes with the same assurance they would the most beautiful, and perform ev'ry thing with a confidence that secures 'em of success.[12]

Musick is become exceeding common in Italy; the Italians sing from their cradles, they sing at all times and places; a natural uniform song is too vulgar for their ears. Such airs are to them like things tasteless, and decay'd. If you would hit their palate, you must regale it with variety, and be continually passing from one key to another, though you venture at the most uncommon, and unnatural passages. Without this you'll be unable to keep 'em awake, or excite their attention. But let us continue this comparison, and bring forth the different characters of their airs.

As the Italians are naturally much more lively than the French, so are they more sensible of the passions, and consequently express 'em more lively in all their productions. If a storm, or rage, is to be describ'd in a symphony, their notes give us so natural an idea of it, that our souls can hardly receive a stronger impression from the reality than they do from the description; every thing is so brisk and piercing, so impetuous and affecting, that the imagination, the senses, the soul, and the body itself are all betray'd into a general transport; 'tis impossible not to be borne down with the rapidity of these movements. A symphony of furies shakes the soul; it undermines and overthrows it in spite of all; the violinist himself, whilst he is performing it, is seiz'd with an unavoidable agony; he tortures his violin; he racks his body; he is no longer master of himself, but is agitated like one possessed with an irresistible motion.

12. Le Cerf de la Viéville responded to this description (*Comparison*, pt. 1, pp. 37–38): "But these kinds of adornments should not be so extravagant, and in making them so, the Italians break the rules at every moment. . . . The first time one hears them in the works of Italian composers, they are enchanting; the second time, they are painful; the third, offensive; the fourth time, revolting. They do everything to excess."

If, on the other side, the symphony is to express a calm and tranquility, which requires a quite different style, they however execute it with an equal success. Here the notes descend so low, that the soul is swallow'd with 'em in the profound abyss. There are bow strokes of an infinite length, ling'ring on a dying sound, which decays gradually 'till at last it absolutely expires. Their symphonies of sleep insensibly steal the soul from the body, and so suspend its faculties, and operations, that being bound up, as it were, in the harmony, that entirely possesses and enchants it, it's as dead to every thing else, as if all its powers were captivated by a real sleep.

In short, as for the conformity of the air with the sense of the words, I never heard any symphony comparable to that which was performed at Rome in the Oratory of St. Jerome of Charity, on St. Martin's Day in the year 1697, upon these two words—"Mille saette," a thousand arrows.[13] The air consisted of disjointed notes,[14] like those in a jigg, which gave the soul a lively impression of an arrow; and that wrought so effectually upon the imagination, that every violin appear'd to be a bow, and their bows were like so many flying arrows, darting their pointed heads upon every part of the symphony. Nothing can be more masterly, or more happily express'd. So that be their airs either of a sprightly or gentle style, let 'em be impetuous or languishing, in all these the Italians are equally preferable to the French. But there is one thing beyond all this, which neither the French, nor any other nation, besides themselves, in the world, ever attempted; for they will sometimes unite in a most surprizing manner, the tender with the sprightly, as may be instanced in that celebrated air, "Mai non si vidde ancor più bella fedeltà," &c.,[15] which is the softest and most tender of any in the world, and yet its symphony is as lively, and piercing as ever was composed. These different characters are they able to unite so artfully, that, far from destroying a contrary by its contrary, they make the one serve to embellish the other.

But if we now proceed from the simple airs to a consideration of those pieces that consist of several parts, we there shall find the mighty advantages the Italians have over the French. I never met with a master in France, but what agreed, that the Italians knew much better how to turn, and vary a trio than the French. Among us the first upper part is generally beautiful enough; but then the second usually descends too low to deserve our attention. In Italy the upper parts are generally three or four notes higher than in France; so that their seconds are high enough to have as much beauty as the very first with us.[16] Besides, all their

---

13. San Girolamo della Carità was a meeting place of the first Oratorians under St. Philip Neri beginning in 1552. It was a venue for musical performances open to the public through the seventeenth century.
14. "Notes pointées," or staccato.
15. From the opera *Camilla* by Giovanni Bononcini; see No. 31, p. 164, n. 3.
16. Le Cerf replied to this objection of Raguenet in his Second Dialogue (*Comparison*, pt. 1, pp. 64–65): "The first upper parts of the Italians squeak because they are too high; their second upper parts have the fault of being too close to the first and too far from the bass, which is the third part."

three parts are so equally good, that it is often difficult to find which is the subject. Lully has composed some after this manner, but they are few in number, whereas we hardly meet with any in Italy that are otherwise.

But of compositions consisting of more parts than three, the advantages of the Italian masters will still appear greater.[17] In France, it's sufficient if the subject be beautiful, we rarely find that the parts which accompany it are so much as coherent. We have some thorough-basses, indeed, which are good grounds; and which, for that reason, are highly extoll'd by us. But where this happens the upper parts grow very poor; they give way to the bass, which then becomes the subject. As for the accompaniments of the violin, they are for the most part nothing but single strokes of the bow, heard by intervals, without any uniform coherent musick, serving only to express, from time to time, a few accords. Whereas in Italy, the first and second upper part, the thorough-bass, and all the other parts that concur to the composition of the fullest pieces, are equally finish'd. The parts for the violins are usually as beautiful as the air it self. So that after we have been entertain'd with something very charming in the air, we are insensibly captivated by the parts that accompany it, which are equally engaging and make us quit the subject to listen to them. Everything is so exactly beautiful that it's difficult to find out the principal part. Sometimes the thorough-bass lays so fast hold of our ear, that in list'ning to it we forget the subject; at other times the subject is so insinuating, that we no longer regard the bass, when all on a sudden the violins become so ravishing, that we mind neither the bass, nor the subject. 'Tis too much for one soul to taste the several beauties of so many parts. She must multiply herself before she can relish and digest three or four delights at once, which are all beautiful alike; 'tis transport, inchantment, and ectasie of pleasure; her faculties are upon so great a stretch, she's forced to ease her self by exclamations; she waits impatiently for the end of the air that she may have a breathing room; she sometimes finds it impossible to wait so long, and then the musick is interrupted by an universal applause. These are the daily effects of the Italian compositions, which everyone who has been in Italy can abundantly testifie; we meet with the like in no other nation whatsoever. They are beauties improv'd to such a degree of excellence, as not to be reach'd by the imagination, 'till master'd by the understanding; and when they are understood our imaginations can form nothing beyond 'em.

17. Compare Le Cerf (*Comparison*, pt. 1, pp. 70–71): " 'Is it in the choruses that the advantage of the Italians is supposed to lie? . . . Everyone knows that choruses are out of use in Italy, indeed beyond the means of the ordinary Italian opera house. . . . How many singers do you suppose an Italian company has?'
'Say twenty or twenty-five, Monsieur, as in our own.'
'Nothing of the sort, Madame; usually six or seven or eight. Those marvelous opera companies in Venice, Naples, and Rome consist of seven or eight voices. . . . When the composer of an opera aspires to the glory of having included a chorus in his work, as a rarity, it is these seven or eight persons as a group who form it, all singing together—the king, the clown, the queen, and the old woman.' "

32 Jean Laurent Le Cerf de la Viéville

Lord of Freneuse and Keeper of the Seals for the parliament of Normandy, Jean Laurent Le Cerf de la Viéville (1674–1707) quickly rose to defend French music in his *Comparison between Italian and French Music,* published in 1704 explicitly as a refutation of François Raguenet's pro-Italian comparison of 1702. In the face of reviews and Raguenet's subsequently published defense of his opinions, Le Cerf quickly brought out a second edition of his *Comparison* with new sections, including a "Treatise on Good Taste" (Brussels, 1705). An additional volume published in 1706 compared French and Italian sacred music and also included a response to Raguenet's *Defense of the Parallel.* Le Cerf began his criticism by attacking Raguenet's spelling of musical terms and ended with a detailed examination of cantatas by Giovanni Bononcini, which he judged only on the basis of a printed score, having had no opportunity to hear them performed.

Le Cerf characterized French music in general as "sage, unie & naturelle," that is, as orderly, even, and natural, as opposed to the "forced, disjointed, incoherent and unnatural taste" of the Italians. Italian music was fine in small portions, but for extended works like operas, French music was to be preferred, as white meat was preferable to ragouts. His standard for good taste in music required that music be natural, expressive, and harmonious. For Le Cerf an expressive air was one in which "the notes are perfectly suited to the words," as he states in dialogue 6 from the *Comparison* (p. 302). This primacy of the text, including its vocables, it intonation, its own rhythm, and its grammar, as well as its meaning and significance, meant that for him music would always be judged as an imitation of language and not as those sonorous forms inspired by language over which Raguenet had rhapsodized. When Jacopo Peri had advocated a close adherence of music to its text a hundred years earlier, he had helped transform musical style. Le Cerf's similar position was now a conservative one. His view of what is expressive in music and what music expresses was stated most clearly in his "Letter to Monsieur de la ***" from part 1 of the *Comparison.*

FROM *Comparison between Italian and French Music*

(1704)

LETTER TO MONSIEUR DE LA °°°

What do reason and the good authors[1] tell us about what is beauty in paint-ing, the art of the painter? To represent things perfectly, as they are. It is to paint grapes so well, like Zeuxis, that birds come and peck at them; it is to paint a curtain so well, as did Parrasius, that Zeuxis himself stretches out a hand to lift it. What is the beauty of poetry? It is doing with words what a painter does with colors. *Ut pictura poesis erit.*[2]

And you know that Aristotle in his *Poetics*[3] speaks only of imitating, which is to say, painting. All the genres of poetry, according to him, are just different *imitations* of different pictures. Perfection in poetry consists of describing the things of which it speaks with terms so appropriate and exact that the reader can imagine that he sees them. Thus when Virgil describes a serpent that a passerby happened upon unawares, *Improvisum aspris*, etc.,[4] I have fear and I am ready to flee like the passerby. When the feelings of the heart are painted so vividly, the reader, struck by what another has felt or knows, can feel them himself and share all the passions that the poet grants his heroes. Thus when Virgil portrays for me Dido agitated by a growing love that she fights in vain, I am disturbed, I am anxious, and I hope along with her. She becomes alarmed, then furious at the departure of her lover, she despairs, she stabs herself: I cannot blame Aeneas, because he is forced to leave her by the gods, but I almost hate him at that moment, and I feel pity, and I weep at Dido's pyre, as did St. Augustine, who did not control his tears when reading such touching poetry.

What, at the present time, is the beauty of the music of opera? It lies in rendering the verse of these operas into a painting that actually speaks. It is, so to speak, giving the finishing touches by applying the final colors.[5] Now how

---

TEXT: *Comparaison de la musique italienne, et de la musique françoise*, part 1, 2d ed. (Brussels: Fr. Foppens, 1705; repr. Geneva: Minkoff, 1972), pp. 151–83; this excerpt, pp. 167–73. Translation by Margaret Murata.

1. The ancient writers.
2. Horace, *The Art of Poetry* [Au.], line 361: "Poetry is like painting."
3. Πᾶσαι τυγχάνουσιν οὖσαι μιμήσεις τὸ σύνολον. Omnes sunt imitatio in universam. Aristotle, *Poetics* 6.1 [Au.]: "They are all in their general essence, modes of imitation" (1447a, lines 15–16).
4. *Aeneid* 1.2 [Au.]: "A rude surprise."
5. Traditional painting in oils built up forms and figures in precise stages that had been practiced since the Renaissance. Design and modeling were executed in monochrome or with a limited palette before colors were employed. The basic procedures are articulated in Giorgio Vasari's

does music *re-paint* the poetry, how do they mutually serve each other, unless they are exactly matched and blended together in the most perfect agreement? The single secret is to apply such proportionate tones to the words that the verse is indistinguishable from and lives again in the music. This carries the feeling of all that the singer says right to the heart of the listener. *Voilà,* this is what we call expression.

Expression is the common goal of painting and of poetry retouched by music. On this footing, if a musician adds a musical idea to some verse that does not suit it at all, it will not matter whether this idea is new and learned or whether the basso continuo resolves the dissonances elegantly. If the poetry and music are badly joined, they will separate from each other, and my attention will wander at this division, and the pleasure which my ears could have from the harmonies will be unknown by my heart—and from that moment, be completely cold. Painting differently is not painting more, which is why it is bad. When the musician plays and fools around on unimportant or serious words by adding runs and roulades, I know at once that the sense does not require these niceties at all. This is not a harmonious representation, and so it is worthless. If, however, the musician sets the words vividly and exactly, the object is doubly represented by the poetry and by the music. Only when they are equal can I be happy with this arrangement.[6] This is painting and it is good. When there are feelings, burning passions, and the musician maintains them, or rather, when he once more rekindles their fire with tones of quickening precision, my heart will feel them, whether it has them or not. This is marvelous painting and it is excellent.

But, you say to me, here we have only common harmonies. So be it. Provided that these harmonies are not at all defective and do not disfigure the beauty of the expression, the listener could want no more. An accompaniment that is wrong or too dull does not necessarily commit a perceptible offense on the subject, as happens when one impermissibly uses a poor word to express the happiest thought. But also as soon as my thought pleases on its own, makes an impression and conveys a feeling, I have no need at all to go on searching for an elegant phrase. It is sufficient that the words do convey the sense. It follows that expression, which must be the goal of the musician, is therefore the most important thing in music, because of all the things in the world, it is this that succeeds in achieving its aim. To express well is to paint well. This is the masterpiece, this the highest peak, *voilà,* everything. Though it can cost the musician to achieve this by the appearance of sterility, of learning disregarded, he will always gain enough. If he does not succeed, learning and productiveness, no matter how sustained, will not take the place of that value in the mind of a

---

Lives of the Painters (1550, 1568); see in *Vasari on Technique,* trans. L. S. Maclehose (London, 1907; repr. New York: Dover, 1960), "Of Painting," ch. 7: "Of painting in oil or on panel or canvas."

6. "Cette convenance," as in a marriage of convenience, or arranged marriage.

reasonable listener. If it is absent, they will not excuse it. Your hero is dying of love and from grief, he says, and what he sings says nothing, isn't expressive at all: I will not be the least interested in his pain, which is what was wanted. . . . But should the accompaniment cleave the rocks. . . . pleasant recompense! Is it the orchestra who is the hero? . . . No, it is the singer . . . Well then, if the singer himself moves me, if a tender and expressive song portrays that he is suffering and if it spares no pains to move me on his behalf, as to the orchestra, it is only there on forgiveness and by accident.

> Si vis me flere, dolendum est
> Primum ipsi tibi.[7]

If the orchestra unites with the singer in order to touch me and to move me, so much the better, for then there are two means of expression instead of one. But the first and the most essential is that of the singer. Reason and experience lead us to find it so essential that once again, nothing compares with it. The power of something beautifully expressed diffuses into an entire scene, and its effect is as general as it is fixed. It is enjoyed by the ignorant, by the connoisseur, by men and by women. It is imprinted on the minds of the audience, who leave thinking about it. That is why, upon leaving our operas, everyone sings something that he has remembered. Certain airs travel from mouth to mouth; they become familiar to those at court, in the city, and in the provinces. Who will not know it? In contrast, one hardly ever remembers an Italian instrumental work, even if it has been heard ten times. Our ears that receive the airs of Lully so quickly and easily do not accept those of the Italian masters the same way without study and trouble. Why is this? It is, one would say, because we are French, not Italians. . . . And you boast that more than half the musicians in France have become Italian by inclination, and that a thousand folk know Italian. Thus neither the country nor the language matters much. But rather it is that the great beauties, beautiful things drawn from nature's breast, the really truthful expressions make themselves felt by all men, and that false beauties are far from having this privilege.

•   •   •   •   •

7. Horace, *The Art of Poetry* [Au.], lines 102–3: "To make me weep, you must first yourself feel grief."

33 Joseph Addison

Joseph Addison (1672–1719), the great English essayist and man of letters, was the leading contributor to the periodicals *The Tatler, The Spectator,* and *The Guardian,* published by his friend Richard Steele from 1709 to 1713. Particularly important are Addison's contributions to *The Spectator,* a paper that stood for reason and moderation in an age of bitter party strife. In his essays, Addison showed himself an able painter of life and manners. His witty, distinguished writings exerted an important influence on criticism, not only in England but also in France and Germany.

In the present essay he demonstrates that agreed-upon artifices are essential to representation in the theater by showing that "shadows and realities ought not be mixed together." His own opera *Rosamond,* set to music by Thomas Clayton in 1707, has been forgotten by history. More memorable are his reactions to a landmark Italian opera by Handel, who had arrived in London at the end of 1710.

FROM *The Spectator*
(1711)

Spectatum admissi risum teneatis?—Hor[ace][1]

An opera may be allowed to be extravagantly lavish in its decorations, as its only design is to gratify the senses, and keep up an indolent attention in the audience. Common sense, however, requires, that there should be nothing in the scenes and machines which may appear childish and absurd. How would the wits of King Charles's time have laughed to have seen Nicolini[2] exposed to a tempest in robes of ermine, and sailing in an open boat upon a sea of pasteboard! What a field of raillery would they have been let into, had they been entertained with painted dragons spitting wildfire, enchanted chariots drawn by Flanders mares, and real cascades in artificial landscapes![3] A little skill in

---

TEXT: From *The Spectator* for Tuesday, March 6, 1711, as edited by G. Gregory Smith for Everyman's Library (London, 1907), vol. 1, pp. 20–23. Especially useful are the annotations in the edition by Donald F. Bond (Oxford: Clarendon Press, 1965), vol. 1, pp. 22–31.

1. "If you were admitted to see this, could you hold back your laughter?" The quotation is from line 5 of *The Art of Poetry* by Horace. Addison expected his readers to remember its context: a painting of a human head on a horse's neck, with feathers on randomly affixed limbs and the upper torso of an attractive woman whose body ends in that of a black fish.
2. Nicolò Grimaldi (1673–1732), known as Nicolini, who sang in London at the Theatre in the Haymarket during the seasons of 1708 to 1712 and 1715 to 1717, created the principal castrato roles in Handel's operas *Rinaldo* (1711) and *Amadigi* (1715).
3. These references are without exception to the stage machinery of Handel's *Rinaldo.*

criticism would inform us, that shadows and realities ought not to be mixed together in the same piece; and that the scenes which are designed as the representations of nature, should be filled with resemblances, and not with the things themselves. If one would represent a wide champaign country[4] filled with herds and flocks, it would be ridiculous to draw the country only upon the scenes, and to crowd several parts of the stage with sheep and oxen. This is joining together inconsistencies, and making the decoration partly real and partly imaginary. I would recommend what I have here said to the directors, as well as to the admirers, of our modern opera.

As I was walking in the streets about a fortnight ago, I saw an ordinary fellow carrying a cage full of little birds upon his shoulder; and, as I was wondering with myself what use he would put them to, he was met very luckily by an acquaintance, who had the same curiosity. Upon his asking him what he had upon his shoulder, he told him, that he had been buying sparrows for the opera. Sparrows for the opera! says his friend, licking his lips; what, are they to be roasted? No, no, says the other; they are to enter towards the end of the first act, and to fly about the stage.

This strange dialogue awakened my curiosity so far, that I immediately bought the opera,[5] by which means I perceived the sparrows were to act the part of singing birds in a delightful grove; though, upon a nearer inquiry, I found the sparrows put the same trick upon the audience, that Sir Martin Mar-all practised upon his mistress;[6] for, though they flew in sight, the music proceeded from a consort of flagelets and bird-calls[7] which were planted behind the scenes. At the same time I made this discovery, I found, by the discourse of the actors, that there were great designs on foot for the improvement of the opera; that it had been proposed to break down a part of the wall, and to surprise the audience with a party of an hundred horse; and that there was actually a project of bringing the New River into the house, to be employed in jetteaus[8] and water-works. This project, as I have since heard, is postponed till the summer season; when it is thought the coolness that proceeds from fountains and cascades will be more acceptable and refreshing to people of quality. In the meantime, to find out a more agreeable entertainment for the winter season, the opera of *Rinaldo* is filled with thunder and lightning, illuminations and fireworks; which the audience may look upon without catching cold, and indeed without much danger of being burnt; for there are several engines filled with water, and ready to play at a minute's warning, in case any

4. A plain.
5. Its libretto.
6. A character in John Dryden's comedy of the same name. In act 5, Sir Martin acts out the singing of a serenade to the lute, while the actual singing and playing is done in an adjoining room by his man. The scheme miscarries.
7. Almirena's cavatina "Augelletti che cantate" ("Little birds who sing," *Rinaldo* act 1, scene 6) has an accompaniment for flauto piccolo (or "flageolett" as Handel calls it in his autograph score), two flutes, and strings.
8. "Jetto," English for *jet d'eaux*, or fountain.

such accident should happen. However, as I have a very great friendship for the owner of this theatre, I hope that he has been wise enough to insure his house before he would let this opera be acted in it.

It is no wonder that those scenes should be very surprising, which were contrived by two poets of different nations,[9] and raised by two magicians of different sexes. Armida (as we are told in the argument) was an Amazonian enchantress, and poor signor Cassani (as we learn from the persons represented) a Christian conjuror (Mago Christiano).[10] I must confess I am very much puzzled to find how an Amazon should be versed in the black art; or how a good Christian (for such is the part of the magician) should deal with the devil.

To consider the poets after the conjurors, I shall give you a taste of the Italian from the first lines of his preface: *Eccoti, benigno lettore, un parto di poche sere, che se ben nato di notte, non è però aborto di tenebre, mà si farà conoscere figliolo d'Apollo con qualche raggio di Parnasso.* "Behold, gentle reader, the birth of a few evenings, which, though it be the offspring of the night, is not the abortive of darkness, but will make itself known to be the son of Apollo, with a certain ray of Parnassus." He afterwards proceeds to call Mynheer Hendel the Orpheus of our age, and to acquaint us, in the same sublimity of style, that he composed this opera in a fortnight. Such are the wits to whose tastes we so ambitiously conform ourselves. The truth of it is, the finest writers among the modern Italians express themselves in such a florid form of words, and such tedious circumlocutions, as are used by none but pedants in our own country; and at the same time fill their writings with such poor imaginations and conceits, as our youths are ashamed of before they have been two years at the university. Some may be apt to think that it is the difference of genius which produces this difference in the works of the two nations; but to show there is nothing in this, if we look into the writings of the old Italians, such as Cicero and Virgil, we shall find that the English writers, in their way of thinking and expressing themselves, resemble those authors much more than the modern Italians pretend to do. And as for the poet himself,[11] from whom the dreams of this opera are taken, I must entirely agree with Monsieur Boileau, that one verse in Virgil is worth all the clinquant or tinsel of Tasso.[12]

But to return to the sparrows; there have been so many flights of them let loose in this opera, that it is feared the house will never get rid of them; and that in other plays they make their entrance in very wrong and improper scenes, so as to be seen flying in a lady's bed-chamber, or perching upon a

9. Aaron Hill and Giacomo Rossi.
10. Giuseppe Cassani (fl. 1700–1728), an alto castrato.
11. Torquato Tasso (1544–1595), from whose epic poem *Gerusalemme liberata* the story of Rinaldo is drawn.
12. Nicholas Boileau (1636–1711), *Satire 9*, lines 173–76: "Tous les jours à la Cour un Sot de qualité / Peut juger de travers avec impunité: / À Malherbe, à Racan, préférer Theophile, / Et le clinquant du Tasse, à tout l'or de Virgile."

king's throne; besides the inconveniences which the heads of the audience may sometimes suffer from them. I am credibly informed, that there was once a design of casting into an opera the story of Whittington and his cat, and that in order to do it, there had been got together a great quantity of mice; but Mr. Rich, the proprietor of the playhouse,[13] very prudently considered, that it would be impossible for the cat to kill them all, and that consequently the princes of the stage might be as much infested with mice, as the prince of the island was before the cat's arrival upon it; for which reason he would not permit it to be acted in his house. And indeed I cannot blame him: for, as he said very well upon that occasion, I do not hear that any of the performers in our opera pretend to equal the famous pied piper, who made all the mice of a great town in Germany follow his music, and by that means cleared the place of those little noxious animals.

Before I dismiss this paper, I must inform my reader, that I hear there is a treaty on foot with London and Wise (who will be appointed gardeners of the playhouse) to furnish the opera of Rinaldo and Armida with an orange-grove; and that the next time it is acted, the singing birds will be impersonated by tom-tits: the undertakers[14] being resolved to spare neither pains nor money for the gratification of the audience.

13. Christopher Rich, the former proprietor of the Drury Lane Theatre.
14. Producers.

34 Pier Jacopo Martello

The earliest writings of Pier Jacopo Martello (1665–1727) were occasional poems, pastorals, tragedies, and at least three operas. Much of this work was published in collected editions of 1709 *(Teatro)* and 1710 *(Versi e prose)*. Both volumes were issued in Rome, when Martello was serving as the Bolognese representative to the Vatican. He spent most of 1713 as a member of a papal legation in Paris. There, in the literary circle around Antonio Conti, he participated in the arguments over the relative merits of French and Italian theater. These encounters prompted Martello to write a dialogue on ancient and modern tragedy, which was seen into print by Conti in 1714, after Martello had returned to Rome. The spirit of Aristotle (in the guise of an old traveler) and the classicizing tendencies of the new Arcadian reformers of literature and theater inform the discursive text—hardly a conversation between opposing views, as "Aristotle" appears as an authority on both the ancients and the moderns. Martello soon brought out an Italian edition (1715), whose fifth section, or "session," concerns contemporary opera. He demonstrates the extent to which opera is a nonliterary genre and asserts that it should therefore not be criticized in the same way as drama. With a somewhat sardonic tone, "Aristotle" nevertheless proceeds to describe the construction of a turn-of-the century libretto—from the meters of the verse to the placement of arias in the acts. These elements are considered only in terms of general formal effectiveness, because Martello first lays down the premise that music is by nature expressive and pleasurable purely as sound. Beyond the beauty of sound, the conventions of opera admit and order musical variety: "whether it is verisimilar is not material." Jean Laurent Le Cerf de la Viéville thought of music as colors added to poetry. For Martello, "the musical composition is the very substance of operas, and all the other parts are incidental, poetry among them."

FROM *On Ancient and Modern Tragedy*
(1715)

I shall inquire then, whether, in order to delight, opera must have the help of words and poetry: and I will frankly declare it does not. When, at night, I listen to one or several nightingales singing and almost conversing in song, I find that this drama of unseen birds delights me and draws me away from all troubling thoughts, so that I will sit long and listen to them; yet Nature limits their warbling to but a few strains, which are much the same if not identical. A serenade of instruments, too, can make a man appear on the balcony and spend several hours there, unconsciously, while the music lasts; and his delight is greater, since the players with their various instruments can produce symphonies as diverse as those of the nightingales were similar. And just as we find it more pleasant to listen to the chirping of birds or the play of instruments within a green wood or in sight of a lovely garden, so are we more refreshed by human voices when we hear them in enchanting surroundings, and even more delighted when the songs alternate amid a wondrous variety of scenes. Consider, further, how much more delightful that songbird will be if it is also beautiful and (O joy!) covered with variegated feathers. Similarly, how much more satisfying is that lute or flute if, having a good sound, it is also handsomely made, inlaid with mother-of-pearl and ivory that add richness to musical perfection. Thus shall we be better pleased by a voice emerging from a shapely mouth, assisted by a pretty complexion and a face of goodly proportions, the whole supported upon a prettily outstretched neck—and even more if it issues

TEXT: *Della tragedia antica e moderna* (Rome: F. Gonzaga, 1715; facs. Bologna, 1978), pp. 18–21, 28–29, 35–44; mod. ed. in his *Scritti critici e satirici*, ed. Hannibal S. Noce (Bari: G. Laterza e figli, 1963), Sessione quinta, pp. 270–96, trans. by Piero Weiss in "Pier Jacopo Martello on Opera (1715): An Annotated Translation," in the *Musical Quarterly* 66 (1980): 378–403, which translates all of Session 5. Reprinted by permission of Oxford University Press.

from a woman whose bosom, heaving to fetch the breath that is to form the song, prefigures it, so to speak, her breasts all atremble. And we shall enjoy ourselves better to see that lovely body clothed in rich, charming, whimsical garments; these shall be her feathers, her precious inlays.

Behold, then, our entertainment, delightful enough in itself, enhanced by scenery, personal beauty, and costumes. But see how insatiable we are, especially when wallowing in pleasure! Knowing that birds can whistle and instruments sound but that man alone can reason, we insist that to the sweetness of human song be added the sweetness of words to tell us of the inner motions of the soul; so that here is one more delight come to assist our entertainment, and here, finally, is Poetry. But poor Poetry cuts quite another figure here than she does in tragedy and comedy. In those she has the principal place, in opera the lowest; there she commands as mistress, here she attends as servant. But let us not abase Poetry by lending her name to such slavish verses.

·   ·   ·   ·   ·

But if (said I) under a Prince's patronage a Poet may write *melodrammi* not entirely to the distaste of the literati, let me have some norms at least for these, for it is not impossible that, for reasons of convenience or out of obligation, I should find it necessary to write such a work. Let me add that in my city the operas, though commercial, are sometimes subsidized by the nobility, who put sufficient restraints upon the Impresario's greed to prevent it from wholly swallowing up those elements which please honest people and the literati, of whom Bologna is the fatherland. And so I await a system from you, be it what it may, by which a skillful Poet may trace a drama that can be read as well as listened to.

Then Aristotle said: Since you ask me to present you with some rules for a type of composition which, in order to be pleasing, should be devoid of rules, I will mention some to you, and they shall be based on observation and experience rather than reason; and to satisfy you I will endeavor to combine the tasks of choragus, composer of the music, singer, and poet, almost forgetting that I am a philosopher.

·   ·   ·   ·   ·

Before you cut the cloth of the acts into scenes, I exhort you to show it all to the composer and ask him which voice, in his judgment, you should place at the beginning, middle, and end of each act. You must, however, stipulate (he will not object) that each act shall contain one *scena di forza*, so called because of some violent or unusual opposition of contrary passions, or some untoward event unexpected by the audience. Thus laid out, the opera, I warrant, will be successful; and now you will have nothing left to do but to cast your drama into verse.

It must be entirely made up of recitative and ariettas, or canzonettas, as they are also called. Every scene must contain either recitative, or an arietta, or (the usual case) both one and the other. Anything in the way or narration or unimpassioned expression should be expressed in recitative verse. But whatever is motivated by passion or somehow reflects greater vehemence tends toward the canzonetta. The recitative we prefer to have short enough so that it will not put us to sleep with its tediousness, and long enough so that we will understand what is happening. Its sentences and construction must be easy, and compact, rather than extended; this will make it more useful for the composer of the music, the singer, and the listener: for the composer, because he will then be able to enliven the recitative (a dead thing in itself) with a variety of cadences; for the singer, since he will thus be able to catch his breath when he sings it and renew his vocal powers at the rests; and for the listener (unaccustomed to the transformation wrought by music in the ordinary sound of words), because he will have to strain less than if the meaning had to be wrested from a tangle of inverted phrases. The recitative must be contained in verses of seven and eleven syllables, alternated and mixed as seems best; and if the cadences, at least, are rhymed, it will enhance the charm of the music. What I have said regarding the brevity of recitatives must suffer some qualification in the scenes I have termed *scene di forza:* for there the recitative must predominate at the expense of the ariettas, since it is better able to convey the pulse of the action and place it in the foreground. And here the Poet may vent himself somewhat and offer a modest sample of his talent; a prudent musical composer will allow it; nor will the singers, themselves expert at staging, refuse him; and the Impresario will be obliged to like it.

Canzonettas are either simple or compound. We shall call them simple when they are sung by one voice only, compound when sung by two or more voices. Those sung by two voices we will call duets; those sung by more may be termed choruses. Of the simple arias, we shall call some entrances, others exits, and others intermediate. From these expressions their use can be deduced. Entrances are used when a character enters upon the stage, and these tend to be acceptable in soliloquies; and the apostrophizing figure[1] is of their very essence. But of these you shall make sparing use. The same caution is advisable for the intermediate [arias]; for they have a chilling effect when, in mid-scene, mute actors are obliged to stand about and listen while another actor sings away at his leisure. Here, therefore, we should have some concomitant action, so that the others may at least be given something to do and not stand idle; in that case these [arias] will produce an excellent effect. [Intermediate arias] are the only type in which the questioning mode may occasionally be tolerated; this is odious in all other types, since it gives no occasion for variety in the music. Exit arias must close every scene, and no singer may exit without first warbling a canzonetta. Whether 'tis verisimilar is not material. It is much too pleasant to hear a scene end with spirit and vivacity. Mind, however, that when you end a scene with an exit aria you do not begin the very next one with an

---

1. Addresses to persons or entities not present.

entrance aria. That would rob the music of its chiaroscuro. The instrumental *ricercate* would tumble over each other and instead of helping would hinder the effect.[2] Hence it is that entrance arias usually make their best effect at the beginning of an act.

Duets are heard with pleasure in mid-scene because they afford action to more than one actor; but I should also like to see a duet at the end of the second act. Choruses at the end of the last act are inescapable, since the public enjoys hearing the combination of all the voices which it applauded singly in the course of the opera; and the noise made by singers and instruments causes everyone to rise and leave feeling replete and elated with the music they have heard, and wishing to come back for more.

These ariettas, or canzonettas, must be so distributed that the singers with the highest standing receive an equal number, for the singers' professional jealousy is inflexible and punctilious; and for that matter it is useful to the production of the drama that the best voices should be displayed equally to the audience.

These ariettas are composed in different meters,[3] as you Italians put it. Let the eight-syllable verse, which is the most sonorous, have pride of place above the others; namely,

> Innamora amor le belle.
> [Love loves beautiful women.]

Be sure to keep in mind that every aria must have its refrain *(intercalare)*. Refrain is what the professionals call the first part of an aria which is later repeated by the singer; for since it is here that the composer displays the full glitter of his musical artifice, he takes pleasure in its repetition. The singers take pleasure in it, too, as does the public. . . . But oh, the disjointed meters your versifiers have invented, meters incapable of good harmony which I do not advise you to use. But these will succeed better if you will adapt them to the passions that are best expressed by their means. Rage is best, nay almost exclusively conveyed in its full horror by the ten-syllable verse.[4] . . . The six-syllable line with the accent on the antepenult portrays very well the enfeebled state of a soul given over to amorous languor.[5] . . .

We must still treat of the style best suited to opera. I believe this type of composition, such as it is, calls for moderation and charm rather than gravity and magnificence; music, an art invented to delight and lift the spirits, needs to be buttressed by words and sentiments clothed in the spirit of delightfulness.

---

2. If each aria has its own ritornello music, then the closing ritornello of an exit aria would go right into the opening ritornello of an ensuing aria.
3. That is, the texts of the arias have differing poetic meters.
4. His example is: Sibillanti dell'orride Eumenidi / veggio in campo rizzarsi le vipere, / minacciando di mordermi il sen (Hissing vipers of the horrid Furies I see arise upon the field, threatening to bite my breast).
5. His example, with the antepenultimate syllables indicated: Le luci ténere / della mia Vénere / mi fan languir (The tender eyes of my Venus make me languish).

This is not to say that from time to time you may not introduce magnificence, if only to set off the charming element: for a bit of sour mixed with the sweet adds a piquancy that is most welcome to the palate; but if the sourness is overwhelming, pleasure turns to disgust, and delicate damsels will spit it out. Let me repeat, therefore, that your constructions must be easy, your sentences clear and not long, the words plain and attractive, the rhymes not insipid, the verses fluent and tenderly sonorous. In the arias I advise you to use similes involving little butterflies, little ships, a little bird, a little brook: these things all lead the imagination to I know not what pleasant realms of thought and so refresh it; and just as those objects are charming, so too are the words that conjure them up and portray them to our fancy; and the musical composer always soars in them with his loveliest notes; and you will have noticed that even in the worst operas, singers win particular applause in these arias, to which the diminutives (so hateful to the French language and temperament) add much grace. Fix it in your mind, too, that the more general the sentiments in an aria, the more pleasing they will be to the public; for, finding them veri-similar or true, they store them up to make honest use of with their ladies and to sing them as daily occasion arises between lovers for jealousy, indignation, mutual promises, absences, and the like; and this will also be most convenient for you, since Poets find it much easier to treat in generalities, and can fill their poetic wardrobes with them while out walking, and later use them to dress up the recitatives of operas. But in the action arias, you must avoid generalities and concentrate entirely on the particulars, for if the action is not to cool off, then the words must lend it life and be perfectly suited to it and to none other.

35 Jean-Philippe Rameau

When his epoch-making *Treatise on Harmony* appeared in 1722, Jean-Philippe Rameau (1683–1764) had a resumé of changing employment as an organist and teacher but few credentials as a composer. It would be another ten years before he would settle in Paris and write *Hippolyte et Aricie,* the first of his thirty operas. His great first treatise was succeeded by five more major theoretical volumes, most immediately the *New System for Music Theory* (1726) and the *Generation of Harmony* (1737). Together these books examined, explored, and codified the harmonic principles of European music, with a focus on chords rather than counterpoint. Although musicians had been performing from figured bass lines for over a hundred years, it was Rameau who conceptualized the fundamental bass—that is, a theoretical bass made up of the "roots" of chords—and the tonal grammar of late Baroque harmony.

In the two chapters offered here, Rameau recognizes the purely melodic nature of the music of the ancient Greeks and Romans, affirms the primacy of harmony in the generation of melody, reminds his readers that music is a language learned "by ear," and ends by discussing some expressive properties of consonance and dissonance.

FROM *Treatise on Harmony*
(1722)

BOOK TWO

CHAPTER NINETEEN. CONTINUATION OF THE PRECEDING CHAPTER, IN WHICH IT APPEARS THAT MELODY ARISES FROM HARMONY

It would seem at first that harmony arises from melody, since the melodies produced by each voice come together to form the harmony. It is first necessary, however, to find a course for each voice which will permit them all to harmonize well together. No matter what melodic progression is used for each individual part, the voices will join together to form a good harmony only with great difficulty, if indeed at all, unless the progressions are dictated by the rules of harmony. Nonetheless, in order to make this harmonic whole more intelligible, one generally begins by teaching how to write a melodic line. No matter what progress may have been made, however, the ideas developed will disappear as soon as another part has to be added. We are then no longer the master of the melodic line. In looking for the direction a part should take with respect to another part, we often lose sight of the original direction, or at least are obliged to change it. Otherwise, the constraining influence of this first part will not always permit us to give the other parts melodic lines as perfect as we might wish. It is harmony then that guides us, and not melody. Certainly a knowledgeable musician can compose a beautiful melodic line suitable to the harmony, but from where does this happy ability come? May nature be responsible? Doubtless. But if, on the contrary, she has refused her gift, how can he succeed? Only by means of the rules. But from where are these rules derived? This is what we must investigate.

Does the first division of the string offer two sounds from which a melody may be formed? Certainly not, for the man who sings only octaves will not form a very good melodic line. The second and the third divisions of the string, from which harmony is derived, provide us with sounds which are no more

TEXT: *Traité de l'harmonie reduite à ses principes naturels* (Paris, 1722), bk. 2, chaps. 19–20, pp. 138–43; trans. by Philip Gossett (New York: Dover, 1971), pp. 152–56; reprinted with permission. Both chapters are also translated into English in E. Fubini, *Music and Culture in Eighteenth-Century Europe*, ed. Bonnie J. Blackburn (Chicago: University of Chicago Press, 1994), pp. 136–40.

suitable to melody, since a melodic line composed only of thirds, fourths, fifths, sixths, and octaves will still not be perfect. Harmony then is generated first, and it is from harmony that the rules of melody must be derived; indeed this is what we do by taking separately the aforementioned harmonic intervals, and forming from them a fundamental progression which is still not a melody. But when these intervals are put together above one of their component sounds, they naturally follow a diatonic course. This course is determined by the progression they follow, when each serves as a foundation for the others. We then derive from these consonant and diatonic progressions all the melody needed. Thus, we have to be acquainted with harmonic intervals before melodic ones, and the only melodic line we can teach a beginner is one consisting of consonant intervals, if indeed these can be called melodic. We shall see furthermore in chapter 21 that the ancients derived their modulation from melody alone, whereas it really arises from harmony.

Once this consonant progression is grasped, it is as simple to add three sounds above the sound used as bass as it is to add only one. We explain this as follows: It is possible, and sometimes compulsory, to place a third, a fifth, or an octave above the bass. Now, in order to use any one of them, we must understand them all. When we understand them all, however, it is no more difficult to use them together than separately. Thus, the part which has formed the third will form the fifth when the bass descends a third; this can be explained in no other way. But when in these different progressions of a bass we find the third here, the octave there, and the fifth in a third place, then we must always know how each interval should proceed according to the different progressions of the bass. Thus, without being aware of it, we teach four-part composition while explaining only two-part composition. Since each of the consonances is met alternately, the progression of each individual consonance with respect to the different progressions of the bass should be known. It is thus no more difficult to use them together than separately. It is all the better, for if we cannot distinguish them when they are all together, we need only consider them individually. Thus, by one device or another we can find the means of composing a perfect harmony in four parts from which we can draw all the knowledge necessary to reach perfection. In addition, the explanation which we add keeps us from being misled. We may cite the experience several people have had; knowing no more at first than the value of the notes, after reading our rules twice, they were able to compose a harmony as perfect as could be desired. If the composer gives himself the satisfaction of hearing what he has written, his ear will become formed little by little.[1] Once he becomes sensitive to perfect harmony, to which these introductory studies lead, he may be certain of a success which depends completely on these first principles.

There can be no further doubt that once four parts are familiar to us, we can reduce them to three and to two. Composition in two parts can give us no

1. It is partly for this reason that we give rules of accompaniment. [Au.]

knowledge, however, for even if we understood it perfectly, which is almost impossible, there is no fundamental to guide us. Everything that may be taught in this manner is always sterile, whether because our memory is insufficient or because the subject may be covered only with great difficulty. At the end, we are obliged to add the words: *Caetera docebit usus.*[2] If we wish to pass from two to three or to four parts, we find that what has been said is of such little substance that genius and taste as fully developed as that of these great masters would be necessary in order to understand what they wish to teach us. Zarlino says that composition in four parts can hardly be taught on paper, and he leaves four-part writing to the discretion of those composers who can achieve this on the basis of his preceding rules concerning two and three parts.[3] Our opinion is quite the opposite, for as we have said harmony may be taught only in four parts. Everything in harmony may then be found in just two chords (as we have indicated everywhere) and it is very simple to reduce these four parts to three or to two. Zarlino, on the other hand, does not even give a clear definition of these two or three parts, and he claims that he is unable to define four parts. He says this even though he is convinced that a perfect harmony consists of four parts, which he compares to the four elements.[4] In conclusion, we affirm that though it has been impossible to understand fully the rules given until now concerning harmony, the source we have proposed will certainly lead to an understanding which is all-embracing.

CHAPTER TWENTY. ON THE PROPERTIES OF CHORDS

Harmony may unquestionably excite different passions in us depending on the chords that are used. There are chords which are sad, languishing, tender, pleasant, gay, and surprising. There are also certain progressions of chords which express the same passions. Although this is beyond my scope, I shall explain it as fully as my experience enables me to do.

Consonant chords can be found everywhere, but they should predominate in cheerful and pompous music. As it is impossible to avoid using dissonant chords there, these chords must arise naturally. The dissonance must be prepared whenever possible, and the most exposed parts, i.e., the treble and bass, should always be consonant with one another.

Sweetness and tenderness are sometimes expressed well by prepared minor dissonances.

Tender lamentations sometimes demand dissonances by borrowing and by supposition, minor rather than major. Any major dissonances present should occur in middle parts rather than in the extremes.

---

2. "Experience will teach the rest."
3. [Zarlino, *Istitutioni harmoniche,*] pt. 3, chap. 65, p. 320 [Au.]: "Necessary observations on compositions for four and more voices."
4. [Zarlino,] chap. 58, p. 281 [Au.]: "The method to be followed in composing music for more than two voices and the names of the parts."

Languor and suffering may be expressed well with dissonances by borrowing and especially with chromaticism, of which we shall speak in the following book.

Despair and all passions which lead to fury or strike violently demand all types of unprepared dissonances, with the major dissonances particularly occurring in the treble. In certain expressions of this nature, it is even effective to pass from one key to another by means of an unprepared major dissonance, as long as the ear is not too greatly offended by an overly large disproportion between the two keys. Hence, this must be done discerningly, just like everything else, for to pile up dissonance upon dissonance every time that a dissonance might occur would be a defect infinitely greater than to use only consonances. Dissonance should be employed only with great discretion. Sometimes we should even avoid its use in chords from which it should ordinarily not be separated, suppressing it skillfully when its harshness is unsuited to the expression, and distributing those consonances which form the rest of the chord through all the parts. We should remember that the seventh, from which all dissonances arise, is only a sound added to the perfect chord, that it consequently does not destroy the fundamental of this chord, and that it may always be suppressed when this is judged appropriate.

Melody has no less expressive force than harmony, but giving definite rules for its use is almost impossible, since good taste plays a greater part in this than anything else. We shall leave to privileged geniuses the pleasure of distinguishing themselves in this domain on which depends almost all the strength of sentiment. We hope that those able men to whom we have said nothing new will not bear us ill-will for having revealed secrets of which they wished perhaps to be the sole trustees. Our little knowledge does not permit us to argue with them about this last degree of perfection, without which the most beautiful harmony may become insipid. In this manner they are always in a position to surpass others. This does not mean that when we know how to arrange appropriately a succession of chords we are unable to derive from it a melody suitable to our subject, as we shall see later; but good taste is always the prime mover here.[5]

In the use of melody, it seems that the Ancients surpassed us, if we may believe what they say. Of this one it is claimed that his melody made Ulysses weep; that one obliged Alexander to take up arms; another made a furious youth soft and human. On all sides, we see the astounding effects of their music. Zarlino comments very sensibly, saying first that the word harmony often signifies only a simple melody to them, and that all these effects arise more from an energetic discourse, whose force is increased by the manner in which they declaim the text while singing, [rather] than from melody alone; for their melody could certainly not have profited from all the diversity which the perfect harmony unknown to them procures for us today. Their harmony, Zarlino says further,[6] consisted of a perfect chord above which they sang their

5. In French this expression is "le premier moteur," an interesting metaphysical metaphor. [Tr.]
6. [Zarlino, *Istitutioni*], pt. 3, chap. 79, p. 356 [Au.]: "Of the things which contribute to the composition of the genera."

different sorts of airs (as with our bagpipes or hurdy-gurdies); Zarlino called this *Sinfonia.*[7]

A good musician should surrender himself to all the characters he wishes to portray. Like a skillful actor he should take the place of the speaker, believe himself to be at the locations where the different events he wishes to depict occur, and participate in these events as do those most involved in them. He must declaim the text well, at least to himself, and must feel when and to what degree the voice should rise or fall, so that he may shape his melody, harmony, modulation, and movement accordingly.

7. "Musettes," "vielles," and "hurdy-gurdy." All these instruments involve drones above which the singer moves with greater freedom. Rameau could be referring either to the instruments or to the characteristic pieces styled on them. [Tr.]

36 Johann Mattheson

In the many conflicts between "ancients" and "moderns" that characterize the Baroque era, Johann Mattheson (1681–1764) took a modernist side against those Lutheran conservatives who deplored both the new Italianate music associated with the theater and the French *galant* style of instrumental music. In their view, both were destroying the rational and well-established foundations of German composition. Mattheson's musical experiences—as opera singer, organist, music director at the Hamburg cathedral for thirteen years (1715–28), composer of operas, oratorios, and chamber music, polemicist, and pedagogue—all contributed to his massive treatise of 1739, *Der vollkommene Capellmeister* (*The Complete Music Director*), which is subtitled *Basic Information about All Those Things That Anyone Who Wants to Direct a Chapel Honorably and Successfully Must Understand, Be Able to Do, and Bring to Perfection.* The volume was not modeled on traditional theoretical treatises and is peppered throughout with Mattheson's rejection of precepts derived from classical writers, his refutations of some newer ideas (such as those of Rameau on harmony), and his practical sense. His aim was not to educate an ordinary professional but to help invent a modern one. That a knowledge of instrumental music was deemed essential for the new musician is shown by the extent to which Mattheson discusses it. The excerpts here from part 2 describe and try to explain affect in instrumental music by means of specific references to tempo and intervals, and also by an examination of phrasing and motivic recurrences.

FROM *The Complete Music Director*
(1739)

PART TWO

CHAPTER 12: THE DIFFERENCE BETWEEN VOCAL AND INSTRUMENTAL MELODIES

All music making is either vocal or instrumental, and the latter is made on certain tools suited for it which are usually called instruments. The human voice likewise has its own natural tools, though these are different from the artificial. The latter are made while the former are inborn. From this it follows that essentially there must be two different classes of melodies, which are called vocal and instrumental. For one must deal differently with things that are made through artifice than with the natural and inborn.

•   •   •   •   •

The first of seventeen differences between a vocal and instrumental melody is that the former is, in a manner of speaking, the mother, but the latter is her daughter. Such a comparison shows not only the degree difference but also the type of relationship. For just as a mother must necessarily be older than her natural daughter, so also vocal melody no doubt existed earlier in this netherworld than did instrumental music. Hence the former not only has rank and privilege, but also directs the daughter to conform to her motherly precepts as best as possible, in order to make everything beautifully graceful and flowing, so that one might hear whose child she is.

Through such observation we can easily perceive which instrumental melodies are true daughters and which are produced as if out of wedlock, according to how they take after the mother, or deviate from her type. On the other hand, just as the motherly quality requires much modesty and reservation, the childlike is more lively and youthful. From this it can be seen how improper it would be if the mother were to deck herself out with the attire of the daughter; and if the latter were to select the attire of the matron. It is best to have each in its proper place.

The second difference between singing and playing follows automatically from this principle. That is, the former precedes, and the latter follows. As natural as this rule seems to be, indeed, as reasonable as it is, things are almost always done in the opposite manner. For who, when he sets out to instruct others in the art of composition begins with a vocal melody? Does not everyone

TEXT: *Der vollkommene Capellmeister* (Hamburg, 1739; rpt. Kassel, 1954), pt. 2, pp. 203–4, 207–10, 223–24, 227–28, 230–31, and 233–34. Translation by Ernest C. Harriss for this edition. For a translation of the complete treatise, see his *Johann Mattheson's* Der vollkommene Capellmeister, *a Revised Translation with Critical Commentary* (Ann Arbor, 1981).

first reach for all sorts of instrumental pieces, sonatas, overtures, etc., before he knows how to sing and write down a single chorale correctly, much less to elaborate on one artistically?

•   •   •   •   •

The twelfth and most familiar difference between our vocal and instrumental melodies is this: that instrumentalists do not have to deal with words, as do singers. But here there is something quite unknown, or at least unobserved. Namely, that instrumental melodies can do without the words themselves, but not without the affections. I do not know how most of our present-day concertizers and fathers of notes will respond on this point. They would deny the basic principles of music and would rather displace its true purpose rather than yield in this, which they can indeed do in *practice* yet never in *theoretice*.

So since the true goal of all melody can only be a type of diversion of the hearing through which the passions of the soul are stirred, no one will accomplish this goal who is not intent upon it, who is not himself moved, and who scarcely thinks of a passion at all, unless it were of the sort that emerges involuntarily. But if he is moved in a nobler manner and also desires to move others with harmony, then he must know how to express sincerely all of the emotions of the heart merely through the selected sounds themselves and their skillful combination, without words, in a way that the auditor might fully grasp and clearly comprehend the impetus, the sense, the meaning, and the expression, as well as all the pertaining divisions and caesuras, as if it were an actual narration. Then what a joy it is! Much more art and a more powerful imagination is required if one wants to achieve this without, rather than with, words.[1]

Now one would scarcely believe that the affections would have to be as greatly differentiated even in little, disesteemed dance melodies, as light and shadow can be. I give only one illustration of this; e.g., the affect is a good bit more sublime and stately in a chaconne than in a passacaglia. The affection of a courante is directed toward a tender longing. I am not speaking of an Italian violin corrente. A dogged seriousness is the only thing encountered in a sarabande. The purpose is pomp and conceit in an *entrée,* and pleasant joking in a rigadoun. The aim is contentment and pleasantness in a bourée, liveliness in a rondeau, vacillation and instability in a passepied, ardor and passion in a gigue, exulting or unrestrained joy in a gavotte, temperate diversion in a minuet, etc.

As regards the jubilant joy of dancing, it occurs to me that the wise Spartans would sometimes have very drunk slaves dance and rejoice[2] in front of their children in order to teach them to abhor immoderation. This is a use[3] of the

---

1. Harmony can express, personify, and articulate everything, even without the help of words. [J. B. Louis Gresset], *Discours sur l'harmonie* (Paris, 1737) p. 76. One can see from this that the wise French are also of my opinion in this respect: as if we had come to agreement about it. [Au.]

2. As a strong man rejoices who comes from drinking. Psalm 78:66. [Au.]

3. In short, the dance itself, which at first glance seems to be nothing but pleasure, also conceals useful lessons, [Gresset], *Disc[ours]sur l'harm[onie]*, p. 79. Though anger, rage, despair, weakness, sensual pleasure, and voluptuousness are also represented by dance. [Au.]

art of dancing and its melodies which is well worth paying special attention to, since some ugly passions and depravities are thereby made despicable, while other praiseworthy affections and virtues are awakened.

This uncommon diversity in the expression of the affections as well as the observation of all caesuras of musical rhetoric can even more clearly be perceived when examining larger and more imposing instrumental pieces, if the composers are of the right kind, e.g., where an *Adagio* indicates distress, a *Lamento* lamentation, a *Lento* relief, an *Andante* hope, an *Affetuoso* love, an *Allegro* comfort, a *Presto* eagerness,[4] etc. This can happen whether a composer has thought about it or not, if his genius functions properly, which can often occur without our knowledge and assistance.

When listening to the first part of a good overture, I feel a special elevation of the spirit. The second part on the other hand expands minds with great joy; and if a serious ending follows, then everything is brought together to a normal restful conclusion.[5] It seems to me that this is a pleasantly alternating movement that an orator could scarcely surpass. Anyone who is paying attention can see in the face of an attentive listener what he perceives in his heart.

If I hear a solemn *sinfonia* in the church, a prayerful trembling comes over me. If a powerful instrumental choir is also worked in, this causes great admiration within me. If the organ begins to roar and thunder, I am seized with the fear of God. Then if a joyous hallelujah brings everything to a close, my heart leaps in my breast. This occurs even if, on account of the distance or for some other reason, I were to understand neither the meaning of this word nor understand anything else, indeed, even if words were not used, but merely the instruments and expressive sounds.

Now if one cannot really say that a composer measures or counts his phrases and cadences, nor that he always considers in advance whether he should use a musical comma here or a *colon*[6] there, etc., which nevertheless are indispensable for clarity and for stirring the affections, still it is certain that skilled and successful masters always do this, with great diligence in graceful expression or writing, as it should be done without thinking about it. However, one enlightens a student in no small measure when, as here, occasion is given to note such things for him in their artistic form, and to provide, though in an unforced manner, a clear conception of the essential nature of such components, related matters, and differences in melodies.

There will be more opportunity to deal with this in the next chapter, with the presentation of the categories and types of all or at least of most melodies. And thus I mention this only briefly here, for, as we have seen, instrumental melody differs from vocal mainly in the fact that the former, without the aid of

4. It is known that these adjectives that indicate the particular feelings in melodies are often used to differentiate the movements as if they were true nouns. [Au.]

5. Mattheson refers here to the sections in contrasting tempos of the typical French overture.

6. A Latin term for a member of a period: a division of a compound or complex sentence, of which the first part consists of two or more clauses separable by semicolons.

words and voices, attempts to express just as much as the latter does with words. So much for the twelfth difference.

•   •   •   •   •

If we discussed the essential sensitivity and expression of the affections in instrumental melodies above, then it is easy to perceive that the theory on *emphasis* also belongs here,[7] only with the difference that vocal melody derives its emphasis from the words, while instrumental melody derives its emphasis from the sound. And that is the fifteenth difference. This seems to be quite a state of affairs. Yet anyone who will not disdain selecting certain prominent passages from good French instrumental pieces will soon find how the knot would be undone, and how he could make his sounds also speak with good emphasis. Commonly this sounding emphasis is prominent in the ascending half step. E.g.:

It is rather striking that the small intervals generally and much more often must serve for such matters of emphasis than do the larger ones, just about as we have seen above with the seemingly insignificant conjunctions. It is also to be observed here that not every melodic accent contains emphasis; but that the latter so to speak would contain a doubled accent. In the musical example quoted, eight [notes] are accented,[8] and yet only one has true emphasis, where the asterisk stands.

•   •   •   •   •

CHAPTER 13: THE CATEGORIES OF MELODIES AND THEIR SPECIAL CHARACTERISTICS

•   •   •   •   •

As has already been pointed out above, everything has to be said about instrumental pieces which the art of composition requires of vocal melodies,[9] indeed, often more. This will be reinforced as we move on to instrumental melodies and their types. For here one turns first to the affections, which are expressed with sounds alone, without words; then to the caesuras in the musical rhetoric, where the words cannot show us the way because they are not used; third to stress, to emphasis; fourth to the geometric;[10] and fifth to the arithme-

---

7. Mattheson discusses the creation of musical emphasis or stress in vocal melodies through pitch and rhythm in part 2, chapter 8.
8. The tones on the duple divisions of the measure.
9. This section follows 78 paragraphs on vocal music.
10. By geometric, Mattheson means the proportional metric relation of phrases, or *numerum sectionalem.*

tic relationship.[11] Even if one were to examine the smallest melody, this will be found to be true.

· · · · ·

Something fresh and brisk might, in its turn, follow these serious melodies, namely VII.[12] the *Gigue* with its types, which are: the common one, the *Loure,* the *Canarie,* the *Giga.* The common or English gigues are characterized by an ardent and fleeting zeal, a rage that soon subsides. On the other hand, the loures or the slow and dotted ones reveal a proud, arrogant nature. For this reason they are very beloved by the Spanish. Canaries must contain great eagerness and swiftness; but still sound a little simple. Finally, the Italian *gige* [*sic*], which are not used for dancing, but for fiddling (from which their name might also derive),[13] constrain themselves to extreme speed or volatility; though for the most part in a flowing and uninterrupted manner, like the smoothly flowing current of a brook.

All of these new observations are not so much directed toward the full understanding merely of dances as toward the discovery of the riches concealed therein and the skilled application of these, with the multitude of other and seemingly more important things: especially with beautiful vocal pieces and the expression of passions of all sorts; wherein innumerable and indeed unbelievable inventions come forth from these modest sources. One should reflect well on this suggestion.

Here there are, as with some of the other categories of melodies, also ariettas *a tempo di Giga* for singing; principally the *Loures,* which have a not unpleasant effect. Merely with the gigue style I can express four principal affects: passion or zeal; pride; foolish ambition; and the volatile spirit. The simplicity of the Canarie gigues is particularly expressed through the fact that all four sections and repetitions always conclude in the tonic key, and in no other.

· · · · ·

Everyone probably knows that there is a category in instrumental, dancing, and vocal melodies with the name XIII. the *Courante,* or *Corrente.* There are those for dancing, for the keyboard, lute etc., for the violin, and for singing. If the courante is used for dancing, there is an absolutely irrevocable rule to which the composer must precisely attend . . . No other meter but three-two, $\frac{3}{2}$, can be used.

But if the melody is for the keyboard, then it is permitted more freedom. It has almost no bounds on the violin (not excluding the viola da gamba), but seeks fully to justify its name through continuous running, yet so that it is

11. "Arithmetic" refers here to rhythm. When rhythmic motives recur, Mattheson observes their "arithmetic uniformity."
12. Omitted are Mattheson's discussion of sixteen types of vocal melody and the first six types of instrumental melody. He discusses the gigue seventh; the courante is thirteenth, and the sonata, the nineteenth type.
13. In the International Phonetic Alphabet, the pronunciation of *Geige,* the German word for violin, is [gaigə], which Mattheson relates to the Italian *giga* [dʒiga].

pleasant and charming. Vocal courantes come the closest to those for dancing, though they actually only use the *tempo di corrente,* the movement, and not its whole structure.

The lutanists' masterpiece, especially in France, is usually the courante, to which one applies his toil and art to advantage. The passion or affection that should be presented in a courante is that of sweet hopefulness. For there is something of the courageous, something of longing, and something of the cheerful in this melody. Only those things of which hope is composed.

Perhaps because nobody might have said this before or scarcely have thought it, many will think that I seek something in these things that is not to be found there, but that originated in my own mind. Yet I can make it almost palpably obvious to everyone that the above three conditions, and consequently the affection arising from them, are to be encountered and must be in a good courante. Let us select an old, very familiar melody for this, for the modern ones not only go off the beaten path, but one might also object that I had composed it and arranged it according to my conception only to support the above statement on hopefulness. I am quite certain that if the connoisseurs of the lute examine their courantes, they will find it just as true as with the following one.

Courante. Hope.

Up to the middle of the third measure, where the † stands, there is something of the courageous in this melody, especially right in the very first measure. No one can deny that. From there to the middle of the eighth measure, where the same sign of the cross is found, a longing is expressed; above all in the last three and one-half measures, and by means of the repeating cadence in the fifth downwards. Finally, a little joy arises toward the end, especially in the ninth measure.

I have examined a considerable number of courantes in this way, many of which are better and have a more proper geometric relationship. But all are by true and proven composers who have done this from natural instinct, *par instinct,* without plan or intent. And the truth of what I say here on the affection is consistently demonstrated. I could very easily produce and analyze similar examples from all of the other genres; however, then we would far exceed the limitations set for us.

•　•　•　•　•

A much more important piece among the categories of instrumental melodies is occupied by XIX. the *Sonata,* with several violins or on one specific instrument alone, e.g., on the transverse flute, etc. Its aim is primarily towards complaisance or kindness, since a certain *complaisance* must predominate in sonatas that is accommodating to everyone, and with which every listener is served. A melancholy person will find something pitiful and compassionate, a sensuous person something pretty, an angry person something violent, and so on, in the sundry diversities in sonatas.[14] The composer must make such a purpose clear with his *adagio, andante, presto,* etc., then his work will succeed.

For some years rudimentary sonatas for the keyboard have been composed with good success. They do not yet have the right form and tend to be more animated than animating, i.e., they aim more towards the movement of the fingers than of the heart. Yet amazement over uncommon dexterity is also a type of affection that often gives rise to envy, though it is said that its true mother is ignorance. The French are becoming pure Italians, both in this sonata business as well as in their recent cantatas. The result is mainly a patchwork of nothing but pieced-together little phrases, and is not natural.

14. For a further exposition of the human temperaments and music, see Kircher in No. 37 below.

VI

DIFFERENCES NOTED

37 Athanasius Kircher

Born in 1601 or 1602 near Fulda in Germany, Athanasius Kircher received a Jesuit education and became a priest and a teacher of mathematics, Greek, Hebrew, and Syriac at various Jesuit colleges. In 1631, when the Protestant Swedish army besieged Würzburg, Kircher transferred from his university post there and followed an itinerary that led him from Germany to Avignon and on to Rome, in 1635. He remained there as a professor of mathematics, physics, and Oriental languages at the Collegio Romano until his death in 1680.

His Latin treatise *Musurgia universalis* could be called a compendium of harmonic relations in fields as diverse as chemistry, ethics, politics, and the heavenly orders. It speaks as authoritatively about mathematical proportions, acoustics, and the physiology of hearing as it does about the notation of birdsong, the composition of music, and the construction of musical instruments. Topics are presented in the hierarchical format traditional for learned exposition. Kircher's arguments, however, are more essays than they are demonstrations of scientific proof. With 1,500 copies printed, the *Musurgia* must have been known to all later serious writers on music.

In the first part of book 7, the perpetual question of whether ancient or modern music was superior led Kircher to posit general explanations of difference based on what today we call "nature and nurture." According to Kircher, listeners, whether ancient or modern, acquire musical taste according to their essential natures. These are determined by the proportions of the four humors in the body, which differ according to geographical location. Kircher fully believed, furthermore, that the nature, or original inclinations, of individuals and cultures could be altered or modified by exposure to and familiarization with the new or foreign. This was the belief that underlay the strategy of adaptation that enabled the Jesuit order to establish footholds in most of the non-European regions of the world. In the course of discussing the reasons for difference, Kircher listed characterizations of national styles in European music that reappear in many later musical commentaries.

FROM *Musurgia universalis, or, The Great Art of Consonances and Dissonances*

(1650)

VOLUME 1, BOOK 7

INQUIRY V: WHETHER THE EXAMINED MUSIC OF THE ANCIENTS WAS MORE PERFECT AND SUPERIOR THAN THE MUSIC OF THE MODERNS

My first proposition is that the customary style of music in any one place follows from the natural temperament[1] of its people and their constitution, which is particular to any one region. Inasmuch as this is true, nothing further is necessary for proof except some examples themselves. Just as the Phrygians certainly differed from the Dorians in musical style, and the Dorians from the Lydians, so did the latter differ from the Phrygians, as the Dorian, Phrygian, Lydian and Ionian compositions clearly demonstrate, in which indeed each of these nations so firmly kept to its own style. The Dorians thought that allowing anything other than Dorian was impermissible, the Phrygians other than Phrygian, the Lydians other than Lydian. For instance, since the Dorians, who were benevolent and mild by instinct, bore themselves in religious rites with remarkable piety, they cultivated melody consistent with this inclination in everything that was Dorian. The Phrygians, a more lustful kind of people, chose a Phrygian style given to enjoyment and dancing, as being in conformance with their character. And experience teaches us what in modern times is the case in the most civilized nations of the whole world, in all parts of Europe. The Italians have a melodic style different from the Germans; these differ from the Italians and the French. The French and Italians differ from the Spanish, and the English have I know not what sort of strangeness, for each natural temperament there is an appropriate style according to the customs of the nation. The Italians hate the dour seriousness in the German style more than is just. They disdain in the French those frequent graces in their pieces and in the Spanish, a certain gravity both pompous and studied. The French, Germans, and Spanish find fault with the Italians, more than is just, on account of their unchecked

---

TEXT: *Musurgia universalis sive Ars magna consoni et dissoni,* 2 vols. (Rome, 1650; facs. ed. Hildesheim, 1970), tome 1, bk. 7, pp. 542–45. Translation by Margaret Murata.

1. The Latin word here is *complexio.* The English equivalent, "complexion," has changed its meaning since the seventeenth century when it indicated the combination in each person of the four humors of the body. The balance among them was held to determine the temperament of the individual: choleric, sanguine, phlegmatic, or melancholy.

chains of notes, which they call trills and *groppi*,[2] which they think of as unpleasant and tiresome repetitions whose indiscreet application decreases the charm of all their music rather than increasing it. Furthermore, as they say, there are the rustic and confused excesses of goat-like voices which, they also say, move us more to laughter than to feeling. As the old saying goes, "The Italians bleat, the Spanish bark, the Germans bellow, the French warble."[3]

This very difference in musical style of the different nations does not come from anywhere else except either from the spirit of the place and natural tendency, or from custom maintained by long-standing habit,[4] finally becoming nature. The Germans for the most part are born under a frozen sky and acquire a temperament that is serious, strong, constant, solid, and toilsome, to which qualities their music conforms. And just as these qualities are consistent with lower voices, compared to people of the south, the Germans rise to higher pitches with difficulty. Thus from natural propensity they choose that in which they can succeed best, namely, a style that is serious, moderate, sober, and choral. The French on the contrary are more changeable, having been allotted a temperament that is cheerful, lively, and innocent of restraint. They love a style that is similar to this temperament: whence they give themselves for the most part to the hyporchematic style,[5] that is, to ensemble dancing, leaps, and similar very suitable dances (which they present to airs such as galliards, passamezzos, and courantes).[6] The Spanish not only do not stand out so much as

2. For *groppi*, see Caccini in No. 19, p. 104. The criticism of the florid Italian style may refer to the earlier Roman art of vocal embellishment, especially in sacred solo music, as taught in the manuals of Giovanni Conforti and Francesco Severi. See also Pietro della Valle in No. 4, pp. 39–40.

3. This "old saying" was repeated and modified by the later Jesuit writer Claude-François Ménestrier in his *Des Représentations en musique anciennes et modernes* (Paris, 1681; facs. Geneva, 1972), p. 107: "The French warble, the Spanish bark or screech, the Italians bleat like goats and the Germans bellow. . . . One can add that the English whistle and the Turks howl." Ménestrier adds that the German "bellowing" is amplified by their use of serpents and sackbuts in ensembles (p. 108); compare Lady Montagu's observation in No. 39, p. 208. An early characterization of this sort is that by John the Deacon, ninth-century biographer of St. Gregory the Great, in his explanation of the inability of the Germans and Gauls to maintain the "suavity" of Roman chant: "For Alpine bodies, which make an incredible din with the thundering of their voices, do not properly echo the elegance of the received melody" (see *SR2*).

4. Ménestrier repeats Kircher, p. 107: "Each nation has its character in terms of song and music, as for the most part in other things that depend on the differences of the spirit of the place, usage, and customs."

5. From the Greek for a "choral hymn." In the seventeenth century, the term came to indicate music for dancing. The hyporchematic is Kircher's third category of theatrical music (vol. 1, p. 310); it includes "other species such as canzonas, allemandes, galliards, passamezzos, duplas, and sarabandes, most in use by the French and Germans."

6. These national characterizations are passed from writer to writer. In the *Critische Musicus* (rev. ed., Leipzig, 1745) of Johann Adolph Scheibe, for September 17, 1737 one reads: "The French style, or rather the French musical style is completely lively and cheerful. It is brief and very natural. . . . The rhythm and meter are clearly heard all the time (p. 146)," and "One sees that . . . German music is serious, highly worked and artful (*ernsthaft, arbeitsam und künstlich*)," (p. 150).

cultivators of music but they also have very little worthy of comparison with others, if one excepts two men, one in theory, Salinas,[7] and the other in practical music, Christopher Morales,[8] as praiseworthy as any in music. Finally, Italy justly appointed to itself the first place in music from the beginning, for there has not been a single age when all the principal composers did not produce music out of Italy, to the continual wonderment of all, with the most precious works. Composers who met with this most temperate clime thus also arrived at a style completely perfect and temperate that corresponded to their natures, neither a lascivious style with too much hyporchematic dancing nor a vulgar one that uses a hypatodic style.[9] They used all styles appropriately and with the best judgment, and were truly born for music.[10] . . .

As for the fact that the style of the Italians and French pleases the Germans very little, and that of the Germans hardly pleases the Italians or French, I think this happens for a variety of reasons. Firstly, out of patriotism and inordinate affection to both nation and country, each nation always prefers its own above others. Secondly, according to the opposing styles of their innate character and then because of custom maintained by long-standing habit, each nation enjoys only its own music that it has been used to since its earliest age. Hence we see that upon first hearing, the music of the Italians, albeit charming, pleases the French and Germans very little, as being to their suffering ears an unusual style, contrary to themselves and of a particular impetuosity. Or even more plain to see, how the peoples of the East—Greeks, Syrians, Egyptians, Africans sojourning in Rome—could hardly endure the refined music of the Romans. They preferred their confused and discordant voices (you would more truly call it the howling and shrieking of animals) to said music from many parasangs away.[11] All this proceeds, as I have said, due to custom acquired from long use: for if said nations had finally become accustomed to the music of the Romans, they would not only have preferred it to other music, but they would also have desired it avidly and seemed to love it.

7. Francisco de Salinas (1513–1590), organist in the viceregal chapel in Naples, chair of music at the University of Salamanca, and author of a theoretical treatise on music (1577).
8. Cristóbal de Morales (1500–1553), composer of mostly liturgical music who worked at the cathedrals in Ávila, Toledo, and Málaga as well as in the private chapels of the pope and the Duke of Arcos.
9. Probably music of low sounds. G. B. Doni defines a "hypatodia organica" as the *basso continuo* in his *Progymnastica musicae*, bk. 1 (1763), p. 231.
10. Ménestrier, *Des Représentations*, pp. 138–39, condenses Kircher's description relating climate to style: "Each people has its different customs and usages which are naturally subject to the same movements of the soul and to the same passions. Thus, although nature is the same everywhere, the different climates vary so strongly, that customs are not the same in every country . . . A Frenchman will be angered by something else than will a Spaniard, and just as one is almost always excited to violent motions, the other attempts to maintain a false gravity, because he is accustomed to this studied dignity; the other instead is freer and naturally accustomed to not restraining and deceiving himself."
11. A "parasang" is a Persian measure of length, between three and three and one half miles. Being distant many parasangs was a common figurative expression found even in English of the time.

And however different are the styles of different nations, despite the famous competition between them and their contesting for primacy of place, the particular style of each should not therefore be despised; for each nation has its own taste in writing songs. The Germans love the choral style for several voices in their compositions, as they love a variety astonishing in manner. What they cultivate as their most favored are choruses formed ingeniously with suspensions and fugues, with voices artfully following upon each other in the motet style. The French titillate the ears marvelously with clever songs and pieces put together in a variety of ways, embracing the hyporchematic style. The Italians, as I said, make use of every style: the motet, the church style, the madrigalian, the hyporchematic. They do not affect just the ears with this variety, but they also draw out both the torments and the passions of the soul, arousing them in every possible way with great power.

My second proposition is that just as the different nations each enjoy a different musical style, so in each nation people of diverse temperament are affected by diverse styles, each principally in conformance with their natural propensities. Hence all do not equally enjoy the same compositions, just as not everything edible is eaten with equal pleasure. The melancholy find pleasure in settings that are grave, dense, and mournful. The sanguine, because their spirits are easily agitated and titillated, are indiscriminately affected by the hyporchematic style. The choleric, because of the force of their bubbling bile, have an appetite for similar musical motion. Hence the military man, accustomed to trumpets and drums, seems to dislike all music that is more refined. Phlegmatics are affected by high women's voices in chorus, inasmuch as the high sound affects the phlegmatic humor favorably, whence its pleasure and charm. Here again certain airs will have rather great power over one person, and none over another. One person will be affected by this mode, another by that one, since all things depend on the different make up of the temperaments, as will be demonstrated later more amply. What indeed is the case is not only that different people enjoy different music but, rather, different intervals. There are those whom thirds please; several are delighted by sixths. Not absent also are those who would be attached to the harsh and discordant, all of which depends on the character of the nation, its propensities, particular temperament, and the customs it maintains.

• • • • •

38 Richard Ligon

Although Richard Ligon's history of Barbados has served as a primary source for studying the colonial history of the West Indies and their plantation slave economies, the author remains a shadowy figure. He played theorbo and served as executor for the estate of his friend, the composer John Coprario (c.1575–1626). He apparently had connections with London theater musicians, who came upon hard times when the theaters were closed down in 1642. He left England for the New World in 1647 in unexplained dire straits, only to return in 1650 to England and be thrown in debtor's prison, where he wrote the record of his voyage and sojourn. He first published these observations of life on the island of Barbados in 1657. On his voyage, an old expatriate English musician surprised him by his plain style of playing without ornaments, and once on the island, he had many opportunities to hear the music making of the Africans enslaved there.

FROM *A True & Exact History of the Island of Barbados*

(1673)

. . . Upon the sixteenth day of June, 1647, we embark'd in the Downs on the good ship called the *Achilles,* a vessel of 350 tunns, the Master Thomas Crowder of London. And no sooner were we all aboard, but we presently weighed anchor and put to sea in so cold weather as at that time of the year, I have not felt the like. . . . But before we came to St. Iago,[1] we were to have visited a small island called Soll, by the intreaty of a Portugal[2] we carried with us. . . . But when we came within sight of it, it appeared to us full of high and steep rocks (the highest of which were mere stone, without any soil at all) and they of so great a height, as we seldom saw the tops, whilst we lay before it; . . . and on the brow of the hill towards the right hand, a very high and steep precipice of a rock, in which stood the house of the Padre Vagado, fixt on the top of the rock. A house fit enough for such a master; for though he were the chief commander of the island, yet by his port and house he kept, he was more

---

TEXT: *A True & Exact History of the Island of Barbadoes* (2d ed., London, 1673; facs. London, 1970), pp. 1, 7–9, 12, 43, 46–52, 106–7. Punctuation and orthography have been modernized. All ellipses are editorial. See further Christopher D. S. Field, "Musical Observations from Barbados, 1647–50," *Musical Times* 115 (1974): 565–67.

1. One of the ten Cape Verde Islands.
2. A Portuguese named Bernardo Mendes de Sousa.

like a hermit than a governor. His family consisting of a mulatto of his own getting,[3] three negroes, a fiddler, and a wench. . . .

Dinner being nearly half done (the Padre, Bernardo, and the other black attendants waiting on us) in comes an old fellow, whose complexion was raised out of the red sack;[4] for near that colour it was: his head and beard milk white, his countenance bold and cheerful, a lute in his hand, and play'd for us a novelty, the *passeme sares galiard*, a tune in great esteem in Harry the fourth's days.[5] For when Sir John Falstaff makes his *amours* to Mistress Doll Tear-Sheet, Sneake and his Company the admired fiddlers of that age, playes this tune, which put a thought into my head, that if Time and Tune be the composites[6] of musick, what a long time this tune had in sayling from England to this place. But we being sufficiently satisfied with this kind of harmony, desired a song, which he performed in as antique a manner; both savouring much of antiquity: no graces, double relishes, trillos, groppos, or piano forte's, but plain as a packstaff. His lute, too, was but of ten strings, and that was in fashion in King David's days, so that the rarity of this antique piece pleas'd me beyond measure.

Dinner being ended, and the padre well near weary of his waiting, we rose, and made room for better company. For now the padre and his black mistress were to take their turns—a negro of the greatest beauty and majesty together that ever I saw in one woman.

• • • • • •

The island [of Barbados] is divided into three sorts of men, *viz.*, masters, servants, and slaves. The slaves and their posterity, being subject to their masters for ever, are kept and preserv'd with greater care than the servants, who are theirs but for five years, according to the law of the Island. . . . It has been accounted a strange thing that the negroes, being more than double the numbers of the Christians that are there, . . . should not commit some horrid massacre upon the Christians, thereby to enfranchise themselves and become masters of the island. But there are three reasons that take away this wonder; the one is, they are not suffered to touch or handle any weapons; the other, that they are held in such awe and slavery, as they are fearful to appear in any daring act. . . . Besides these, there is a third reason, which stops all designs of that kind, and that is, they are fetch'd from several parts of Africa, who speak several languages, and by that means, one of them understands not another: for some of them are fetch'd from Guinny and Binny, some from Cutchew, some from Angola, and some from the River of Gambia.[7] . . .

3. Though a priest, Padre Vagado was the father.
4. Red wine.
5. Ligon attributes this galliard on the chord pattern called the *passamezzo* to the early fifteenth century, because he associates it with Shakespeare's play *Henry IV*, part 2, in which "Sneak and his company" appear.
6. Components.
7. Guinea, Benin, Cacheu (Guinea-Bissau), and the other places are all on the west coast of the African continent.

We had an excellent negro in the plantation, whose name was Macow and was our chief musician, a very valiant man and was keeper of our plantain grove. . . . On Sunday [the slaves] rest and have the whole day at their pleasure, and most of them use it as a day of rest and pleasure. But some of them who will make benefit of that day's liberty, go where the mangrove trees grow and gather the bark, of which they make ropes, which they truck away for other commodities, as shirts and drawers.

In the afternoons on Sundays, they have their musick, which is of kettle drums, and those of several sizes. Upon the smallest the best musician plays, and the other come in as choruses. The drum, all men know, has but one tone; and therefore variety of tunes have little to do in this musick, and yet so strangely they vary their time, as 'tis a pleasure to the most curious ears, and it was to me one of the strangest noises that ever I heard made of one tone. And if they had the variety of tune, which gives the greater scope in music, as they have of time, they would do wonders in that art. And if I had not fallen sick before my coming away, at least seven months in one sickness, I had given them some hints of tunes, which being understood, would have serv'd as a great addition to their harmony; for time without tune is not an eighth part of the science of music.

I found Macow very apt for it of himself, and one day coming into the house (which none of the negroes use to do, unless an officer, as he was), he found me playing on a theorbo, and singing to it, which he hearkened very attentively to. And when I had done, he took the theorbo in his hand and strook[8] one string, stopping it by degrees upon every fret, and finding the notes to varie, till it came to the body of the instrument; and that the nearer the body of the instrument he stopped, the smaller or higher the sound was, which he found was by the shortening of the string. [He] considered with himself how he might make some tryal of this experiment upon such an instrument as he could come by, having no hope ever to have any instrument of this kind to practice on. In a day or two after, walking in the plantain grove to refresh me in that cool shade and to delight myself with the sight of those plants, which are so beautiful, . . . I found this negro (whose office it was to attend there) being the keeper of that grove, sitting on the ground, and before him a piece of large timber, upon which he had laid cross, six billets, and having a handsaw and a hatchet by him, would cut the billets by little and little, till he had brought them to the tunes[9] he would fit them to. For the shorter they were, the higher the notes, which he tryed by knocking upon the ends of them with a stick which he had in his hand. When I found him at it, I took the stick out of his hand and tried the sound, finding the six billets to have six distinct notes, one above another, which put me in a wonder, how he of himself should, without teaching, do so much.[10] I then shewed him the difference between flats and sharps, which he presently

8. Stroked.
9. Pitches.
10. Macow had constructed an instrument recognizable as the African xylophone known as the *balafo*.

apprehended, as between *Fa* and *Mi:* and he would have cut two more billets to those tunes, but I had then no time to see it done and so left him to his own enquiries. I say thus much to let you see that some of these people are capable of learning arts.

. . . On Sundayes in the afternoon, their musick playes and to dancing they go, the men by themselves and the women by themselves, no mixt dancing. Their motions are rather what they aim at, than what they do; and by that means, transgress the less upon the Sunday, their hands having more of motion than their feet, and their heads more than their hands. They may dance a whole day and ne'r heat themselves; yet, now and then, one of the activest amongst them will leap bolt upright and fall in his place again, but without cutting a caper. When they have danc'd an hour or two, the men fall to wrestle (the musick playing all the while). . . .

When any of them dye, they dig a grave, and at evening they bury him, clapping and wringing their hands, and making a doleful sound with their voices. . . . Some of them, who have been bred up amongst the Portugals, have some extraordinary qualities, which the others have not; as singing and fencing. . . . For their singing, I cannot much commend that, having heard so good in Europe; but for their voices, I have heard many of them very loud and sweet.

· · · · · ·

Some other kinds of pleasures they have in England, which are not so fully enjoyed in the Barbadoes, as smooth champion[11] to walk or ride on, with variety of landscapes at several distances; . . . As for musick and such sounds as please the ear, they [the colonists] wish some supplies may come from England, both for instruments and voices, to delight the sense, that sometimes when they are tir'd out with their labor, they may have some refreshment by their ears; and to that end, they had a purpose to send for the Musick that were wont to play at the Black-Fryars,[12] and to allow them a competent salary to make them live as happily there as they had done in England. And had not extream weakness by a miserable long sickness made me uncapable of any undertaking, they had employed me in the business, as the likeliest to prevail with those men, whose persons and qualities were well known to me in England. And though I found at Barbadoes some who had musical minds, yet, I found others whose souls were so fixt upon and so riveted to the earth and the profits that arise out of it, as their souls were lifted no higher. And those men think and have been heard to say that three whip-sawes, going all at once in a frame or pit, is the best and sweetest musick that can enter their ears; and to hear a cow of their own, or an assinigo[13] bray, no sound can please them better. But these men's souls were never lifted up so high as to hear the musick of the spheres, nor to be judges of that science as 'tis practised here on earth; and therefore we will leave them to their own earthly delights.

11. Grassy lawn.
12. Musicians who played at the Blackfriars Theatre in London, demolished in 1655.
13. A little ass.

39 Lady Mary Wortley Montagu

Mary Pierrepont (1689–1762), whose father was the fifth earl and first Duke of Kensington, taught herself Latin as a girl, eloped with Edward Wortley Montagu at the age of twenty-three, and four years later accompanied her husband to Turkey, where he served as ambassador to the Sublime Porte. Some of her writing appeared anonymously or in pirated editions during her lifetime, but it was the posthumous publication of her Turkish Embassy letters in 1763 that established her reputation as a fine writer and as a sympathetic and straightforward observer of her own and others' ways. Further volumes of her letters soon appeared, and a collected edition of her letters and works was issued in 1837. The present extracts describe musical performances and her thoughts about them as taken from letters written from abroad in 1717 and 1718. One relates privileged visits to the wives of the grand vizier and of the *kâhya* (the second in command of the Ottoman Empire). Her correspondents here are her sister, Lady Frances, Countess of Mar; Lady Elizabeth, Countess of Bristol; and the poet Alexander Pope.

FROM Letters of 1717–1718

To Lady————. Vienna, Jan. 1, 1717

... You may tell all the world in my name that they are never so well inform'd of my affairs as I am myself, and that I am very positive I am at this time at Vienna, where the carnival is begun and all sort of diversions in perpetual practise except that of masqueing, which is never permitted during a war with the Turks. The balls are in public places, where the men pay a gold ducat at entrance, but the ladies nothing.[1] I am told that these houses get sometimes a 1,000 ducats on a night. They are very magnificently furnish'd, and the music good if they had not that detestable custom of mixing hunting horns with it that almost deafen the company, but that noise is so agreeable here they never make a consort without 'em.[2] The ball always concludes with English country dances to the number of 30 or 40 couple, and so ill danc'd that there is very little pleasure in 'em. They know but half a dozen, and they have danc'd them

TEXT: Lady Mary's Turkish letters have appeared many times in print and reprints. Robert Halsband's edition returned to manuscript sources in the Harrowby Manuscript Trust, Stafford, in *The Complete Letters of Lady Mary Wortley Montagu*, 3 vols. (Oxford, 1965), in which the Turkish letters appear in volume 1 with extensive annotations. In the present text most spelling and capitalization have been modernized. Ellipses are all editorial.

1. The ducat at this time was worth four florins. When Antonio Caldara was appointed to the Imperial court in 1716 his annual salary was 1,600 florins; Johann Joseph Fux, the director of music at court received a salary of 3,100 florins from 1715.
2. See No. 37, p. 201, note 3.

over and over this 50 year. I would fain have taught them some new ones, but I found it would be some months labor to make them comprehend 'em.

Last night there was an Italian comedy acted at Court. The scenes were pretty, but the comedy itself such intolerable low farce without either wit or humor, that I was surpriz'd how all the Court could sit there attentively for 4 hours together. No women are suffer'd to act on the stage, and the men dress'd like 'em were such awkward figures they very much added to the ridicule of the spectacle. What completed the diversion was the excessive cold, which was so great I thought I should have died there. It is now the very extremity of the winter here.

•   •   •

To Alexander Pope, Adrianople, April 1 [1717]

... The summer is already far advanced in this part of the world and for some miles round Adrianople the whole ground is laid out in gardens and the banks of the river set with rows of fruit trees, under which all the most considerable Turks divert themselves every evening, ... drinking their coffee and generally attended by some slave with a fine voice, or that plays on some instrument. ... I have often seen them and their children sitting on the banks of the river and playing on a rural instrument, perfectly answering the description of the ancient fistula;[3] being composed of unequal reeds with a simple but agreeable softness in the sound. Mr. Addison[4] might here make the experiment he speaks of in his travels, there not being one instrument of music among the Greek or Roman statues that is not to be found in the hands of the people of this country.

... I read over your Homer[5] here with an infinite pleasure, and find several little passages explain'd that I did not before entirely comprehend the beauty of, many of the customs and much of the dress then in fashion being yet retain'd; and I don't wonder to find more remains here of an age so distant than it is to be found in any other country. ... Their manner of dancing is certainly the same that Diana is sung [sic] to have danced by [the] Eurotas.[6] The great Lady still leads the dance and is follow'd by a troop of young girls who imitate her steps, and, if she sings, make up the chorus. The tunes are extremely gay and lively, yet with something in 'em wonderful soft. The steps are varied according to the pleasure of her that leads the dance, but always in exact time and infinitely more agreeable than any of our dances, at least in my opinion. I sometimes make one in the train, but am not skilful enough to lead. These are Grecian dances, the Turkish being very different.

3. Normally *fistula* refers to a pipe; Lady Mary's description fits a syrinx or panpipes.
4. Joseph Addison; see No. 33.
5. Pope's translation of Homer's *Iliad* into English. In this part of her letter Lady Mary finds continuity between Homer's Greeks and the customs and dress she sees around her. Charles Fonton, in the next reading, also believed that remnants of ancient music were preserved in the music of the peoples of the Turkish Empire.
6. A river in the Greek Peleponnese.

• • •

To Lady Mar, Adrianople, April 18 [1717]

. . . To confess the truth my head is so full of my entertainment yesterday that 'tis absolutely necessary for my own repose to give it some vent. Without farther preface I will then begin my story.

I was invited to dine with the Grand Vizier's Lady[7] and 'twas with a great deal of pleasure I prepar'd myself for an entertainment which was never given before to any Christian. . . . She entertain'd me with all kind of civility till dinner came in. . . . The treat concluded with coffee and perfumes, which is a high mark of respect. Two slaves kneeling cens'd my hair, clothes, and handkerchief. After this ceremony she commanded her slaves to play and dance, which they did with their guitars in their hands, and she excus'd to me their want of skill, saying she took no care to accomplish them in that art. I return'd her thanks and soon after took my leave.

I was conducted back in the same manner I enter'd, and would have gone straight to my own house, but the Greek lady with me earnestly solicited me to visit the Kahya's Lady, saying he was the 2nd Officer in the Empire. . . . I had found so little diversion in this harem that I had no mind to go into another, but her importunity prevail'd with me, and I am extreme glad that I was so complaisant. All things here were with quite another air than at the Grand Vizier's, and the very house confess'd the difference between an old devote[8] and a young beauty. It was nicely clean and magnificent. I was met at the door by 2 black eunuchs who led me through a long gallery between 2 ranks of beautiful young girls with their hair finely plaited almost hanging to their feet, all dress'd in fine light damasks brocaded with silver. . . .

[Fatima's] fair maids were ranged below the sofa to the number of 20, and put me in mind of the pictures of the ancient nymphs. I did not think all nature could have furnish'd such a scene of beauty. She made them a sign to play and dance. Four of them immediately begun to play some soft airs on instruments between a lute and a guitar, which they accompanied with their voices while the others danc'd by turns. The dance was very different from what I had seen before. Nothing could be more artful or more proper to raise certain ideas, the tunes so soft, the motions so languishing, accompanied with pauses and dying eyes, half falling back and then recovering themselves in so artful a manner that I am very positive the coldest and most rigid prude upon earth could not have look'd upon them without thinking of something not to be spoke of. I suppose you may have read that the Turks have no music but what is shocking to the ears, but this account is from those who never heard any but what is play'd in the streets, and is just as reasonable as if a foreigner should take his

7. The wife of Arnavut Hacı Halil paşa.
8. The grand vizier's wife had told Lady Mary that "her whole expense was in charity and her employment praying to God."

ideas of the English music from the bladder and string, and marrow bones and cleavers. I can assure you that the music is extremely pathetic. 'Tis true I am enclin'd to prefer the Italian, but perhaps I am partial. I am acquainted with a Greek lady who sings better than Mrs Robinson,[9] and is very well skill'd in both, who gives the preference to the Turkish. 'Tis certain they have very fine natural voices; these were very agreeable.

When the dance was over 4 fair slaves came into the room with silver censers in their hands and perfum'd the air with amber, aloes wood and other rich scents. After this they serv'd me coffee upon their knees in the finest Japan china with soûcoupes of silver gilt.

*　*　*

To Alexander Pope, Belgrade Village, June 17 [1717]

. . . I have already let you know that I am still alive, but to say truth I look upon my present circumstances to be exactly the same with those of departed spirits. The heats of Constantinople have driven me to this place which perfectly answers the description of the Elysian fields. I am in the middle of a wood consisting chiefly of fruit trees, water'd by a vast number of fountains . . . within view of the Black Sea, from whence we perpetually enjoy the refreshment of cool breezes that makes us insensible of the heat of the summer. The village is wholly inhabited by the richest amongst the Christians, who meet every night at a fountain 40 paces from my house to sing and dance, the beauty and dress of the women exactly resembling the ideas of the ancient nymphs as they are given us by the representations of the poets and painters. . . . To say truth, I am sometimes very weary of this singing and dancing and sunshine, and wish for the smoke and impertinencies in which you toil, though I endeavor to persuade my self that I live in a more agreeable variety than you do, and that Monday setting of partridges, Tuesday reading English, Wednesday studying the Turkish language (in which, by the way, I am already very learned), Thursday classical authors. Friday spent in writing, Saturday at my needle, and Sunday admitting of visits and hearing music, is a better way of disposing the week than Monday at the Drawing Room,[10] Tuesday Lady Mohun's,[11] Wednesday the Opera, Thursday the Play, Friday Mrs. Chetwynd's,[12] etc.: a perpetual round of hearing the same scandal and seeing the same follies acted over and over, which here affect me no more than they do other dead people. I can now hear of displeasing things with pity and without indignation.

*　*　*

9. Anastasia Robinson (1692–1755), soprano, then contralto of the London stage. She sang leading roles in operas by Handel, Alessandro Scarlatti, and Giovanni Bononcini between 1714 and 1724, retiring from the stage upon her marriage to the Earl of Peterborough.
10. At St. James's Palace, the residence of the English royal family.
11. Elizabeth Lawrence (d. 1725), widow of the fourth Baron Mohun, mother of Lady Rich.
12. Mary Berkeley (d. 1741).

To Lady Bristol, [Constantinople, 10 April 1718]

. . . I had the curiosity to visit one of [the monasteries] and observe the
devotions of the dervishes, which are as whimsical as any in Rome. These fellows have permission to marry, but are confin'd to an odd habit,[13] which is only
a piece of coarse white cloth wrapp'd about 'em, with their legs and arms
naked. Their order has few other rules, except that of performing their fantastic
rites every Tuesday and Friday, which is in this manner. They meet together in
a large hall, where they all stand with the eyes fix'd on the ground and their
arms across, while the imam or preacher reads part of the Alcoran,[14] from a
pulpit plac'd in the midst; and when he has done, 8 or 10 of them make a
melancholy consort with their pipes, which are no unmusical instruments.[15]
Then he reads again and makes a short exposition on what he has read, after
which they sing and play till their superior (the only one of them dress'd in
green) rises and begins a sort of solemn dance. They all stand about him in a
regular figure; and while some play, the others tie their robe (which is very
wide), fast round their waists and begin to turn round with an amazing swiftness and yet with great regard to the music, moving slower or faster as the
tune is played. This lasts above an hour without any of them shewing the least
appearance of giddiness, which is not to be wonder'd at when it is consider'd
they are all us'd to it from infancy, most of them being devoted to this way of
life from their birth, and sons of dervishes. There turn'd amongst them some
little dervishes of 6 or 7 years old who seem'd no more disorder'd by that
exercise than the others. At the end of their ceremony they shout out: "There
is no other God but God, and Mahomet is his prophet;" after which they kiss
the Superior's hand and retire. The whole is perform'd with the most solemn
gravity. Nothing can be more austere than the form of these people. They
never raise their eyes and seem devoted to contemplation, and as ridiculous as
this is in description, there is something touching in the air of submission and
mortification they assume.

·   ·   ·   ·   ·

13. Type of clothing.
14. The Koran.
15. The Turkish *ney*.

40 Charles Fonton

Next to nothing is known about the Frenchman Charles Fonton, except that he had studied "Oriental" languages and was clearly interested in the music and the musical instruments he encountered in Constantinople in the mid-eighteenth century. Recognizing that all peoples have their own customs and preferences, he hoped to dispel some of the ignorance and "universal prejudgment" with which "Oriental"—that is Persian, Arabic, or Turkish music—was heard by Europeans. His views survive in a manuscript dated 1751 whose full title reads: "Essay on Oriental Music as Compared with European Music, which attempts to give a general idea of the music of the peoples of the East, of their specific tastes, and of their rules of melody and combining tones, with a summary of their principal instruments." For the latter he provided pen and ink illustrations annotated in Turkish. The nineteenth-century critic and historian François-Joseph Fétis noted in his biographical dictionary of 1835–44 that he thought Fonton's information fairly useless; the essay, however, articulates some notable views clearly. In his introduction Fonton asks whether "most things are not relative and arbitrary, as far as what is true and beautiful." In the second section, given in full here, he nonetheless goes on to judge difference on grounds other than those of truth and beauty. He states that a present practice that has undergone little change must come from a less developed stage of culture, even if in this case it originates from the "ancients," and he equates Eastern music with his perception of Turkish culture as "effeminate," according to his notions of masculine and feminine traits.

FROM *Essay on Oriental Music Compared to the European*
(1751)

ARTICLE II. OF THE MUSIC OF THE ORIENTALS AND OF THEIR PARTICULAR TASTE

Since all peoples in general, however different their customs and character, nevertheless agree about the victorious charm of music and are responsive to it, it follows necessarily that each separate people should have a kind of music that is its own and is capable of moving them. Indeed, the tender and passionate Italian sighs in his airs and paints his passions. The lively and joyful Frenchman, is pleased by the agreeable sounds of a music that is playful and gay. The

TEXT: "Essay sur la musique orientale compareè a la musique européenne," in Bibliothèque national, Fonds fr. nouv. acq. 4023, pp. 37–45. Translation by Margaret Murata. A translation into Turkish by Cem Behar was published in 1987 (Istanbul: Pan Yayancalak).

spirited and hot-headed Englishman lends himself only to harmonies fitting his character. Any others than these would hardly touch him. The dour and heavy German, satisfied by sounds less sweet and affected, does not get excited by great delicacy in harmony. In a word, each country has, down to the least things, some trait that characterizes it and makes it different from the others. The Orientals also make a separate picture. Distant from our manners and customs in everything, they do not come close to us any the more in their music, which bears no relation to that of any European peoples. We also do not need to know the music of the ancients well to be able to assess that it is absolutely the same case with it. But at least there is room to believe that if some vestige of it remains, it must be among the Orientals, among whom the most part of their arts has been preserved much as it was since their beginnings, almost without any development or improvement.

Several prejudgments seem to authorize this opinion. The simplicity and naturalness that reign in Oriental music; the same taste universally widespread among the different peoples of the Orient; certain airs and certain dances which are spoken of in well-known ancient authors and up to the present by people of this land. All this forms the presumption that one can regard this, if not as proof of, then at least as traits of resemblance between the music of the ancients and modern Oriental music.

However the case may be, it is an established fact that this music is hardly so much to be rejected as one imagines, nor is it so disagreeable that one could not comprehend it. In the judgment of connoisseurs, it has the beauty of its species. But it is difficult to give a just and precise idea of it, because music is the kind of thing of which one feels the effect and does not express it. Everything that one can say in general, and in spite of its critics, is that it is passionate and moving.[1] It inspires feeling (le sentiment) and gives birth to pleasure. Adapted to the Asiatic genius, it is like the nation, soft and languorous, without energy and strength, and has neither the vivacity nor the spirit of ours. The great defect of which it can be accused is that of being too uniform. It is unaware of the admirable variety in art that imitates nature and that knows how to rouse and present all the passions without confusing one with another. As different in the tender and the graceful as in the grand and sublime, the impressions that music makes should not be the same. The soul changes situation and object according to the different movements that harmonies produce in it and which it obeys without coercion. It is this successive passing from one feeling to another, this undergoing of different transformations, that keeps it in a continual agitation, constantly providing the intelligence (l'esprit) with new perceptions and perpetuating the intoxication and enchantment of our senses.

It is rare to find in Oriental music this effect of variety which originates in the diversity of our sensations. The uniformity and monotony that reigns in it poses an obstacle. There is only, so to speak, one part of ourselves that is sus-

---

1. Fonton's phrase is "pathetique et touchante."

ceptible, because there is only one of our faculties that operates. The soul is moved, but not in all its capacity. It is true that this music excels in the chromatic genus, of which it is fond. I can swear that it does move and penetrate and make one feel tender, perhaps more than does any other music. It is a pleasure that one experiences, but it is one of a thousand that one could experience. Even this pleasure ceases, on account of its continuousness, and it often degenerates into a languidness and inevitable ennui.

Indeed, if a music is monotonous, admirable as it may be otherwise, it will inevitably cause drowsiness and sleep. Reiteration of the same impressions on the fibers of the organ of hearing slow down the movement of the animal spirits by suspending activity and action, not allowing any other change and, by natural consequence, promoting sleep. What contributes further to this deadening in relation to us, is the effeminacy of most Oriental airs,[2] so contrary to our inclinations. Our attention does not know how to be captivated for long, if it is not wakened at times by something lively and animated. European ears require the strongest impressions, the most manly sounds and the most muscular, less of the melancholy and more of the gay. The people of the Orient are susceptible to the opposite sentiments. The same difference that nature has placed in our tendencies and our characters, she has also placed in the object of our likes and desires. All things provide us daily with new proofs. Since we are divided in everything else, we would be pretending in vain to be united by the usual charms that music exerts. This would be allying two incompatible things and putting some badly assorted figures in the same picture. Oriental music is compared by its partisans to a peaceful, tranquil stream, whose sweet and soothing murmuring enchains the soul and puts it to sleep in the bosom of pleasure. If I may be permitted to express myself exactly, I would say, following this comparison, that European music is a great and majestic river that sends forth its waters judiciously, measures its course by the needs of the lands that it waters, and carries with itself everywhere riches and abundance. I leave it to the connoisseurs to decide the justness of the parallel.

2. Fonton's phrase is "la moleste effeminée" or literally "effeminate molestation." Traits that he considers "feminine" are apparent throughout the essay.

41 Jean Baptiste Du Halde

A moment of intersection between European and Chinese music occurred under the reign of the Manchurian Emperor Kangxi (1662–1722), whose court produced—among various monumental collections of Chinese scholarly knowledge—*The True Meaning of Tones,* a treatise published in 1723 in a compendium along with other calendrical and acoustic subjects. The emperor's interest in music was spurred by his musical encounters with Jesuit missionaries, especially Tomas Pereira (1645–1708), who arrived in Beijing in 1673 and who eventually lived at the palace and wore the emblem of the Imperial dragon, and Teodorico Pedrini (1670–1746), who arrived in Beijing in 1711 and taught music to the children at court.

Jean Baptiste Du Halde (1674–1743), the Jesuit who served in Paris as secretary for correspondence from missionaries abroad, compiled an encyclopedic four-volume treatise on China and Chinese history and civilization. Published in 1735, the book appeared in English as early as 1736, in German from 1747 to 1756, and in Russian in 1770. It was based on the extensive missionary reports Du Halde had received, and it testifies to the Jesuit presence at the imperial court at a time of high scholarly activity. Kangxi appears prominently with regard to music, which Du Halde treats as it had been handled in his sources: anecdotally in association with the emperors of China (whose reigns are described in chronological order) and as documentary history in a section of transcriptions compiled on Kangxi's orders and preserved with the emperor's comments. One example of such an ancient declaration is given here. The longest treatment of music occurs as part of a section on the "other sciences," where the discussion of music follows sections on logic and rhetoric.

FROM *Geographical, Historical, Chronological, Political, and Physical Description of the Empire of China and of Chinese Tartary*

(1735)

THE KNOWLEDGE OF THE CHINESE IN THE OTHER SCIENCES

As one takes a look at the great numbers of libraries that are found in China, all magnificently built, equally decorated, and enriched by a prodigious quantity of books; when one considers the astonishing multitude of their doctors, and colleges established in all the cities of the empire, their observatories and the attentiveness with which they make observations; when, in addition, one reflects on the fact that study is the unique way to achieve rank and that one is raised only in proportion to one's abilities; that for more than four thousand years, there has not been, according to the laws of the empire, any but men of letters who govern the cities and provinces and who are appointed in all the posts of tribunals and of the court, then one will be tempted to believe that of nearly all the nations in the world, the Chinese nation is the most spiritual and learned.

Meanwhile in the short time one visits there, one is soon disillusioned. It is true, and one cannot forbear from acknowledging that the Chinese have much intellect: but is it with this intellect that one invents, analyzes, excavates, and investigates? They have made discoveries in all the sciences, and yet they have not perfected any of those that we call speculative and which demand some subtlety and analysis. Nevertheless, I do not wish to speak ill of the essence of their intellect nor, even less, to assert that they lack the intelligence and that cleverness that understands different subjects, seeing that they succeed in other areas which demand as much genius and understanding as our speculative sciences. But two principal obstacles oppose the progress that could have been made in these kinds of knowledge. That is, first, that there is nothing within or without the empire to stimulate and support competition; and in second place, that those who could gain distinction have no reward awaiting them. . . .

TEXT: *Description géographique, historique, chronologique, politique, et physique de l'empire de la Chine et de la Tartarie chinoise*, 4 vols. (Paris, 1735), 2: 405; 3: 264–68. Translation by Margaret Murata. Excerpts from the English translation of London, 1738–41, are in Frank Ll. Harrison, *Time, Place and Music: An Anthology of Ethnomusicological Observation, ca. 1550 to ca. 1800* (Amsterdam, 1973), pp. 161–66.

OF THEIR MUSIC

If you will believe the Chinese, they are the first inventors of music, and they boast of having formerly brought it to the highest perfection. But if what they say be true, it must have strangely degenerated, for it is at present so imperfect that it scarcely deserves the name, as may be judged by some of their airs, which I have notated to give some idea of them [see Example].

Chinese airs

Indeed in former times, music was in great esteem, and Confucius, their greatest sage, undertook to introduce its rules into every province[1] whose government he was entrusted with. The Chinese themselves of today greatly bewail the loss of these ancient books which dealt with music.

At present music is seldom used but at plays, certain holidays, weddings, and on such like occasions. The *bonzes*[2] employ it at funerals, but when they sing, they never raise and lower their voices a semitone, but only a third, a fifth, or an octave, and this harmony is very charming to the ears of the Chinese. In like manner the beauty of the concerts does not consist at all in variety of tones or of differences between parts. They all sing the same air, as is the practice throughout Asia. European music does not displease them, provided there be only one voice singing, accompanied by some instruments. But what is most marvelous in this music—I mean the contrast of different voices, of low and high sounds, sharps, fugues, and suspensions (*syncopes*)—is not at all to their taste, and seems to them a disagreeable confusion.

1. Confucius lived in the late sixth century B.C.E. Du Halde calls "the provinces" those regions that were generally separate kingdoms before the Han dynasty, c. 200 B.C.E.
2. Although the term *bonze* generally refers to the Buddhist priesthood, Du Halde probably did not intend any sectarian designation.

Unlike us they have no musical notation, nor any signs that mark the difference of pitches, the rising or falling of the voice, and all the other variations that constitute harmony; they have, however, certain characters[3] that allow one to recognize the different tones. The airs that they sing or play upon their instruments are only learned by practice after hearing them sung. Nevertheless, they make new ones from time to time, and the late Emperor Kangxi composed some himself. These airs, well played upon their instruments or sung by a good voice, have something in them that will please even a European ear.

The ease with which we are able to retain an air at only one hearing by means of notation surprised the late Emperor Kangxi extremely. In the year 1679, he called Father Grimaldi and Father Pereira[4] to the palace to play upon the organ and the harpsichord that they had formerly given him. He enjoyed our European airs and seemed to take great pleasure in them. Then he ordered his musicians to play a Chinese air upon one of their instruments and played it himself with much grace. Father Pereira took his notebooks and wrote down all the melody while the musicians were performing; and when they had finished, the Father repeated it without missing a note, as if he had practiced it a long time. The Emperor had such difficulty believing it, he seemed surprised. He bestowed great praise on the justness, beauty, and fluency of European music. He admired above all the fact that this Father had in so short a time learned an air which had given him and his musicians no small trouble; and that by help of certain signs, he was made so perceptive of it that it was impossible for him to forget it.

To be the more sure of this, he made several further trials. He sang many different airs, which the Father wrote down and repeated immediately after with the greatest exactness. "It must be owned," cried the Emperor, "that European music is incomparable, and this Father," speaking of Father Pereira, "has not his equal in all the empire." This ruler afterwards established an Academy for Music, composed of all those[5] who were most skilled in this area and committed it to the care of his third son,[6] a man of letters who had read a great deal. They began by examining all the authors that had written on this subject, causing all sorts of instruments to be made after the ancient manner and according to settled dimensions. The faults of these instruments emerged and were corrected by more modern rules.

After this they compiled a book in four volumes with the title *The True Doctrine of the Lü Lü, Written by the Emperor's Order.* To these they added

---

3. Ideograms.
4. Filippo Maria Grimaldi and Tomas Pereira, both Jesuits.
5. The other Chinese scholars were He Guozong (d. 1766), Zhang Zhao (1691–1745), Yin Reng (1674–1725), Yin Lu (1695–1767), Yin Zhi (1677–1732), Mei Gucheng (d. 1763), Chen Menglei (1651–?), Zhang Ying (1638–1708), Fang Bao (1668–1749), and Li Guangdi (1642–1718); see Gerlinde Gild-Bohne, *Das Lü Lü Zheng Yi Xubian* (Göttingen, 1991).
6. Yin Zhi, a member of the Academy of Music; see note 5 above.

a fifth, containing all the elements of European music, written by Father Pereira.[7]

The Chinese have invented eight sorts of musical instrument which they think are the closest to the human voice.[8] Some are of metal like our bells; others are made of stone, and one among the rest has some resemblance to our trumpets. There are others of skins like our drums, of which there are several kinds, and some so heavy, that to fit them for beating on they must be propped with a piece of wood. They have huge instruments with strings, but the strings are generally of silk, seldom of gut. Their fiddles (*vielles*), like those played by blind people, are as their violins: both have but three strings which one plays with a bow. But there is one instrument with seven strings, very much esteemed and not disagreeable when played upon by a skillful hand. There are others also, but they are made wholly of wood, being pretty large tablets which they clap against each other. The *bonzes* use a little board, which they touch with much art, and in good time. In short, they do have wind music. Such are their flutes, which are of two or three sorts, and an instrument composed of several pipes, which has some resemblance to our organ and on the whole an agreeable sound, but is very little, being carried in the hand.

·   ·   ·

DECLARATION OF THE EMPEROR AI DI FOR REFORMING MUSIC[9]

At present, three great abuses prevail among us: prodigality in eating and dress, etc., the search for thousands of vain ornaments, and a passion for the tender, effeminate music of Zheng and Wei.[10] From prodigality follows the ruin of families; they fall in the third generation, and the whole empire becomes poorer. The desire for vain ornaments occasions multitudes of people to attend only very useless arts and to neglect agriculture. Finally effeminate tender music inspires licentiousness. To pretend, while these subsist, to intro-

---

7. The title given here is a translation of Du Halde's translation of *Lülü zhengyi*, which he called "La Vraye Doctrine du *Ly lu*." The sense of the Chinese title is "rectifying the meaning of the tones." The fifth, supplementary volume that describes elementary European music theory is the *Houbian* allegedly begun by Pereira and continued by Pedrini. It translates Western terms into Chinese. A modern translation of the supplement into German appears in Gild-Bohne, note 5 above.

8. The "eight sorts of musical instruments" is a conceptual category in Chinese music, that of *bayin* or "eight sounds." The eight are metal, stone, skin, silk, bamboo, wood, gourd, and earth. The "tablets" are the large wooden clappers called *paiban*. The small "pipe organ" mentioned by Du Halde is the *sheng*. The large silk-strung instruments may be the *zheng*; the seven-string instrument is probably the *qin*, whose invention is attributed to Fu Xi, the first emperor of China (see Du Halde, vol. 1, p. 273).

9. Du Halde drew upon the *Imperial Collection Containing Edicts, Declarations, Ordinances and Instructions of the Emperors of Different Dynasties* that Emperor Kangxi had had his scholars assemble. Although Du Halde's immediate source representing this collection is not known, among the documents was an edict on music over 1,700 years old, which he presented with Kangxi's remarks. Du Halde's words are in italics. Ai Di, a Han emperor, reigned 7–1 B.C.E.

10. These are the names of a country, formerly two petty kingdoms. [Tr.]

duce plenty and innocence into a state is to pretend that a muddy spring makes a pure and limpid stream. Confucius was quite right to say that the music of Zheng should be avoided, because it inspired looseness of manners.

By these presents, we discharge our musical establishment and all the officials who were in charge of it. As for the usual music for the ceremony of Tiao,[11] we do not plan to affect them nor the instruments of war. These are things approved in our [jing][12] but no officials are appointed for these purposes. It is our wish that there be an inquiry ascertaining to which of the other officials it will be proper to commit the management of these matters.

•   •   •

The Emperor Kangxi, who loved music and involved himself in it, made the following remarks about this declaration: Music has the virtue to calm the heart, and it is for this that the wise man loves it. Also, while amusing himself, he may take exercise in governing well by a very correct and ready application of government to music.[13] But with regard to wanton music, that admits of no comparison. To what good end is so much expense? Ai Di was right to fire them.[14] *A gloss says that he saved in this regard the appointments and maintenance of 440 persons.*

11. Frederick Lau, whose help with this text has been invaluable, has suggested that, as opposed to *Gong Diao* or "court music," the "ceremony of *Tiao*" is the *jiaosi,* a rite performed only by the emperor. The term implies an offering to nature or to spirits of nature.
12. Ancient books of rules [Tr.]. Du Halde uses the work "King" here; without seeing the Chinese character it is difficult to know what Chinese word was meant in his source. The word "jing," which means "classic," could refer, according to F. Lau (see note 11 above), to the ancient *Lüshi Chunqiu,* which includes sections on the use of music in various ceremonies.
13. Kang Xi is comparing the knowledge and discipline required for musical performance to the just application of laws by a ruler.
14. That is, the officials in charge of the musical establishment.

GLOSSARY OF FOREIGN PERFORMANCE TERMS

accento (It., pl. *accenti;* Lat. *superjectio, accentus*)   A short, local ornament. Vocal illustrations from Zacconi (1592) to Bismantova (1677) suggest they are usually escape tones added to descending passing figures that emphasize the tone to which they move, or anticipations of the next tone in rising step-wise motion. Various writers describe subtle changes of volume and tempo that are part of its execution. Muffat (1698, his Example YY) recognizes six types of single-note accents. The upper accent, the lower accent (Lat. *subsumptio*), and the salterello (in French *sursaut*) come before the second tone (beginning the new bow stroke). He gives the superficial, or common accent; the *calamento* (Fr. *relâchement*), and *dispersione* as subdivisions of the first tone, taken with the same bow. These accent the second tone by leaping to it.

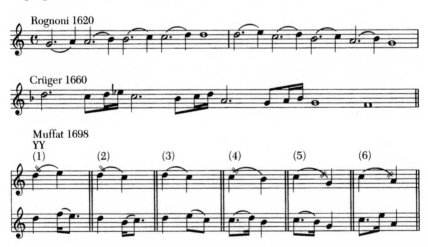

Artusi's examples of *accenti* in the *Imperfections of Modern Music* (1600) resemble more the *portar la voce.* Muffat classes the *port de voix* as a a type of "accentuation." See also PORTAR LA VOCE.

affetto (It., pl. *affetti*)   A general term for short, local ornaments. Apart from its use in music, "affetto" may also refer to an affection, or passion. Both senses come together in a description by Caccini (1614): "Affect, for who-ever sings, is nothing other than the expression of the words chosen to be sung and their ideas, by means of the power of different notes and their varied stresses, tempered by softness and loudness, a power capable of moving the affection of the listener."

craquer (Fr.)   In string playing, to take two or more detached notes in a single bow stroke, usually an up-bow.

esclamazione (It., pl. *esclamazioni*)   As defined first by Caccini in *Le nuove musiche* (1602), a technique for singing longer tones, in which the voice "relaxes" a bit after the first attack and then intensifies for the duration of the note. This intensification is usually translated in modern terms as a gradual *crescendo*. Dotted values appear in many illustrations, with the voice relaxing again for the smaller note or notes that follow the longer one.

gorgia or **gorga** (It., pl. *gorghe*)   A general name for vocal embellishments; related to the verb "gorgheggiare," to warble. In Zacconi (1592, bk. 1, chap. 66), they apply to note values of eighths and sixteenths (*crome, semicrome*).

groppo, gruppo (It., pl. *groppi, gruppi*)   In the earlier seventeenth century, the name for a neighbor-note trill. In most illustrations, it is notated with equally subdivided note values and closes with a turning figure. Whether they are "simple" or "double" seems to depend on their duration.

movimento (It., pl. *movimenti*)   Simple, stepwise figures that fill in pitch intervals of various sizes, subdividing tones of various lengths.

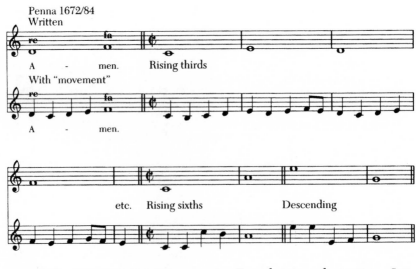

passaggi (It., sing. *passaggio;* Fr. *passages;* Eng. divisions, diminutions; Lat. *variatio, transitus*)   Embellishments created by ornamental subdivisions, often extremely rapid, of melodic tones, usually continuing for a measure or more. Although they originated in the sixteenth century as improvised diminutions, in the early seventeenth century, a number of composers published "motetti passeggiati" and "arie passeggiate" (J. Kapsberger, 1612), "psalmi passeggiati" (F. Severi, 1615), etc. See Francesco Rognoni's *Selva de varii passaggi secondo l'uso moderno* (1620).

portar la voce (It., Fr. *port de voix*)   A re-articulated "accento." The re-articulation of the first tone of the pair can be a subdivision of it, or it can be on the beat of the second tone, delaying and robbing it of a little time. In his *Imperfections of Modern Music,* Artusi illustrates the latter as an example of *accento.* Depending on the affect desired, time and loudness, and perhaps pitch (e.g., in the application of a tremolo or microtonal changes) were adjusted to intensify its effect. Muffat (1698, his Example ZZ) equates *port de voix* with the Italian term "appoggiatura," that is, an *accento* with the re-articulation of the first tone of a pair occurring on the new bow stroke.

raddoppiate (It., sing. *raddoppiata*)   Probably meaning doubled figures or notes in a melismatic embellishment, in two senses: (1) doubling by repetition of the figure itself (which lengthens the embellishment; examples identified in Crüger 1660 are melodic sequences); or (2) mixing subdivisions of differing note values in the same melisma, which increases its speed. The latter sense is implied by the seventeenth-century phrases "double relish" or in French, *double cadence.*

ricercata (It., usually pl. *ricercate*)   A general term for free improvisations on keyboard or plucked string instrument that does not exclude fugal textures; a prelude. This sense is still given in the 1708 *Dictionaire de musique* of S. Brossard. Roger North (1728) called it "a this-way-that-way manner, like searching."

sprezzatura (It.)   In general, ease of manner, with the inborn bearing of good breeding. As used by the Florentine monodists, its achievement in singing

depended on several musical techniques that imparted flexibility, gracious-
ness, and spontaneity in performance. As described by Giulio Caccini (1614),
"*Sprezzatura* is that elegance given to a melody by several incorrect eighths
or sixteenths on different tones, incorrect with respect to their rhythm
(tempo), thus freeing the melody from a certain narrow limitation and dry-
ness and making it pleasant, free, and airy, just as in common speech, elo-
quence and invention make affable and sweet the matters being spoken of."

tenuë (Fr., pl. *tenuës*)   A tone held for the length of a measure or more.

tirata (It., *tirate;* Fr. *tirade,* pl. *tirades)*   A stepwise succession of notes of the
same rhythmic value. Toward the end of the seventeenth century, they were
often of eighth or sixteenth notes, beginning after a rest on the beat.

vaghezza (It., usually pl. *vaghezze)*   A term for ornaments in general.

References

Lodovico Zacconi, *Prattica di musica* (Venice, 1592; repr. 1967, 1982).

Giovanni Maria Artusi, *L'Artusi, overo Delle imperfettioni della moderna musica* (Venice, 1600;
repr. 1968).

Giulio Caccini, *Le nuove musiche* (Florence, 1602); mod. ed. by H. Wiley Hitchcock (Madison,
1970).

Giulio Caccini, *Nuove musiche e nuove maniera di scriverle* (Florence, 1614); mod. ed. by H.
Wiley Hitchcock (Madison, 1978).

Francesco Rognoni, *Selva di varii passaggi secondo l'uso moderno* (Milan, 1620; repr. 1970).

Johannes Crüger, *Musicae practicae praecepta brevia* (Berlin, 1660).

Lorenzo Penna, *Li primi albori musicali* (Bologna 1672; repr. of 4th, 1684 ed. Bologna, 1969).

Bartolomeo. Bismantova, "Compendio musicale," MS dated Ferrara, 1677–79 (facs. ed. Florence,
1978).

Georg Muffat, *Suavioris harmoniae instrumentalis hyporchematicae florilegium secundum* (Passau, 1698), preface; mod. ed. by W. Kolneder (Strasbourg, 1970).

Sébastien de Brossard, *Dictionaire de musique* (Amsterdam, n.d.; repr. Geneva, 1992).

Roger North, "The Musical Grammarian," in *Roger North's The Musical Grammarian 1728,* ed.
by M. Chan and J. C. Kassler (Cambridge, 1990).

INDEX

Note: Numbers in boldface refer to pages where definitions for a term are found, or to the source reading passages themselves.

Academy of Ancient Music (London), 11
Accademia della Crusca (Florence), 15
accento, 18, **22n–23n,** 111, **131n, 223**
Acciaiuoli, Filippo, 164n
accompaniment
   of opera, 46, 68, 121–23, 124
   of sacred concertos, 112–13
   of solo singing, 97, 132–34
acoustics of music, 121–23
acting, 64–66, 124–26
Addison, Joseph, 4, 175, 209n
   The Spectator, **175–78**
affections, 8–10, 16, 41, 44–45, 125–26, 190–91, 192, 194–95. *See also* emotions in music
Affektenlehre, 9
affetto, 54, 104, 133–34, **223–24**
African music, 12, 206
Agazzari, Agostino, 3, 6, 113, 130
   Of Playing upon a Bass with All Instruments and of Their Use in a Consort, 114–20
Agazzari, Camilla ("Camilluccia"), 42
Agnelli, Scipione, *Marriage of Tethys*, 154
Agostini, Piersimone, 11, 45n
Ai Di, Emperor of China, 221–22
Albrici, Vincenzo, 49
Aldobrandini, Cardinal Pietro, 41n
Alterati (Florentine academy), 15
amateurs, 4, 85–93
Amelot de la Houssaie, A.-N., 66
Annibali, Domenico, 71, 72n
arcate mute, **118n**
Archilei, Vittoria, 41n, 42, 98, 153
aria, 44–46
   types of, 10, 181–83
aria di bravura, **44n**
Aristides Quintilianus, 152n
Aristotle, *Poetics*, 172
Aristoxenus, *Harmonics*, 26
Artusi, Giovanni Maria, 10–11, 18, 27, 28–36
   Artusi, or, Of the Imperfections of Modern Music, **18–26,** 34, 223, 225
Athenaeus, *The Deipnosophists*, 87
Augustine, St., 172

Bach, Johann Sebastian, 57
Bach Society edition of, 3
Short but Most Necessary Draft for a Well-Appointed Church Music, **57–61**
Bach Society, 3
balafo, 206n
ballet de cour, 8, 160–62
Banchieri, Adriano, 130
   Conclusioni del suono dell'organo, 113
Banister, John, 79
Barbados, 12, 204–207
Barberini family, 42n
Bardi, Giovanni de', 15, 31n, 97, 100
Bardi, Pietro de', 7, 15
   Letter to Giovanni Battista Doni, **15–17**
Baroni, Caterina, 42n
Baroni, Leonora, 42n
"Baroque," 4
Basile, Adriana, 42n, 156n
Basile, Margherita, 43n, 156n
Basile, Vittoria, 156n
basso continuo, 3, 5–6, 27, 78, 82, 97, 98, 106–108, 109, 113–20, 130, 133–36, 154, 170, 183
Basteris, Gaetano, 72n
Beauchamps, Pierre, 166
Becker, Dietrich, 78
Belli, Giuseppe, 73
Benevoli, Margherita, 105n
Berkeley, Mary, 211n
Bianchi, Francesco, 41n
Bible, 87
Boethius
   De institutione musica, 158n
   Fundamentals of Music, 26
Boileau, Nicholas, *Satires*, 177n
Bolles, John, 126–27
Bolles, Sir Robert, 126
Bonnet, Jacques, 11n
Bonnet-Bourdelot, Pierre, *Histoire de la musique*, 11n
Bononcini, Giovanni, 45n, 163
   cantatas of, 171
   Rinnovata Camilla, Regina de' Volsci, 164n, 169n
   Temistocle in bando, 164n

Bontempi, Giovanni Andrea, 49, 53
Boretti, Guidobaldo, 41n
Borghese, Cardinal Scipione, 42
Boschi, Giuseppe, 45n
Bottrigari, Ercole, 32
Bourdelot, Pierre, *Histoire de la musique*, 11n
bowing, 5, 6–7, 118, 140, 141–46, 165
boy singers, 41, 113
Braccino, Antonio, 18, 28
Brandi, Antonio, 153
Brossard, Sébastien de, *Dictionaire de musique*, 225
Buelow, George, 9
Bukofzer, Manfred, *Music in the Baroque Era*, 3n
Buxtehude, Dietrich, church cantatas of, 3
Buzzolini, Giovanni, 45n

Caccini, Francesca, 43, 105n
Caccini, Giulio, 32, 97, 223–24, 226
    Dedication to *Euridice*, **97–99**
    Deh, dove son fuggiti, 106–108
    Euridice, 17n, 151
    Le nuove musiche, 6, 224
    madrigals of, 98, 100
    monodies of, 15, 16
    Preface to *Le nuove musiche*, 98n, **100–109**
    published works of, 3
    Rapimento di Cefalo, 156n
Caccini, Lucia, 105n
Caccini, Settimia, 105n
cadences, 99, 112, 116, 167
Caldara, Antonio, 208n
Camerata (Florence), 15–17, 100, 151
"Camilluccia." *See* Agazzari, Camilla
Campra, André, *L'Europe galante*, 66
canto alla francese, 34
canzonetta, 181–82
Capellmeister, profession of, 49–53
Capranica, Matteo, 72n
Carissimi, Giacomo, 45n
Cassani, Giuseppe, 177n
castrati, 41, 43, 53n, 68, 71, 73n, 165, 175n, 177n
Cavaliere del Leuto, 38
Cavalieri, Emilio de', 31, 40–41, 151
    La rappresentatione di anima, et di corpo, 41n
    published works of, 3
Cazzati, Maurizio, 78
Cenci, Giuseppino, 40n
Cesi, Anna Maria, 43n
Cesti, Antonio (Pietro), operas of, 3
cetera, **114n**
ceterone, **119n**
chant, mode in, 35
Charles II, King of England, 77
Chen Menglei, 220n

Chiabrera, Gabriele, 97
Chiccheri, Vittorio, 72–73
Chinese music, 12, 216–22
chitarrina, **115n**
Chor-Ton, 147
choragus, 121, 125
Choragus, The (anon.), 6, **121–26**
Chrysander, Friedrich
    Corelli edition of, 3
    Handel edition of, 3
church musicians, Bach's standards for, 57–61
"Ciecolino." *See* Rivani, Antonio
Cini, Francesco, 153
cittern, 119
Claudian, *Against Eutropius*, 86
clavichord, 113
Clayton, Thomas, *Rosamond*, 175
Clemens non Papa, 32
Coli, Francesco, 4, 54
    Pallade veneta, **54–56**
"comedy," **17n**
concerts
    programming of, 80–82
    public, 4, 79–82
concitato, 8, 158n
conducting, 123–24
Conforti, Giovanni Luca, 40n, 201n
Confrérie de Saint-Julien-des-Ménétriers, 73–76
Confucius, 219, 222
consonance and dissonance, 98, 133–34, 152, 167–68, 185, 186–87
    in figured bass realization, 115–16
    second practice style, 18–26, 28, 31–33
    tuning and, 119
consorts, 78
Conti, Antonio, 178
Conti, Gioacchino, "Gizziello," 73n
contracts, 61–63
Coprario, John, 204
Corelli, Arcangelo, 136, 163
    complete works edition of, 3
Cornaro family, 70n
Cornet-Ton, 147
Corsi, Jacopo, 17, 151, 153
counterpoint, 10, 27, 37–39, 120, 130–31
courante, 193–94
craquer, **143n**, 145, **224**
Créquillon, Thomas, 32
criticism, music, 4, 70–73, 175–78

dance. *See also ballet de cour*
    emotion in, 8, 160–61
    Greek, 209
    in opera, 68, 73, 165–66
    Turkish, 210, 212
dance music, 161–62, 190, 193–94, 201
    suites, 78, 136–47

dancing masters, 73–76
Dante Alighieri, *Inferno,* 16
Della Valle, Pietro, 11, 36, 201n
    Carro di fedeltà d'amore, 40n
    Of the Music of Our Time, **37–43**
Derelitti, Ospedale dei (Venice), 54n, 56
dervish ceremony, 212
Descartes, René, *Discourse on Method,* 10n
Descoteaux, René-Pignon, 165n
Desmatins, Mlle. (singer), 65
dissonance. *See* consonance and dissonance
division, 127–30
Dognazzi, Francesco, 156n
Doni, Giovanni Battista, 15–17, 36
    Progymnastica musicae, 202n
    Treatise on Theatrical Music, 15n
double bass, 147
Dresden, 60
drone, 188n
drums, African, 206
Dryden, John, 176n
Du Halde, Jean Baptiste, 12, 216
    *Geographical, Historical, Chronological,
        Political, and Physical Description of
        the Empire of China and of Chinese
        Tartar,* 217–22
Dumanoir, Guillaume, 73–74
    Statutes of the Masters of Dance and Play-
        ers of Instruments, **74–76**
dynamics, in Baroque music, 99, 101–105

embellishments. *See* ornamentation
emotions in music, 7, 8, 11, 157–59, 168–69,
    172–74, 186–88, 193, 203, 215. *See also*
    affections; imitation
English style, 91n, 200, 214
esclamazione, 103–104, **224**

falsetto, **108n,** 113
Fang Bao, 220n
Fattorini, Gabriele, *Sacri concerti a due voci,*
    111n
Ferrotti, Angelo, 41n
Fétis, François-Joseph, 213
figured bass. *See* basso continuo
Fiorini, Hippolito, 19
first practice, 30–35
flute, 165
Fontanella, Alfonso, 31, 153
Fonton, Charles, 9, 11–12, 213
    *Essay on Oriental Music Compared to the
        European,* **213–15**
French style, 9, 11, 137–47, 163–74, 200–203,
    214
Fux, Johann Joseph, 208n

Gabrieli, Andrea, 24, 38
Gabrieli, Giovanni, 24, 38, 50–51

Gagliano, Marco da, *La Flora,* 151
Galilei, Vincenzo, 15–16
    *Dialogo della musica antica e della mod-
        erna,* 16
Galuppi, Baldassare, 70
    Antigona, 72–73
Gasparini, Francesco, 45n
Gastoldi, Giovanni, 24
genera, 158–59
German style, 9, 11, 200–203, 214
Gesualdo, Carlo, 31n
Ghirardi, Lorenzo, 71, 72n
Giorgi, Filippo, 71, 72n
Giovanelli, Ruggiero, 24
Giusti, Jacopo, 154
Gogova, Antonio, 26n
Gombert, Nicolas, 32
gondoliers, 46n, 69
Gonzaga, Ferdinando, 154
Gonzaga family, 42n, 154
Goretti, Antonio, 19
gorgia (or *gorga*), 40, 131n, **224**
Greece, Baroque views of, 16, 30, 31, 33–34,
    85–87, 91, 97–99, 101, 152, 156, 158–
    59, 178, 185, 187–88, 200
Grimaldi, Filipo Maria, 220
Grimaldi, Nicolò, 175n
groppo, gruppo, 99, 104–105, 153, 201, **224**
Grossi, Giovanni Francesco "Sifacio," 45n
Gualtero, Lodovico, 39–40
Guarino Veronese, *Regulae,* 25
Guidiccioni, Lelio, 37

Haas, Robert, *Die Musik des Barocks,* 3n, 6
Handel, George Frideric
    Amadigi, 175n
    Chrysander edition of, 3
    Esther, 77
    Rinaldo, 175–78
harmonic proportions, 21
harmony, 19–36, 114–20, 167, 173, 184–88.
    See also consonance and dissonance
harp, double, 119
He Guozong, 220n
Hill, Aaron, 177n
historiography, 3–4
Homer, *Iliad,* 209n
Horace
    The Art of Poetry, 172n, 174
    Epistles, 29
    Satires, 25
Hotteterre family, 165n
humors, 8–9, 79n, 199, 200n, 203

imitation, 8–10, 16, 158–59, 172. *See also*
    affections
improvisation, 5, 6, 127–30, 133
Incurabili, Ospedale degli (Venice), 54n, 56

inganni, **24n**
Ingegneri, Marc'Antonio, 32
instrumental music, 38–39, 189–95. *See also*
    accompaniment; dance music; *specific*
    instruments
  basso continuo in, 113–20
  Chinese, 221–22
  domestic performance of, 88–93
  emotion in, 8–9
  English, 78–82, 205
  Italian style, 9, 11, 137, 141, 163–74, 200–203,
    213

Jacomelli, Giovan Battista, 153
Lapi, Giovanni, 153
Joachim, Joseph, Corelli edition of, 3
Johann Georg I, Elector of Saxony, 49–53
John the Deacon, 201n
Josquin Desprez, 32
  Masses of, 35

Kangxi, Emperor of China, 216, 220, 221n,
    222n
Kircher, Athanasius, 8–9, 199
  Musurgia universalis, 200–203
Kuhnau, Johann, 60

La Rue, Pierre de, 32
Lapi, Giovanni, 153
Lappoli, Geronimo, 61–63
Lasso, Orlando di, 24
Latilla, Gaetano, 70
  Romolo, 71–72
Lau, Frederick, 222n
"Laudomia." *See* Muti, "Laudomia"
Laurenzi, Filiberto, 63
Lawrence, Elizabeth, 211n
Lazzarini, Gregorio, 41n
Le Cerf de la Viéville, Jean Laurent, 3, 7, 11,
    151, 163, 167n, 168n, 169n, 170n, 171,
    179
  Comparision between Italian and French
    Music, **172–74**
Le Rochois, Marie, 64–66, 162
Li Guangdi, 220n
librettos, 7, 154–57, 178–83
Ligon, Richard, 12, 204
  A True & Exact History of the Island of Bar-
    bados, **204–207**
lirone, **114n**, 118
Lolli, Eleonora, 42
Lolli, Madalena, 42
London
  domestic music-making in, 89–93
  opera in, 175–78
  public concerts in, 77–80
Loret, Jean, 4, 88
  The Historical Muse, **88**
Loss, Christoph von, 51
Lotti, Antonio, 45n

Lucian, *Dialogues*, 86–87
"Luigino" (singer), 45n
Lulier, Giovanni, *Temistocle in bando*, 164n
Lully, Jean-Baptiste, 11, 63, 78, 137, 140, 174
  Armide, 7, 65–66
  Atys, 166n
  Isis, 166n
  operas of, 3, 67, 162, 163, 164n
  Persée, 166
  Proserpine, 64
Lülü zhengyi, 216 220–21
Lupori, Angela Caterina, 54
lute, 118
Luzzaschi, Luzzasco, 19, 32, 38–39

Macque, Jean de, 38
madrigals
  of Caccini, 98, 100
  of Monteverdi, 18–36, 157–59
  of Rore, 30
  of Schütz, 50n
Malvezzi, Cristofano, 16
Mancini, Luigi, 45n
mandore, **88n**
Marenzio, Luca, 11, 32
Marin, Louis, 10n
Marie d'Orléans, 88
Marotta, Cesare, 42n
Martello, Pier Jacopo, 7, 10, 178–79
  On Ancient and Modern Tragedy, **179–**
    83
Mattheson, Johann, 4, 8, 188
  The Complete Music Director, 7, 11, **189–**
    95
Mazarin, Cardinal Jules, 42n, 159
Medici, Caterina de', 154
Medici, Cosimo II de', 42n
Medici, Maria de', 154
Mei Gucheng, 220n
melodia, **27**
melody, 184–95
  Chinese, 218–20
  in *stile rappresentativo*, 16n, 17
Mendicanti, Ospedale dei (Venice), 54–56
Ménestrier, Claude-François, *Des Représenta-*
    tions en musique anciennes et mod-
    ernes, 201n, 202n
Merulo, Claudio, 24, 38n
Metastasio, Pietro, 70
meter. *See* rhythm and meter
modes
  church, 46
  mixed, 35
monody, 15, 16–17, 97
Montagu, Edward Wortley, 208
Montagu, Lady Mary Wortley, 4, 11–12, 201n,
    208–12
Montalto, Cardinal, 40n, 42, 156n
Montalvo, Grazia, 153

Monteverdi, Claudio, 7, 10, 27, 154
  Arianna, 17n, 156n
  Coronation of Poppea, 61
  criticized by Artusi, 18
  Cruda Amarilli, 18, 19–26, 29–31
  Laudate Dominum, 158n
  madrigals of, 18–36, 157–59
  Marriage of Tethys (project), 154–57
  O Mirtillo, 35
  Orfeo, 156n
  Preface to *Madrigali guerrieri, et amorosi,* 8, **157–59**
  Scherzi musicali (1607), 27
Monteverdi, Giulio Cesare, 18, 27
  Explanation of the Letter Printed in the Fifth Book of Madrigals, **28–36**
Monte, Philippe de, 24
Morales, Cristóbal de, 202n
morals and music, 9–10, 92–93, 158
Moreau, Fanchon, 65
Moretti, Lucrezia, 42
Moritz, Landgrave of Hessen-Kassel, 49–50, 51
Morselli, Adriano, *Temistocle in bando,* 164n
Mouton, Jean, 32
movimento, **131n,** 135, 136, **224**
Muffat, Georg, 6, 11, 136–37, 223, 225
  Preface to the *First Florilegium,* **137–30**
  Preface to the *Second Florilegium,* **140–47**
music as a profession, 4
musica ficta, 24n
musicians' guilds, 73–76
Muti, "Laudomia" (singer), 42

Nanino, Giovanni Bernardino, 24
Nanino, Giovanni Maria, 24
national styles, 9, 199, 200–203, 213–15. *See also specific types*
Neri, St. Philip, 169n
Nicolini, Bartolomeo, 41n
non-Western music, 9, 11–12, 202, 204–22, 205–207
North, Roger, 4, 77, 225
  Memoirs of Music, **77–80**
  Notes of Me, **81–82, 89–93**
notation, 137, 138–39
  basso continuo, 3, 97–99, 120

oboe, 165
Ockeghem, Johannes, 32
opera
  early, 15, 16–17, 97–99, 151–57
  emotion in, 7
  French, 64–66, 67, 68
  French *vs.* Italian styles, 163–74
  libretto writing for, 154–57, 178–83
  public performances of, 4
  in Rome, 70–74
  staging of, 6, 121–26, 175–78
  Venetian, 46n, 61–63, 66–70

opera seria, 10
organ, 112, 114, 117, 132–36
ornamentation. *See also specific ornaments*
  glossary of terms, 223–26
  instrumental, 5, 38–39, 116, 118, 127–30, 140, 162
  vocal, 18, 22n–23n, 39–41, 43, 44–46, 54–55, 99, 101–108, 110–13, 153, 201n
overture, French, 191
Ovid
  Amores, 86
  Art of Loving, 86
  Remedies for Love, 86

Padovano, Annibale, 38
Palentrotti, Melchior, 40n, 153
Palestrina, Giovanni Pierluigi da, 24
  Missa Papae Marcelli, 120
  Vestiva i colli, 38
Pallade veneta, 54
Paris
  domestic music-making in, 88
  operas in, 64–66
Partenio, Domenico, 55
Pasqualini, Marc'Antonio, 41n
passaggi, 39–40, 54–55, 98, 100, 101, 111, 116, 118, 131, **224–25**
passamezzo, 205n
passions. *See* affections
patronage, Baroque period, 4, 29, 49–53, 57–61, 77–78, 90, 154, 180
Pecci, Tomaso, 31n
pedagogy. *See also* tutors
  Baroque period, 57–61, 93
Pedrini, Teodorico, 216, 221n
Penna, Lorenzo, 6, 130
  Musical Daybreaks for Beginners in Measured Music, **130–36**
Pereira, Tomas, 216, 220–21
Peretti, Michele, 43n
perfidie, **37**
performance practice, of Baroque music, 5–7, 37–46, 97–147
Peri, Jacopo, 7, 32, 151, 171
  Dafne, 16–17, 153n
  Euridice, 17n, 40, 98n, 156n
  Preface to *Euridice,* **151–54**
  published works of, 3
pertinacia, 37n
Philibert, 165n
Philidor, Anne Danican, 165n
Pietà, Ospedale della (Venice), 54n, 56
Pistocchi, Francesco, 45n
pitch. *See* tuning and temperament
Plato, 30, 32, 91, 100
  Laws, 158n
  Gorgias, 32n
  Republic, 27, 33, 156, 158n, 159n
  Timaeus, 34n

Pope, Alexander, 208, 209
Porta, Costanzo, 24
portar la voce, 18, 22–24, **225**
printing and publishing, of monument editions, 3
Ptolemy, Claudius, *Of Harmonics*, 26
Purcell, Henry
   operas of, 3
   Purcell Society edition of, 3
Purcell Society, 3
Pure, Abbé Michel de, 8, 159–60
   Aspects of Ancient and Modern Spectacles, **160–62**

Quagliati, Paolo, 40n
Quinault, Philippe, 64n, 65n, 164, 166n
Quintilianus, Aristides, 152n

raddoppiate, 98, **225**
Raguenet, François, 4, 7, 9, 10, 151, 162–63, 171
   A Comparison between the French & Italian Musics and Operas, **163–70**
Rameau, Jean-Philippe, 7, 183
   Saint-Saëns edition of, 3
   Treatise on Harmony, 10–11, **184–88**
Rasi, Francesco, 153, 156n
recitative style, 123–26, 133, 151–54, 157, 181
Recupito, Hippolita, 42n
"Relato sincero, Il. *See* "Truthful Reporter, The"
Renzi, Anna, 61–63
rhetoric, 7–8, 192. *See also* affections; emotions in music
rhythm and meter
   in Baroque music, 140
   bowing and, 142, 144–45
   mensuration, 115n
   meter signs, 136, 138–39
   poetic, 182
   unequal notes, 139, 146
   in vocal music, 5, 7, 99, 192–93
ricercata, 38n, 56n, **225**
Rich, Christopher, 178
Riemann, Hugo, *Handbuch der Musikgeschichte*, 3n
Rimbault, Edward F., 77
Rinuccini, Ottavio, 16, 97
   Arianna, 17
   Euridice, 151, 153–54
   Dafne, 17
Rivani, Antonio, "Ciecolino," 45n
Roberts (Robartes), Francis, 78
Robinson, Anastasia, 211n
Roccaforte, Gaetano, 72
Romano, Giulio, 43
Rome, 46n
   domestic music-making in, 85–87
   opera in, 70

oratories, music in, 169
   singers in, 39–43
Rore, Cipriano de, 24, 31, 32
   madrigals of, 30
   Quando, signor, lasciaste, 35
Rosini, Girolamo, 41n
Rospigliosi family, 42n
Rossi, Giacomo, 177n

St. Barbe, Sir John, 126
St. Thomas School (Leipzig), 57–61
Saint-Didier, Alexandre-Toussaint, Sieur de, 66–67
   City and Republic of Venice, **67–70**
Saint-Saëns, Camille, Rameau edition of, 3
salaries
   of instrumentalists and dancing masters, 50, 74–76
   of music directors (Vienna), 208
   of opera singers, 62–63
Salinas, Francisco de, 202n
San Girolamo della Carità (Rome), 169n
Sances, Lorenzo, 41n
Sandrinelli, Bernardo, 56
Sannazaro, Jacopo, *Arcadia*, 97n, 101
Santa (singer), 42
Sauveterre, François, 73n
Savioni, Mario, 41n
Scacchi, Marco, *Breve discorso*, 11
Scarlatti, Alessandro, 45n, 136
scena di forza, 181
Scheibe, Johann Adolph, *Critische Musicus*, 201n
Schelle, Johann, 60
Schütz, Heinrich, 49
   madrigals of, 50n
   Memorandum to the Elector of Saxony, **49–53**
   Spitta edition of, 3
   Symphoniae sacrae, 49
science, seventeenth-century, 8, 10, 199
second practice, 27, 28–36, 157–59
Severi, Francesco, 201n
Shakespeare, William, *Henry IV*, pt. 2, 205n
Simpson, Christopher, 6, 126–27
   The Divison-Viol, **127–30**
   Principles of Practical Musick, 126
singing. *See also castrati;* vocal music
   French, 165, 168
   Italian, 39–46, 68–70, 97–109, 123–26, 166–68
   ornamentation in, 18, 22–23
   tutors for, 6, 130–36
Sofonisba (singer), 42
sonata, 195
sospiro, **55n**
Soto de Langa, Francisco, 41n
Sousa, Bernardo Mendes de, 204n
Spada, Giacomo, 56

Spanish style, 200–203
Spitta, Philip, Schütz edition of, 3
sprezzatura, 98, 100, 108, **225–26**
Stampiglia, Silvio, *Rinnovata Camilla, Regina de' Volsci*, 164n
Steele, Richard, 175
Stella, Santa, "La Santini," 45n
stile rappresentativo, 7, 16–17, 97
Stradella, Alessandro, 11, 45n
Striggio, Alessandro, 154, 155
  Nasce la pena mia, 35
Strozzi, Piero, 153
suppositi, **23n–24n**

tactus, 99, **101n**
Tasso, Torquato, *La Gerusalemme liberata*, 158, 177n
Teatro Argentina (Rome), 70, 72
Teatro Capranica (Rome), 164n
Teatro delle Dame (Rome), 70, 71n, 72
Teatro Grimani (Venice), 61
Teatro Novissimo (Venice), 61–63
tempo, 7, 137, 138–39, 140, 144, 146n, 158
tenuë, **226**
Terradellas, Domingo, 71n
text setting, 7, 119–20, 151–53, 171, 173–74, 192
  in arias, 181–83
  of Caccini, 99–109
  of Monteverdi, 30, 33–34, 35–36
theaters. *See also* acting
  staging techniques for, 121–26
theorbo, 118
theory, 183–95. *See also specific topics*
tirata (also *tirade*), **117n, 162n, 226**
Titon du Tillet, Evrard, 63–64
  Parnassus of France, first Supplement, **64–66**
"Tonina" (Antonia; singer), 54–55
Torri, Carlo de', 155
Tosi, Pierfrancesco, 4, 7, 11, 43
  Observations on the Florid Song, **44–46**
transposition, 119
trills, 29, 104–105, 131n. *See also groppo, gruppo*
"Truthful Reporter," 4, 70
tuning and temperament, 5, 102n, 119, 123, 140–41, 146–47
Turco, Giovanni del, 31n
Turkish music, 9, 11, 210–12, 213
tutors, 5–6
  singing, 130–36
  viol, 126–30
  violin, 140–47

Uberti, Antonio, "Porporino," 71–72
Uberti, Grazioso, 4, 85
  The Musical Disagreement, **85–87**
unequal notes, 139, 146

vaghezza, **226**
Valeria, Anna di, 42n
Vanini, Francesca, 45n
Vasari, Giorgio, *Lives of the Painters*, 172n–73n
Vecchi, Orazio, 153
Venice
  opera in, 46n, 61–63, 66–70
  ospedali in, 54–56
  theaters in, 61
Venturini, Casimiro, 73
Viadana, Lodovico, 109, 130
  Preface to *One Hundred Sacred Concertos*, op. 12, **110–13**
  published works of, 3
Vienna, 208–209
Vinci, Leonardo, 70
viol, 78, 90, 127–30
viola, 147
violin, 78, 136–47
violoncello, 79n, 147
violone, 118
Virgil, *Aeneid*, 85–86, 172
virtuosity, 100. *See also* ornamentation; singing
Vitali, Giovanni Battista, 78
Vitello, Erasmus, 21
Vittori, Cavaliere Loreto, 41n
vocal music. *See also* opera; singing
  counterpoint in, 38
  melody in, 189–92
  ornamentation of, 18, 22n–23n, 38–41, 43, 44–46, 54–55, 99, 101–108, 153, 201n
  sacred concertos, 110–13
voice range, in *stile rappresentativo*, 16n, 17

Wallington, Benjamin, 79
Wert, Giaches de, 24, 32
Willaert, Adrian, 24, 32–33
  Ne projicias nos in tempore senectutis, 35
Wolffersdorff, Gottfried von, 51
women
  as instrumentalists, 55–56, 88, 92–93
  as singers, 41–43, 54–56, 61–66, 85–87, 105, 156

Yin Lu, 220n
Yin Reng, 220n
Yin Zhi, 220n

Zacconi, Lodovico, 224
Zarlino, Gioseffo, 27, 28
  Istitutione harmoniche, 32–33, 34, 35, 186n, 187n
Zhang Ying, 220n
Zhang Zhao, 220n
Ziani, Marc'Antonio, *Temistocle in bando*, 164n
Ziani, Maria Anna, 55–56